POSTCARD HISTORY SERIES

# *Old Orchard Beach*

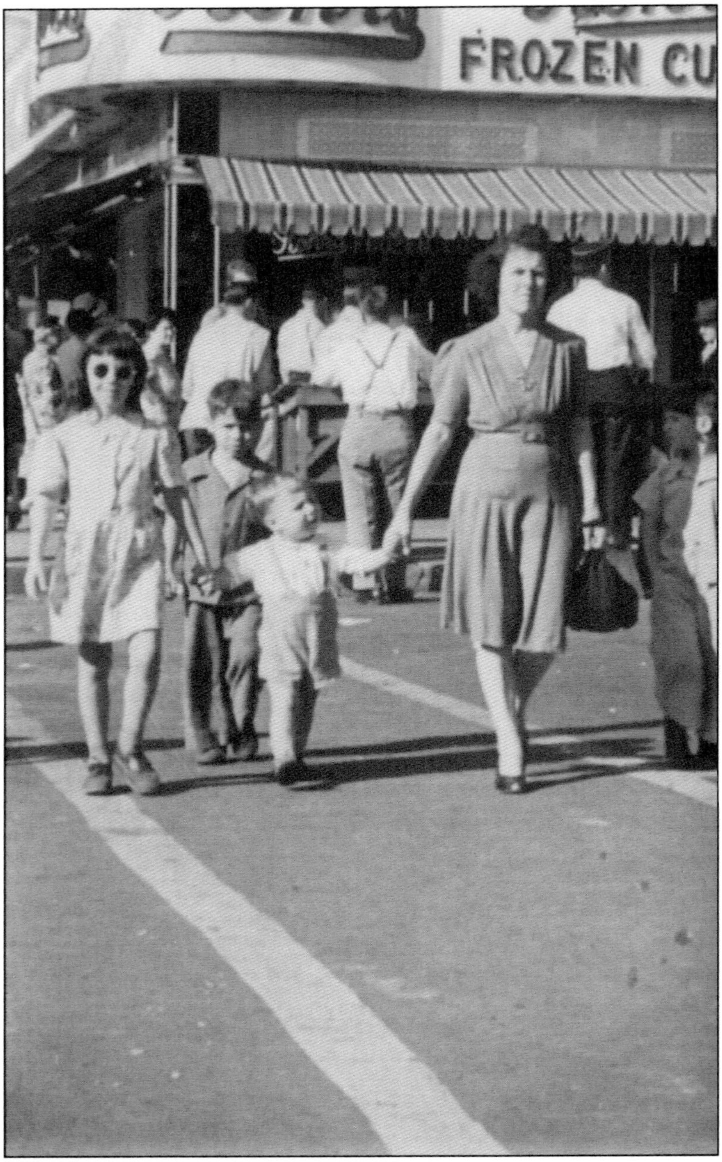


The above real-photo postcard was taken in the summer of 1946 by local downtown street photographer George Coe. It shows the Blaney family crossing lower Old Orchard Street. Seen walking are, from left to right, sister Dorothea B., brother Martin R., the author, mother Rhea E., and brother Richard P. Blaney.

*On the front cover*: Here one can see Old Orchard Beach in the future. This rare *c.* 1907 lithographic postcard shows Old Orchard Beach on the move. This card is the most sought after card by collectors. The author knows of only four copies to exist, of which he owns three. (Author's collection.)

*On the back cover*: This one-of-a-kind, real-photo postcard, shows a well-attired foursome sitting on Googin's Rocks at the foot of Union Avenue in 1913. Their car can be seen in the background. (Author's collection.)

POSTCARD HISTORY SERIES

# Old Orchard Beach

Daniel E. Blaney

ARCADIA
PUBLISHING

ISBN 978-0-7385-4960-6

Published by Arcadia Publishing
Charleston, South Carolina

Printed in the United States of America

Library of Congress Catalog Card Number: 2006935101

For all general information contact Arcadia Publishing at:
Telephone 843-853-2070
Fax 843-853-0044
E-mail sales@arcadiapublishing.com
For customer service and orders:
Toll-Free 1-888-313-2665

Visit us on the Internet at www.arcadiapublishing.com

# Contents

# Acknowledgments

This book and the postcards within are part of a true community effort. In order to make this book as interesting and complete as possible, I sought out the help of those who know much about Old Orchard Beach history. My appreciation to the following, in no particular order: Bernard Emery, Dwight McLeod, John Margarones, Jerome Lepelletier, George and Glen Shorey, Foster Leavitt, Jeffrey Thompson, Ester Willey, Dale Davis, Roger Painchaud, Bob Domingue, Jim Hepburn, and the Old Orchard Beach Historical Society.

A special thanks to my daughter-in-law, Melanie Blaney, who did all the transcription and typing and to my good friend Gary Curtis, who proofread and corrected my grammatical errors—thanks guys. Without their help, the pages within would be pictures without captions. Thanks to everyone for contributing to this endeavor.

Using my collection of postcards as a base, I also borrowed several from other collectors: page 23 lower card, Nancy Barbano collection; page 74 upper and lower cards, Jim Hepburn collection; and page 100 lower card, Les Eastman collection.

Sources for this book include *The Great Steel Pier* (1998) by Peter Dow Bachelder; A Picture Post Card History by Robert Domingue (1981); *A History of Maine Built Automobiles 1834–1934* (1991) by Richard A. and Nancy L. Fraser; *Street Cars to Old Orchard Beach* (1989) by O. R. Cummings and Edward D. Leavitt; miscellaneous news clips from *Portland Evening Express*; miscellaneous news clips from *Biddeford and Saco Journal*; the booklet "The York National Bank" 1803–1953; Saco and Biddeford Savings Institution booklets, miscellaneous years; and "A Biography of a Railroad: the Dummy Line of Old Orchard Beach," a 1969 thesis for the University of Maine by Alton Bryant Cole.

# INTRODUCTION

There are 432 towns, 22 cities, and 34 plantations in the state of Maine. Without a doubt, one of the most interesting, notable, most talked about, most visited, and most liked towns must be Old Orchard Beach. In 1603, explorer Martin Pring walked the sands of Saco Bay. However, Saco Bay was much different when the last glaciation occurred. The ice was estimated to be one mile thick when it reached Old Orchard Beach. Geologists state that Prouts Neck and Wood Island were connected until the weaker rock in between separated and was deposited into the ocean, leaving the sandy deposits on our shore.

In 1636, Thomas Rogers, our first settler, arrived and planted an apple orchard. In 1675, Native Americans destroyed all of Old Orchard, and the community was abandoned for 42 years, until people dared to return. Rogers's old, abandoned orchard became known as the old orchard, hence our name.

In 1776, the men of Old Orchard proudly served in the Revolutionary War. In 1790, the Staples family moved to Old Orchard and took in guests in their house. Stagecoach was the main mode of transportation until the Boston and Maine Railroad built the tracks right through the heart of Old Orchard. With the depot on Old Orchard Street, near the ocean, the tourists came in droves. The 1880s saw the building of many of the large hotels and boardinghouses. In 1898, the great steel pier was constructed. Several years later, during one of the town's best seasons ever, fire struck the downtown area. Many of the large hotels and boardinghouses were destroyed. Reconstruction started immediately, and ideas were born on how to bring the tourists back. Auto racing on the beach was one of these ideas, and visitors came in large numbers. The 1920s saw many transatlantic flights originate on the sands of Old Orchard Beach. In the 1930s, we saw marathon dances, the longest and biggest in New England. The 1930s, 1940s, and 1950s brought all the big bands. From Louis "Satchmo" Armstrong to Si Zenter, Old Orchard was the place to play in all of Maine for big bands.

In 2000, the federal census lists Old Orchard Beach's population at 8,858. In the summertime, our population explodes into hundreds of thousands, who still come to enjoy what Old Orchard Beach has to offer, the beach. Old Orchard Beach can claim itself as the longest, cleanest, sandiest, and busiest beach in the entire Northeast.

Only 127 pages are used in the postcard series books, and it is difficult to show the real Old Orchard Beach. Hopefully the postcards in this book will give the reader a glimpse of the Old Orchard, as it was, in all its glory. I hope you, the reader, enjoy this work as much as I enjoyed preparing it. Enjoy.

—Daniel E. Blaney, November 2006

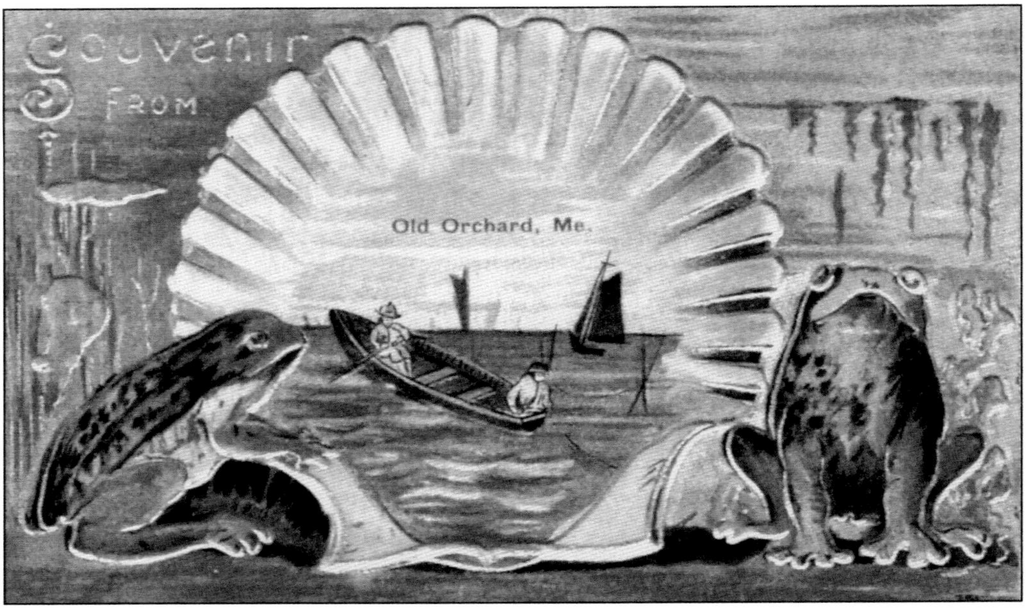


Postcards originated in Europe in the 1860s. The United States government recognized postcards in 1893. In 1898, postcards could be mailed for 1¢ instead of the 2¢ envelope rate. Local historians utilize postcards to study the past.

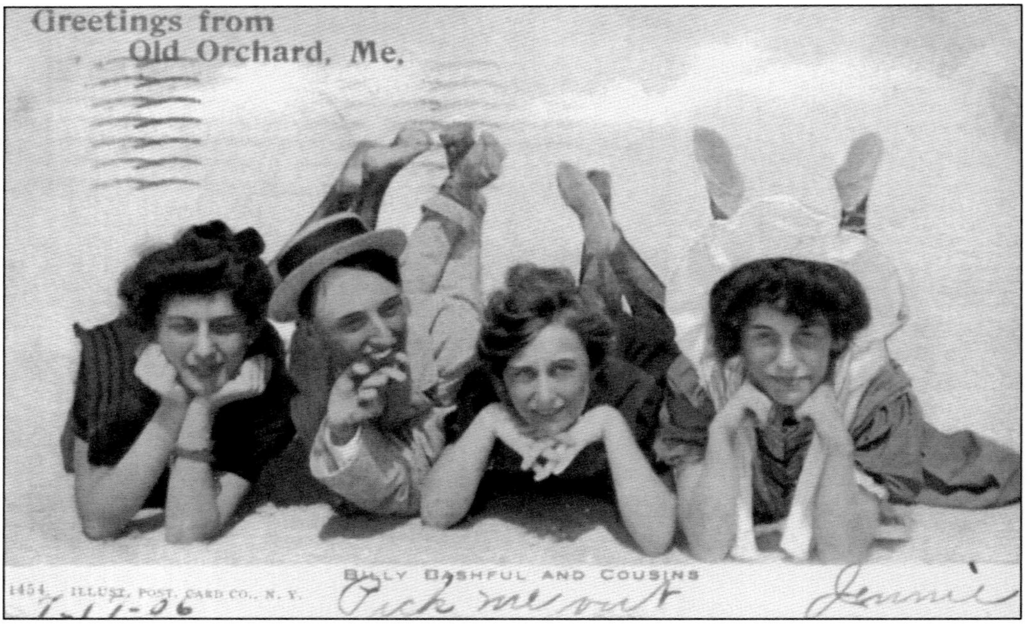


Many postcards were printed in the United States. However, during the golden era, 1900–1915, more than 75 percent were published in Germany. U.S. planes stopped all that during World War I. It is estimated that more than 4,000 different postcards were printed with views of Old Orchard Beach, more than any other town in Maine.

*One*

# Transportation

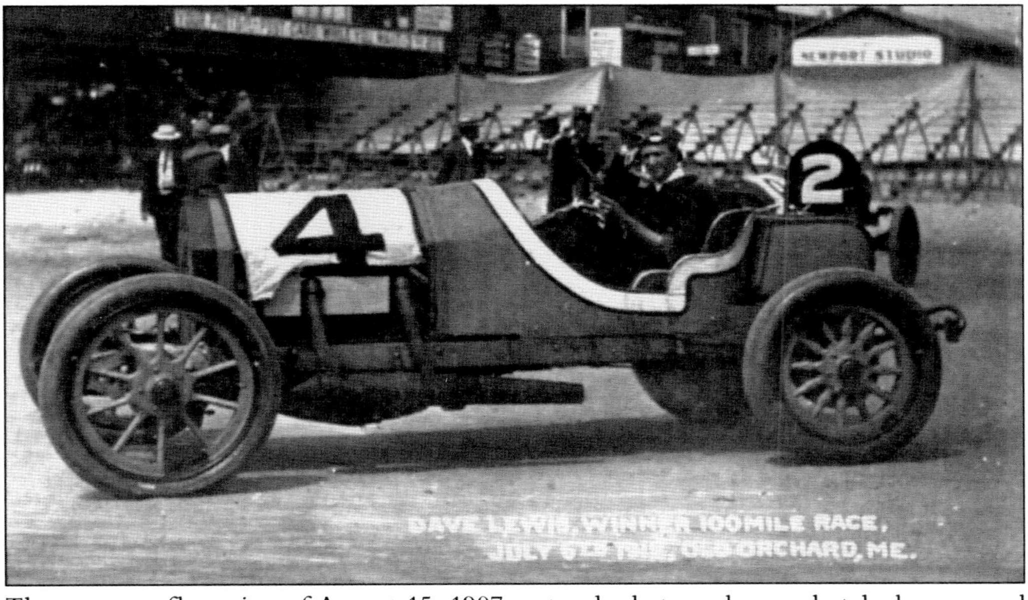


The great conflagration of August 15, 1907, not only destroyed many hotels, houses, and businesses, it put a damper on tourism. A way was needed to bring back the large crowds that once came to Old Orchard Beach, for the day, the week, or the summer. An answer was found in auto racing on the beach. The year was 1911.

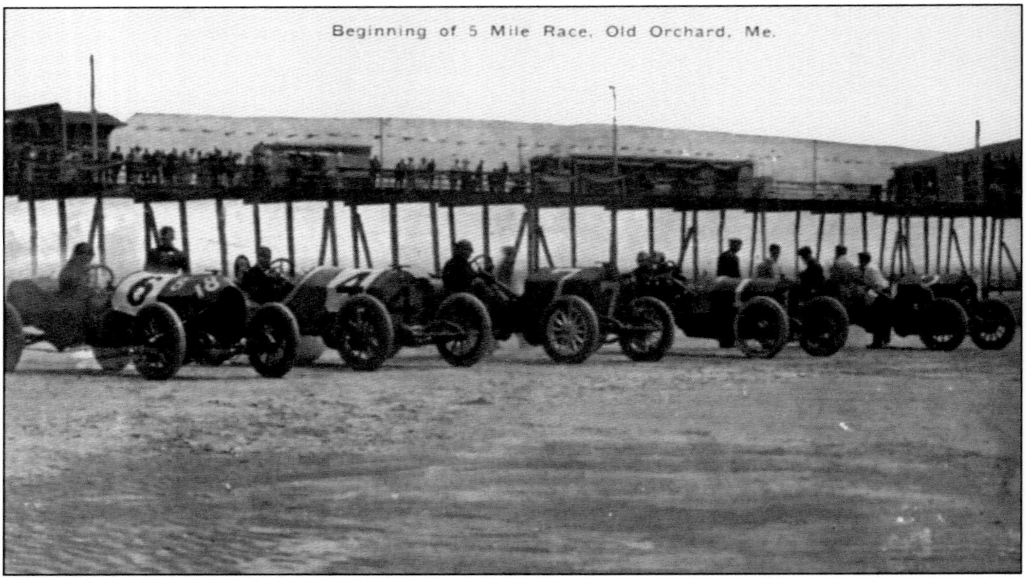


Old Orchard Beach was proclaimed the "fastest auto-course in the world." The first auto races held in Old Orchard Beach were on Labor Day weekend, September 4–6, 1911. Crowds of 50,000 people would come to town for a day of auto racing.

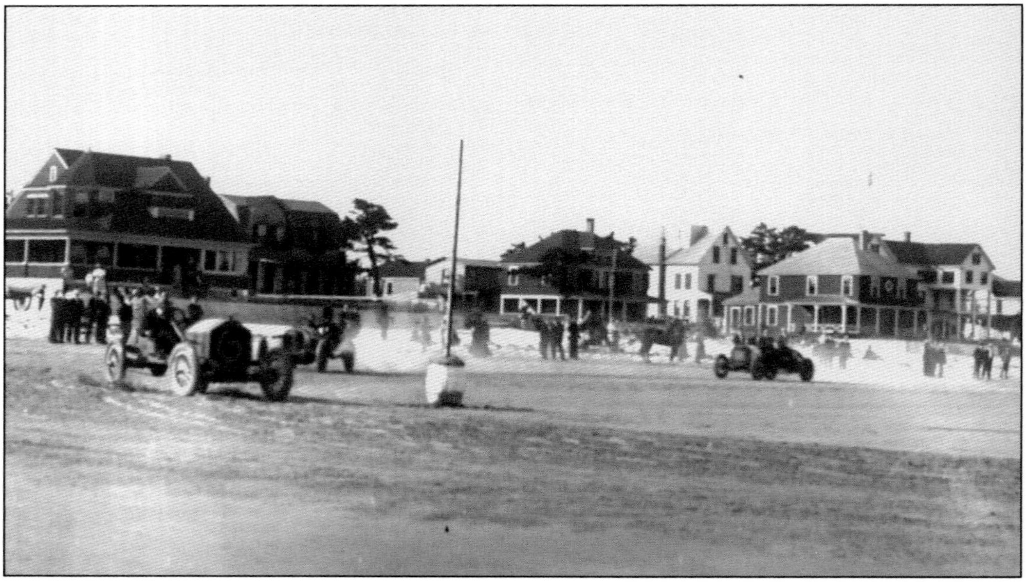

Race cars are seen here turning at the mile-and-a-quarter pole at the foot of Atlantic Avenue. The other pole was located one and a half miles north of the pier. The start and finish line was in front of the grandstand, at the foot of Old Orchard Street. One loop would make a five-mile race. The above race was held on July 4, 1912.

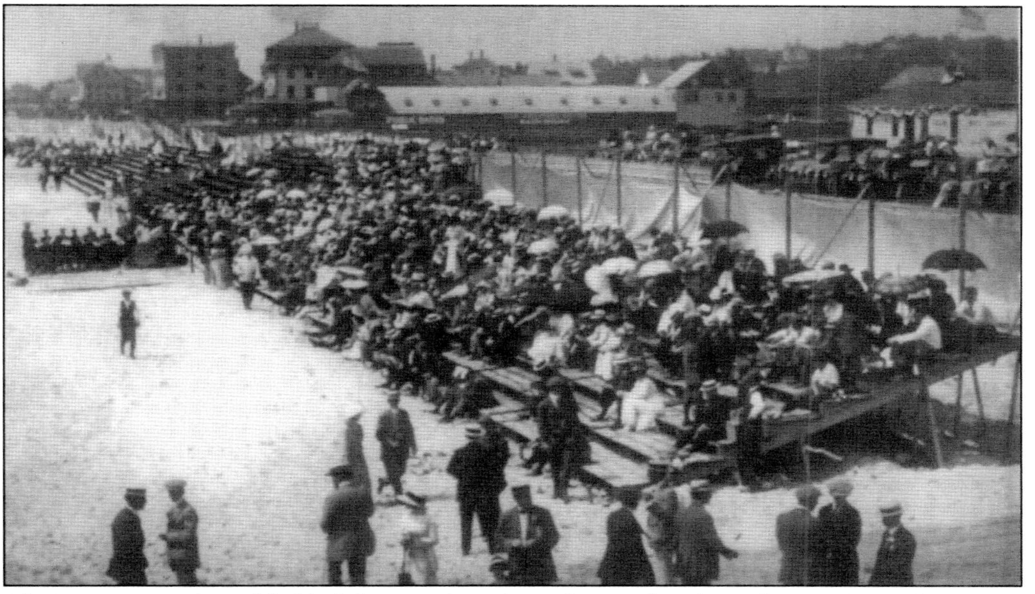

Cloth tarps were draped behind the grandstands to obscure the view of many nonpaying racing enthusiasts. Ropes were strung up and down the beach for five miles to hold back the onlookers. Newspaper stories of the day stated that Boston pickpockets were having a free-for-all.

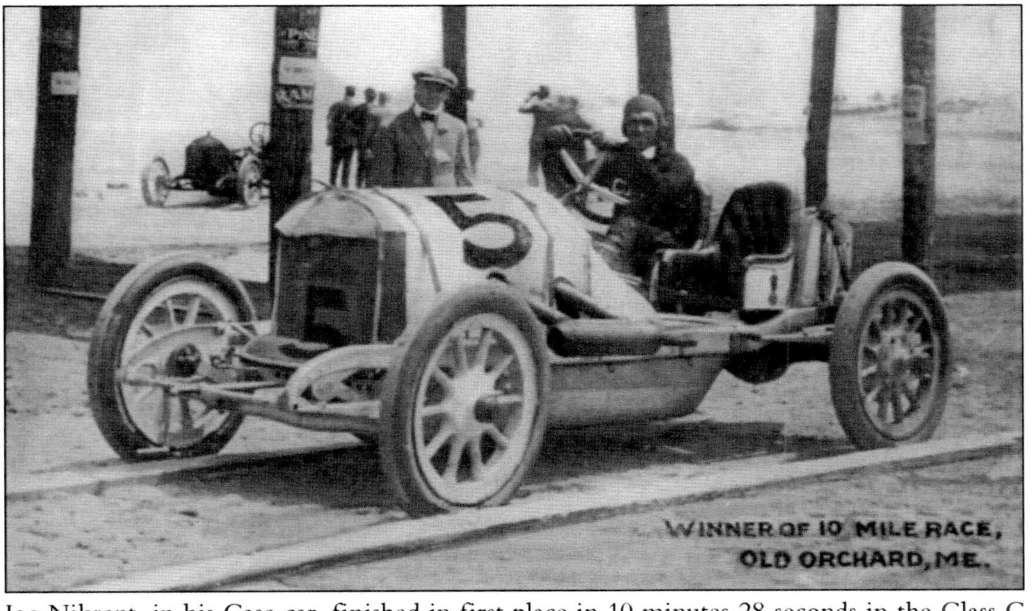


Joe Nikrent, in his Case car, finished in first place in 10 minutes 28 seconds in the Class C division (nonstock) 231-to-300-cubic-inch piston displacement class. His winning speed was slightly less than 60 miles per hour in this 10-mile race.

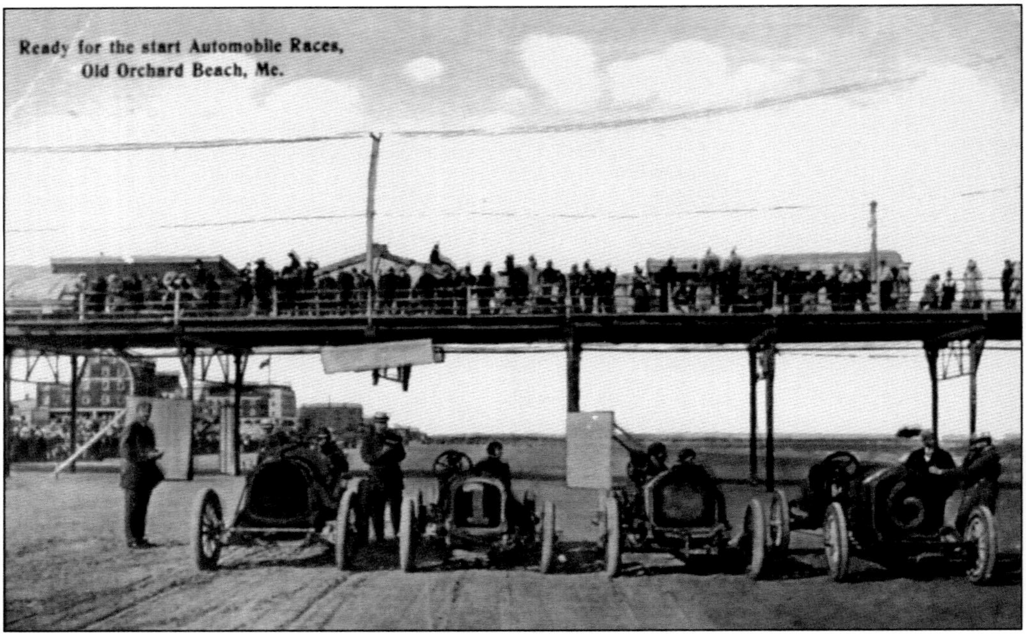


The above postcard shows a section of the steel pilings that were removed to allow race cars to pass under the pier with some margin of safety. Local honorary race referees were town clerk Fred Luce; Judge Percy N. H. Lombard; and well-known local mechanic Harry E. McGrath.

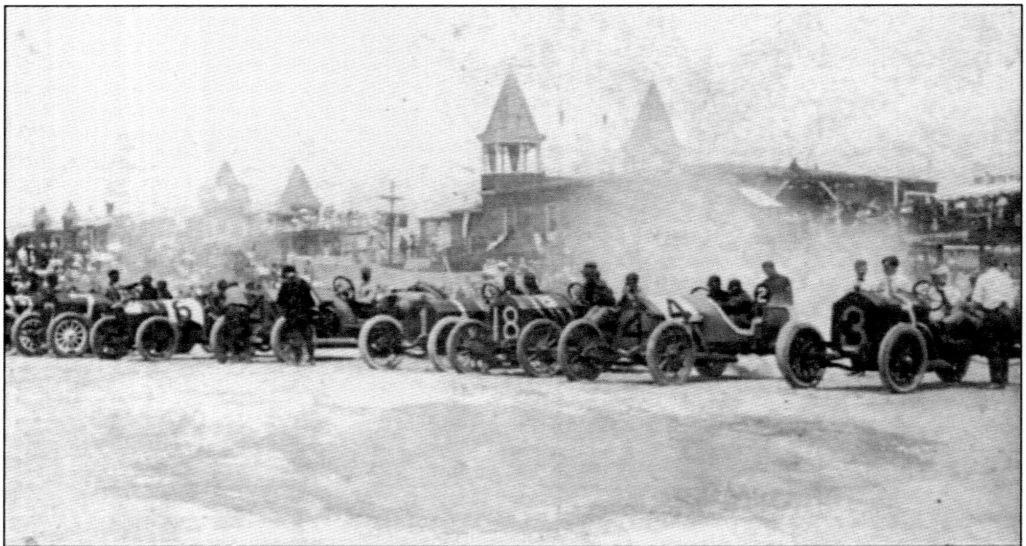

BEGINNING OF THE 100 MILE RACE, OLD ORCHARD, MAINE, JULY 6, 1912

The *Biddeford Daily Journal* of July 3, 1912, stated, "All drivers and mechanics have been instructed to appear, at the town hall this evening at 8 o'clock for their instructions. The main gate to the beach will be opened at 8 o'clock a.m. and a general admission of 50 cents will be charged."

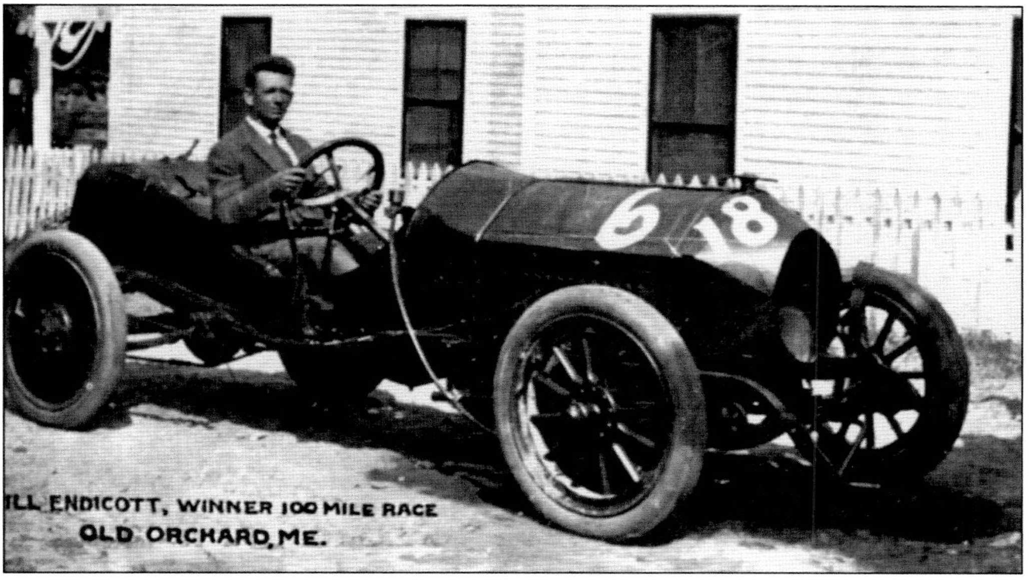


The *Biddeford Daily Journal* dated Tuesday evening, May 3, 1904, stated that a 15-mile race would be held, for the first time, at Old Orchard Beach. This race never materialized. The above postcard shows Bill Endicott, No. 18, winner of the 100-mile race in 1912.

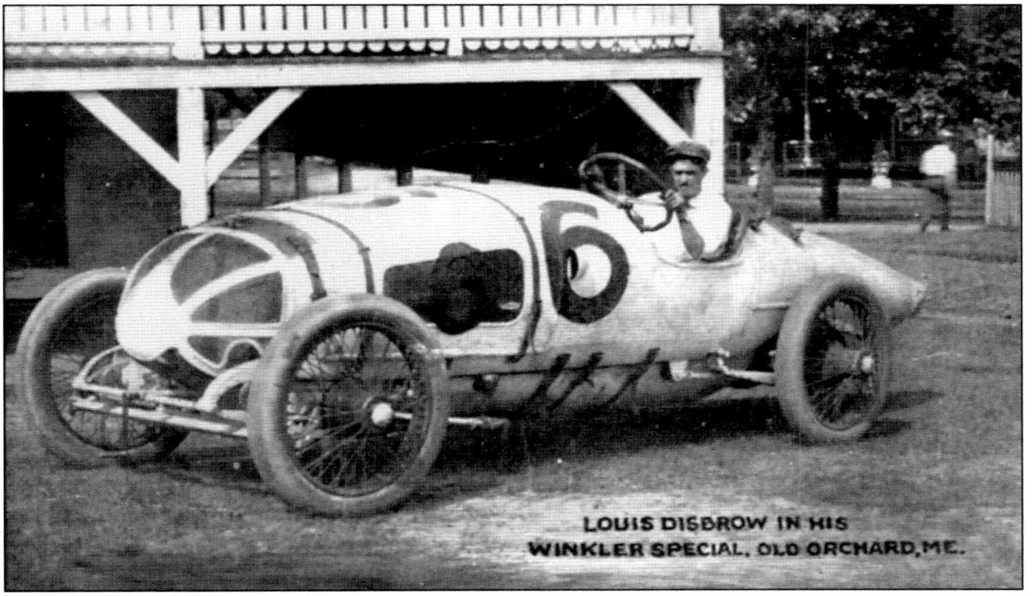


The *Biddeford Daily Journal* of Friday, July 12, 1912, stated, "Disbrow makes Beach Mile record in 35.1 seconds." The previous best time was 39 seconds in 1911. Louis Disbrow came in on the course in his great Jay Eye Eee, a torpedo-shaped affair that attracted great attention for its shape and business-like appearance.

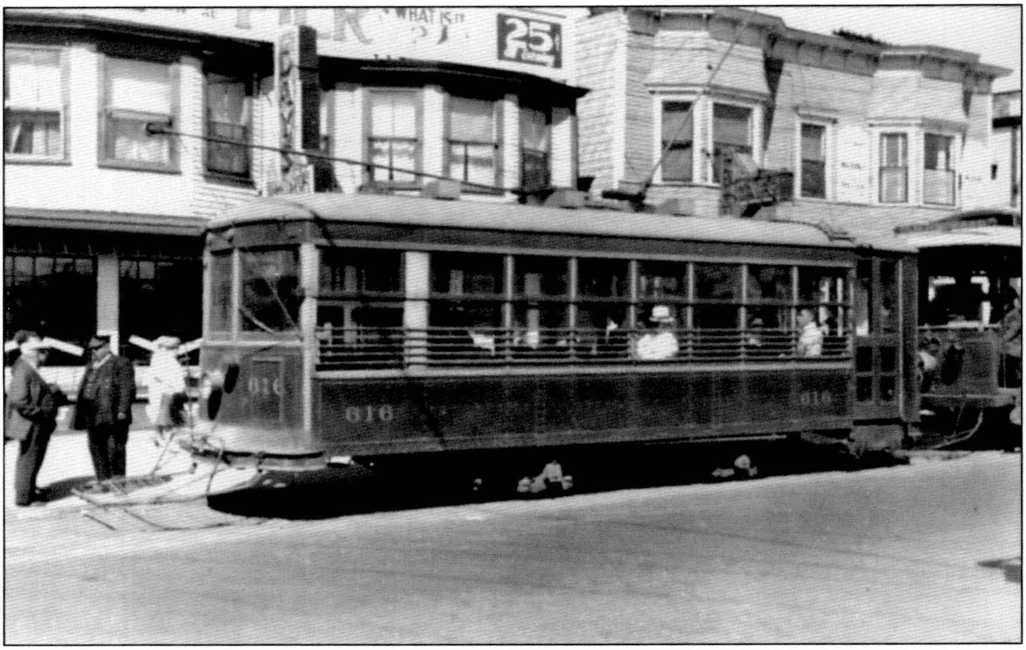

Seen here is Biddeford and Saco Railroad car No. 616 at the end of the line. George Beaudette is seen talking with motorman George Perkins while awaiting passengers on Old Orchard Street. This photograph was taken in 1939.

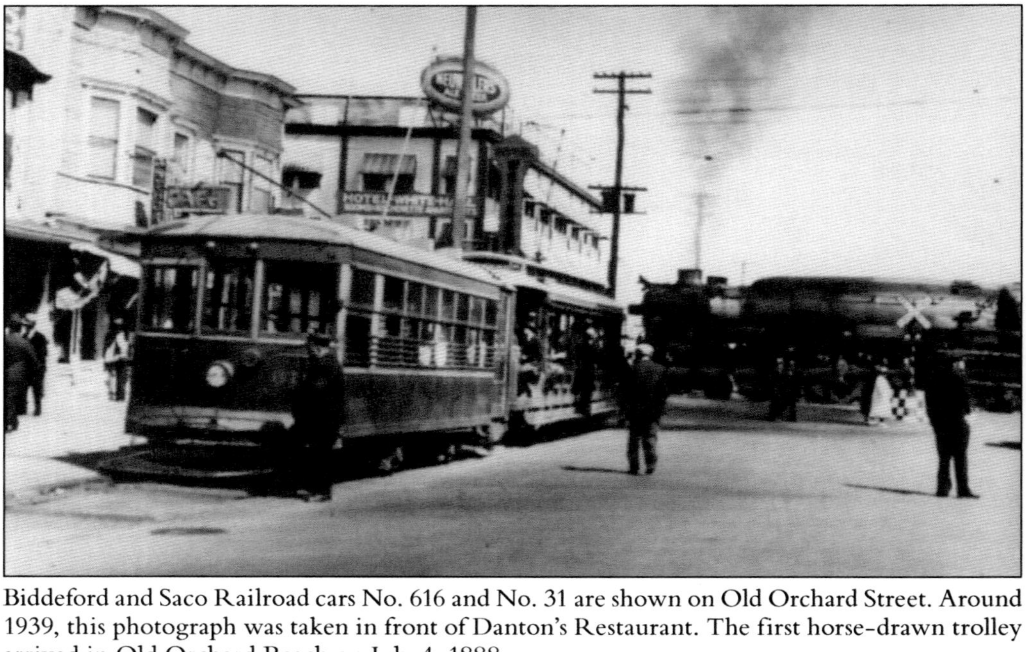

Biddeford and Saco Railroad cars No. 616 and No. 31 are shown on Old Orchard Street. Around 1939, this photograph was taken in front of Danton's Restaurant. The first horse-drawn trolley arrived in Old Orchard Beach on July 4, 1888.

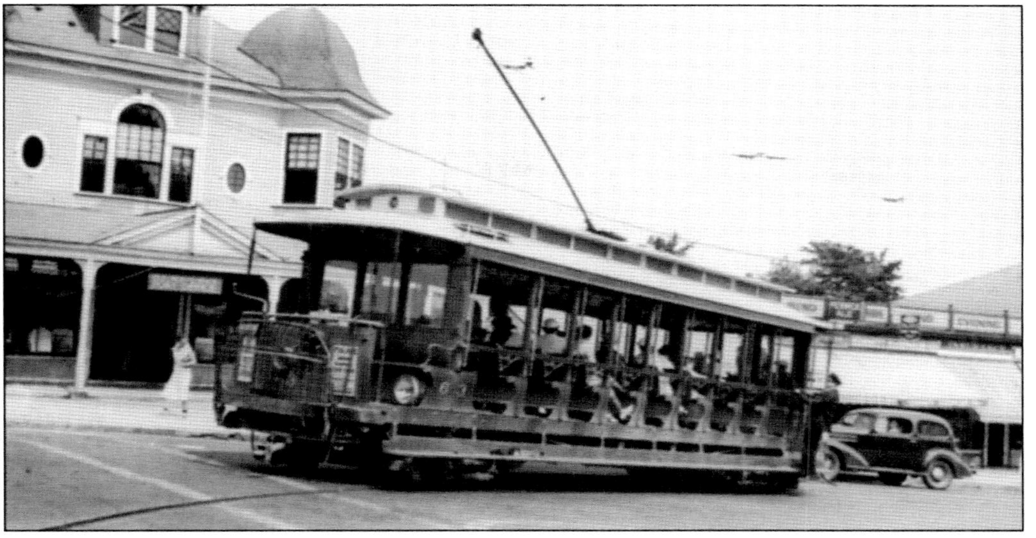

This image shows open car No. 63 turning onto Saco Avenue at the top of Old Orchard Street. The building on the left is the Old Orchard Beach Post Office. In 1892, Biddeford and Saco trolleys became electrified. The final run of the Biddeford and Saco Railroad was on July 5, 1939, as buses took over thereafter.

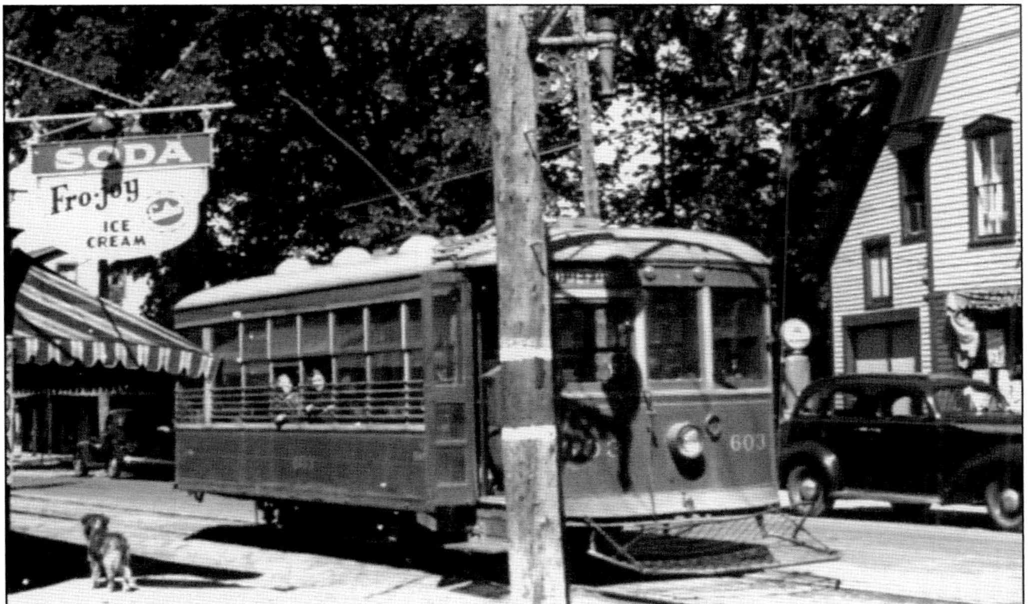


Seen here is closed car No. 603 stopped on Washington Avenue, perhaps for a soda. This photograph was taken in June 1939. The ice-cream/soda shop on the left is Emmons Drug Store. The store on the right is Kennett's Market, formerly Harper's Store and later Wortman's Hardware Store.

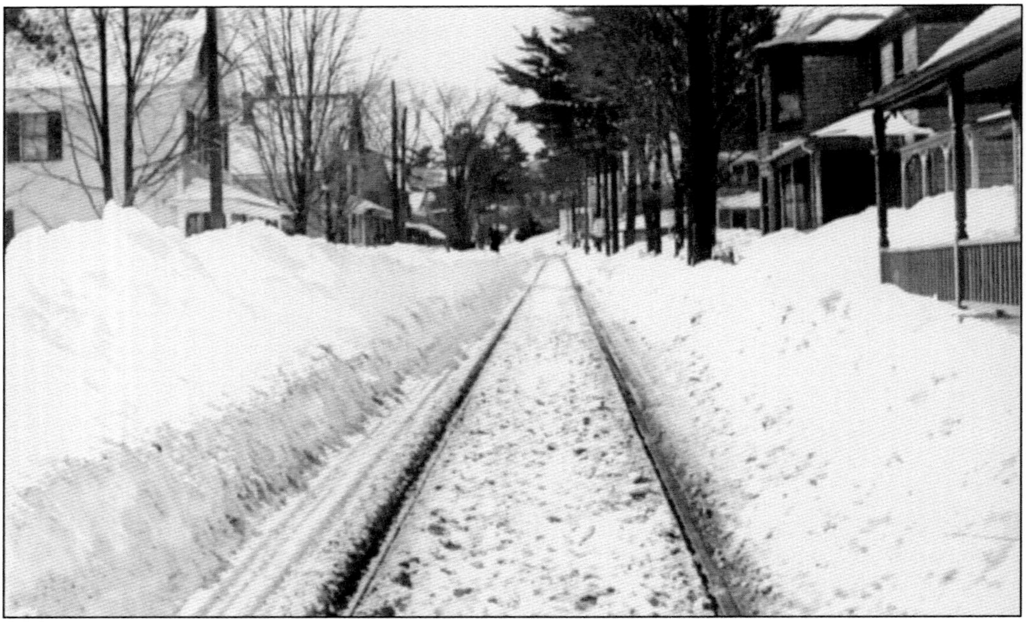

This rare real-photo postcard is looking up Washington Avenue, which looks much the same today, with the exception of trees. Thousands of people daily would take the trolley to Old Orchard Beach to attend the campground meetings.

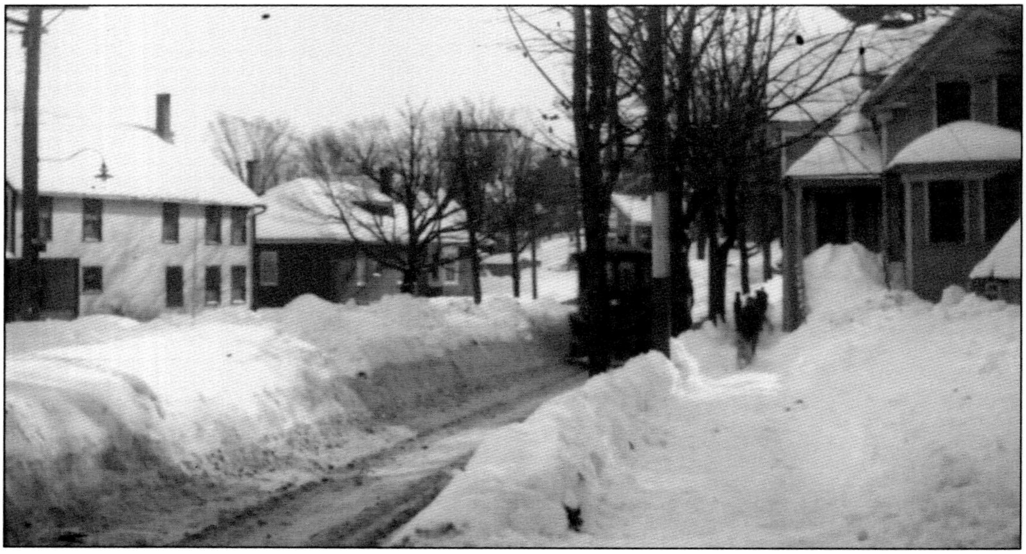

The Taunton four-wheel nose plow coming down Washington Avenue is captured in this *c.* 1925 photograph. The two houses on the left are still there today. The old Hawkins House on the right was razed, and a new building was constructed on the same site.

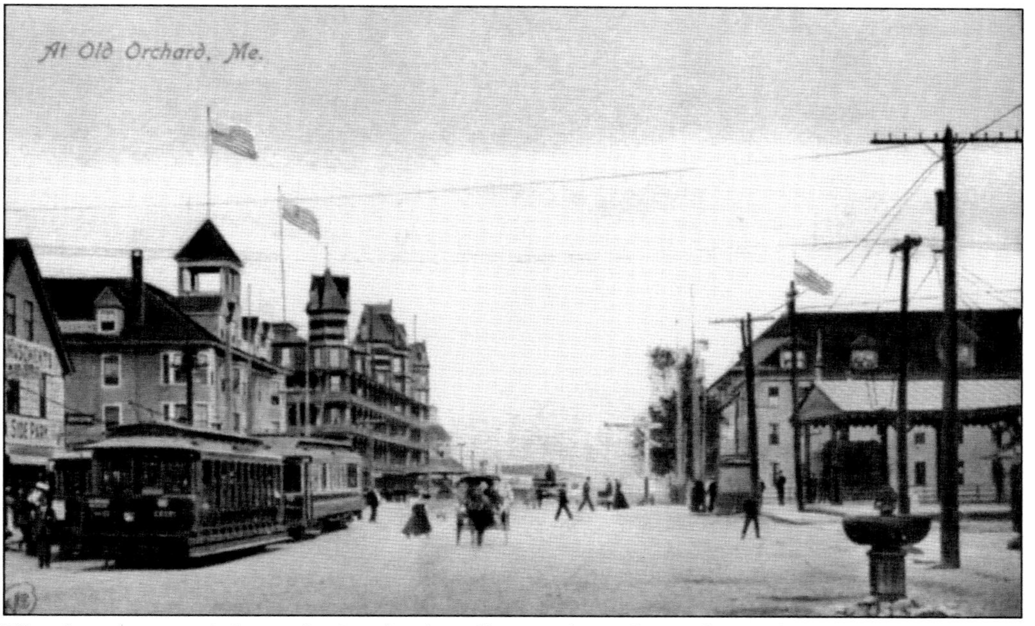


The above postcard shows the Portland Trolley on the right track and the Biddeford and Saco Railroad on the left. This early-20th-century postcard shows the old watering fountain at the intersection of First Street and Old Orchard Street. The days of the horse-drawn wagon were numbered.

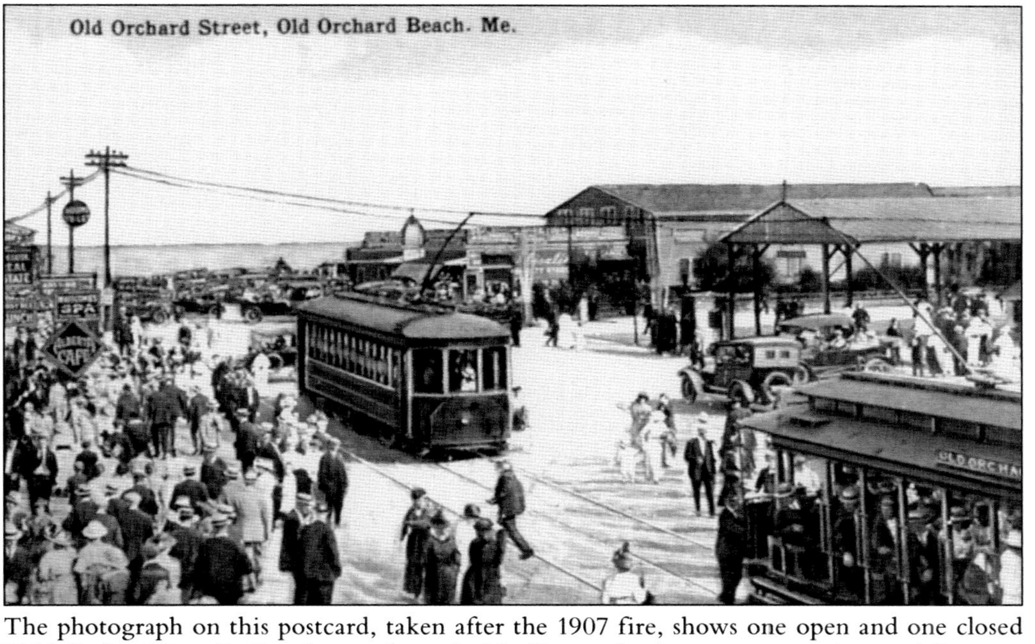


The photograph on this postcard, taken after the 1907 fire, shows one open and one closed Biddeford and Saco Railroad car at the end of the line, at the downtown stop. Automobiles were in and horses were out, compared to the above postcard.

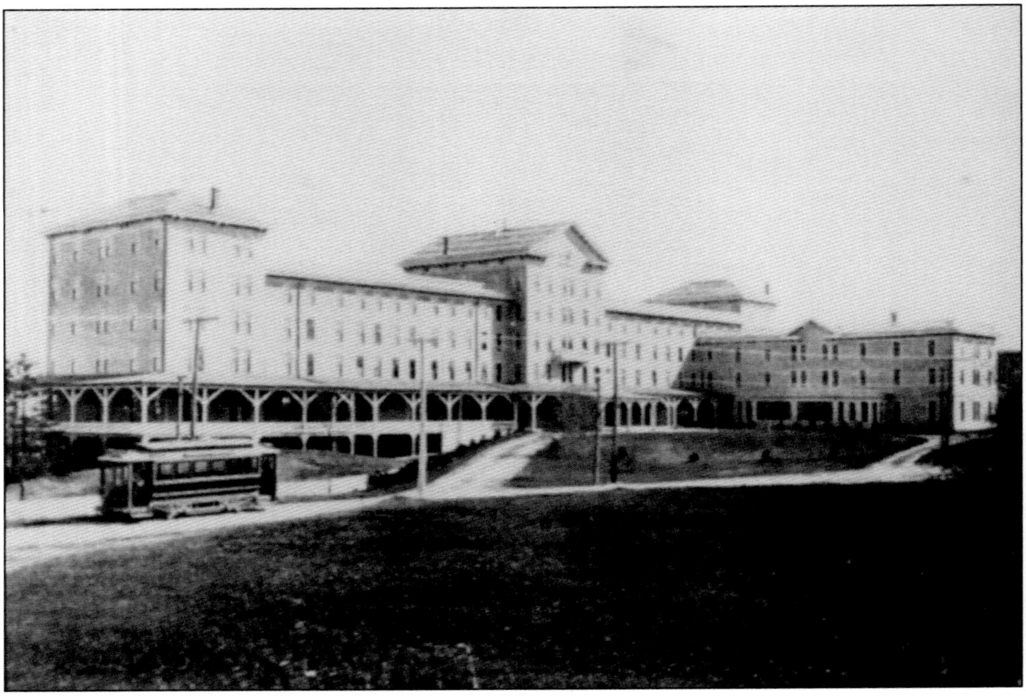

The view in this image is heading downtown on Saco Avenue. Many visitors at the famed Old Orchard House would travel to Saco and Biddeford using the trolley. The Old Orchard House in the foreground, built in 1876, was razed in 1943.

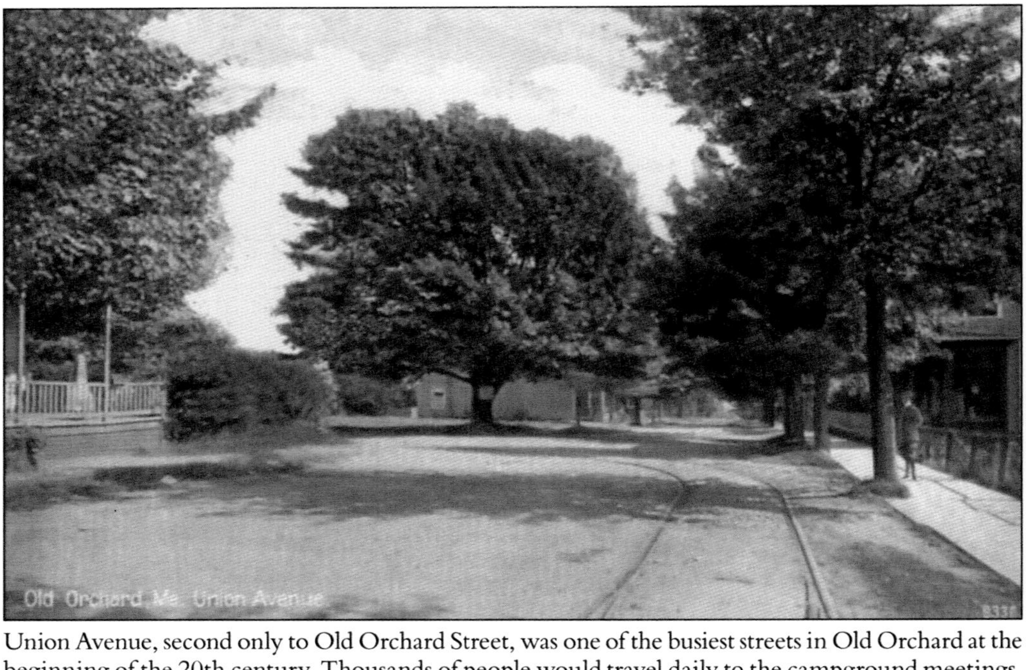


Union Avenue, second only to Old Orchard Street, was one of the busiest streets in Old Orchard at the beginning of the 20th century. Thousands of people would travel daily to the campground meetings. So many in fact there was even a turnout at the Tabernacle to load and offload passengers.

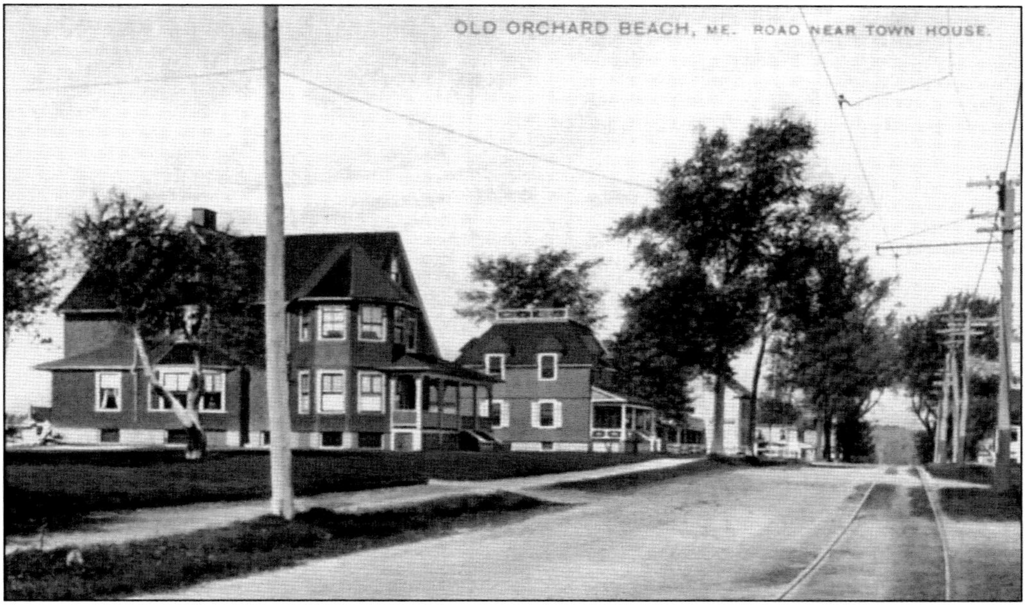


Seen here is a view looking out Portland Avenue around 1910. The Portland Railroad Company sent a letter dated February 15, 1902, to the board of selectman of the Town of Old Orchard for permission to construct a trolley line into Old Orchard. This line lasted 29 years, from 1903 to April 23, 1932. It met the Saco and Biddeford Railroad line at the top of Old Orchard Street and used the same tracks to the end of the line, where each had its own turnout.

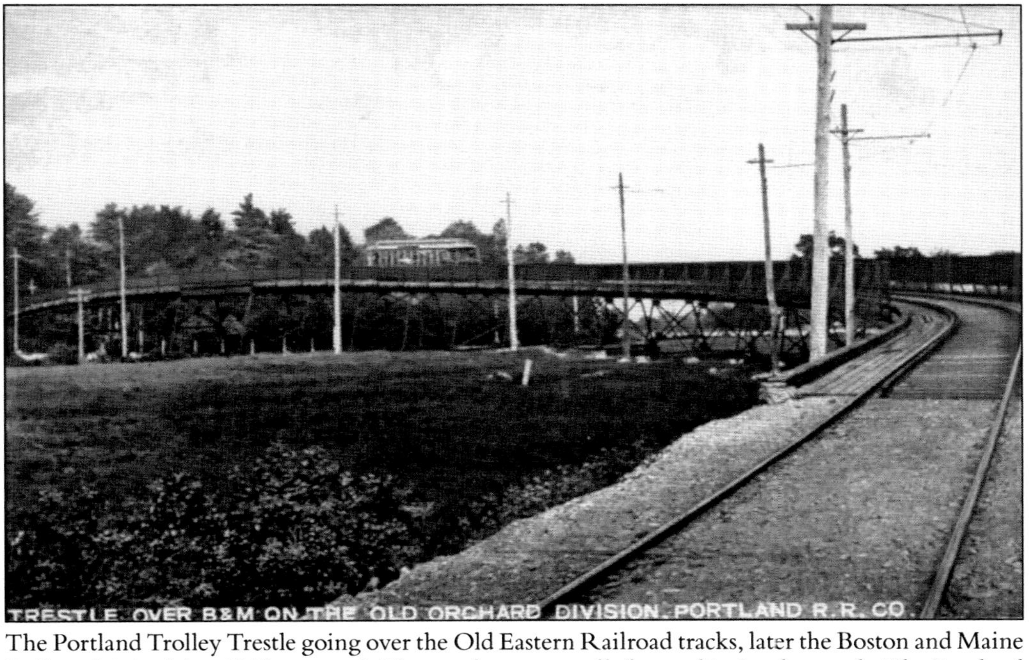


The Portland Trolley Trestle going over the Old Eastern Railroad tracks, later the Boston and Maine Railroad, is in this *c.* 1910 postcard. The trestle was actually located in Scarborough. The Portland Railroad Company ceased operations to Old Orchard Beach in 1932, and shortly thereafter, the S-shaped steel viaduct over the Boston and Maine Railroad line was dismantled.

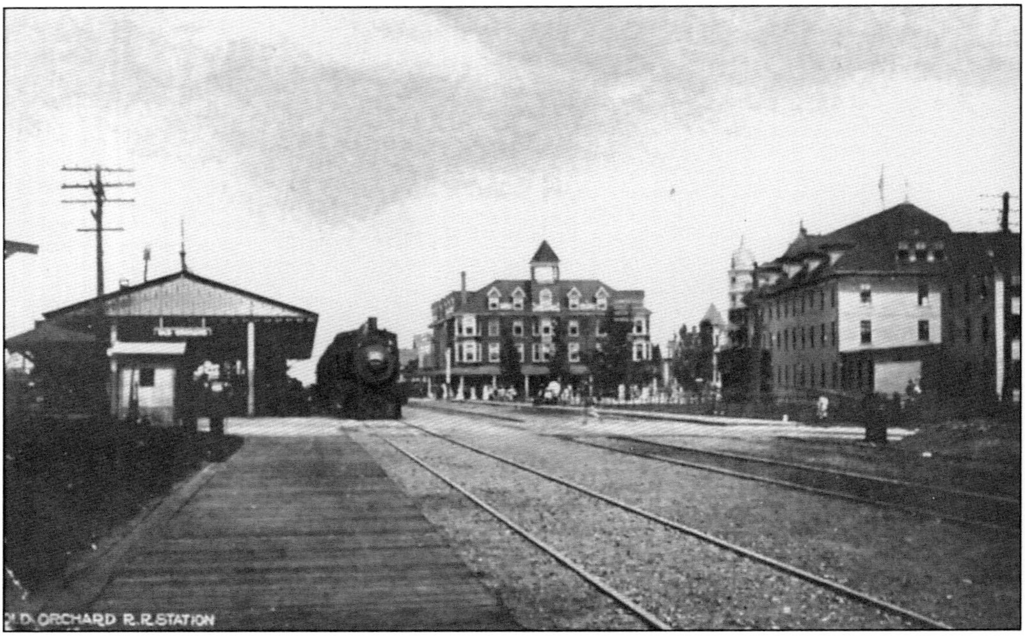


The above postcard shows three tracks. Two are for the Boston and Maine Railroad, northbound and southbound. The track on the right is for the Dummy line. Three prominent hotels stand out in this image taken around 1903: the Alberta; the Velvet, with its left tower showing; and the Seashore House, on the right. The crossing-gate house is seen on the left at the Staples Street crossing.

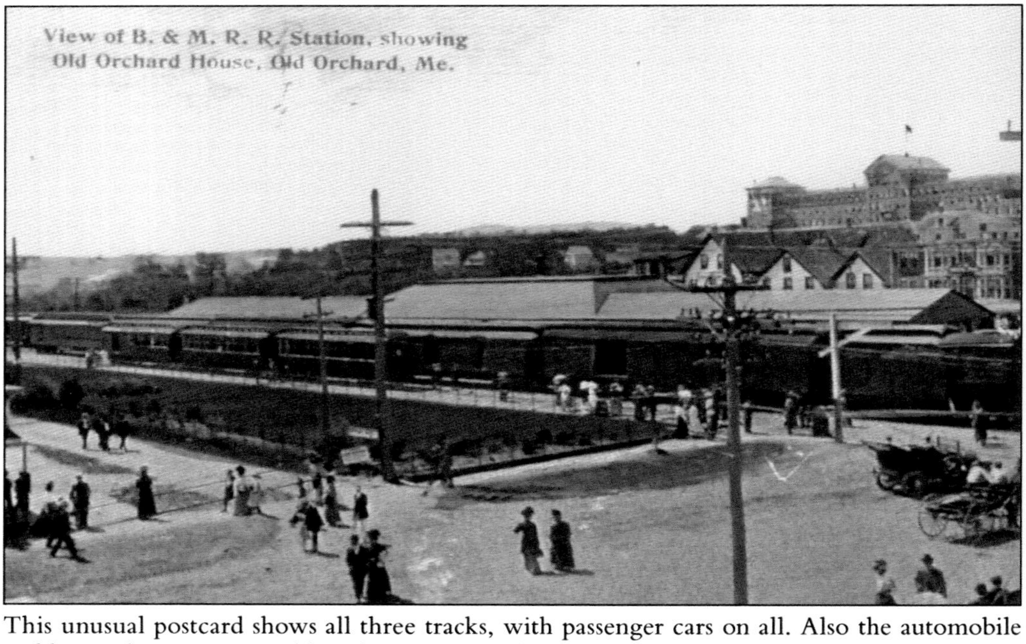


This unusual postcard shows all three tracks, with passenger cars on all. Also the automobile and horse-drawn wagon add to the era. Formerly a small graveyard, the fenced-in area on the left was a park built by Boston and Maine Railroad in 1888.

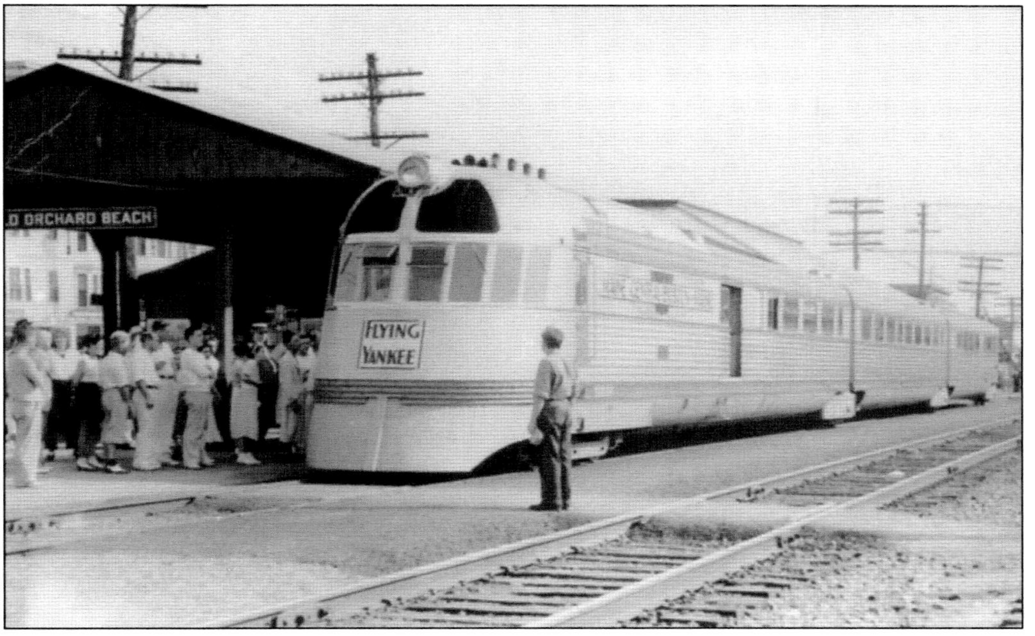


Seen here is the fabulous *Flying Yankee*, stopping at Old Orchard Beach. In 1935, the Boston and Maine Railroad and the Maine Central Railroad, two former rivals, joined forces and provided the first streamline service, on the Boston-to-Portland run. The three-car, diesel-electric passenger train ran until 1957.

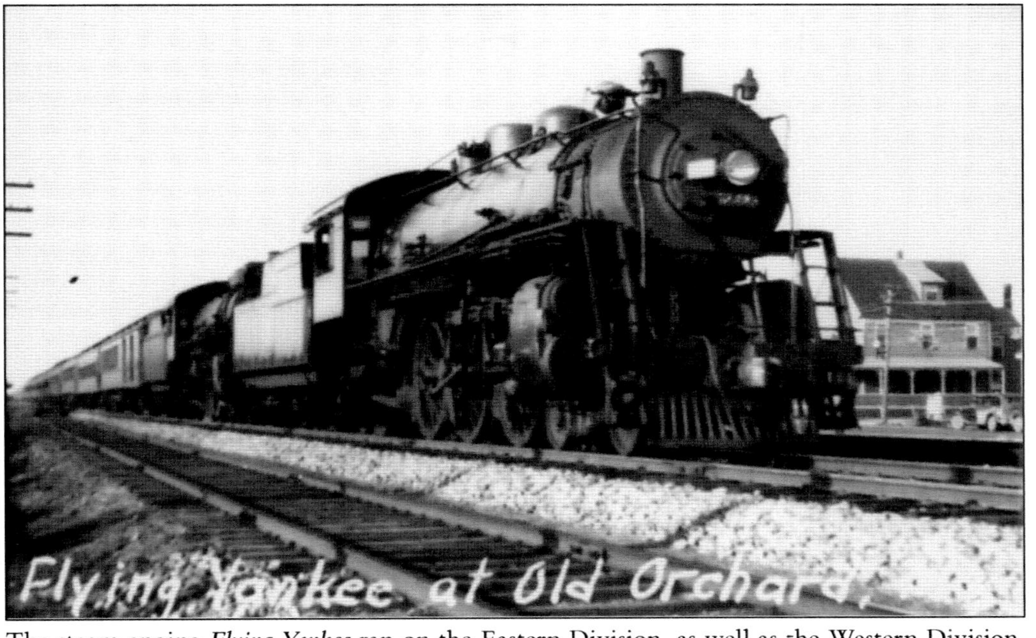


The steam engine *Flying Yankee* ran on the Eastern Division, as well as the Western Division, on its trip through Old Orchard Beach. It ran from April 26, 1926, until April 28, 1946. The last run of the old-style steam engines on the Western Division through Old Orchard Beach was on Sunday, August 22, 1956.

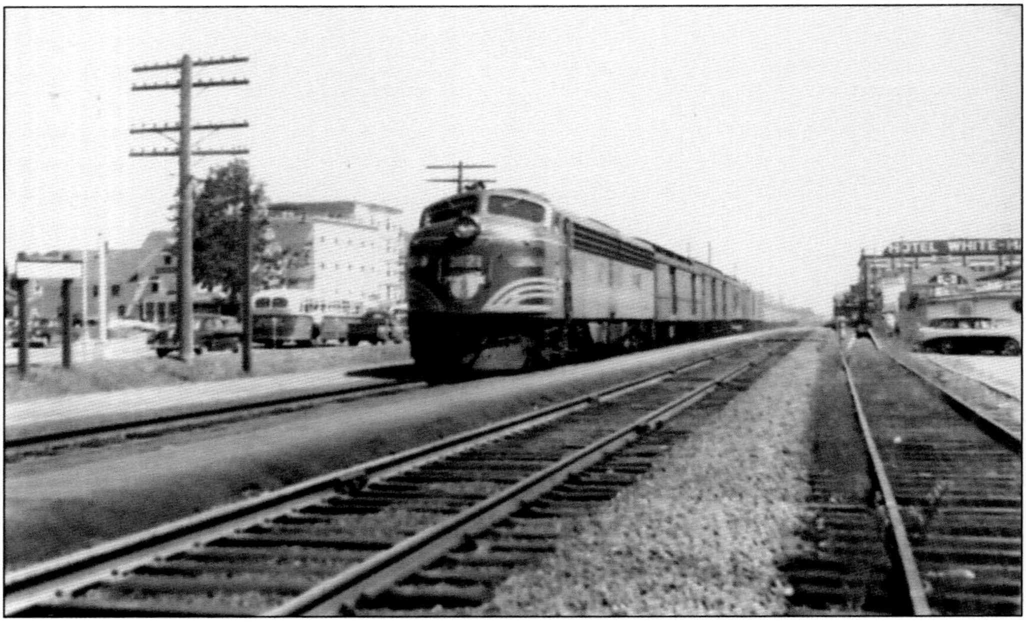

Boston and Maine diesel engine No. 384 is seen here, taking on passengers on July 26, 1956. As more and more people relied on the automobile for transportation, passenger train service to Old Orchard Beach was ceased in the summer of 1964.

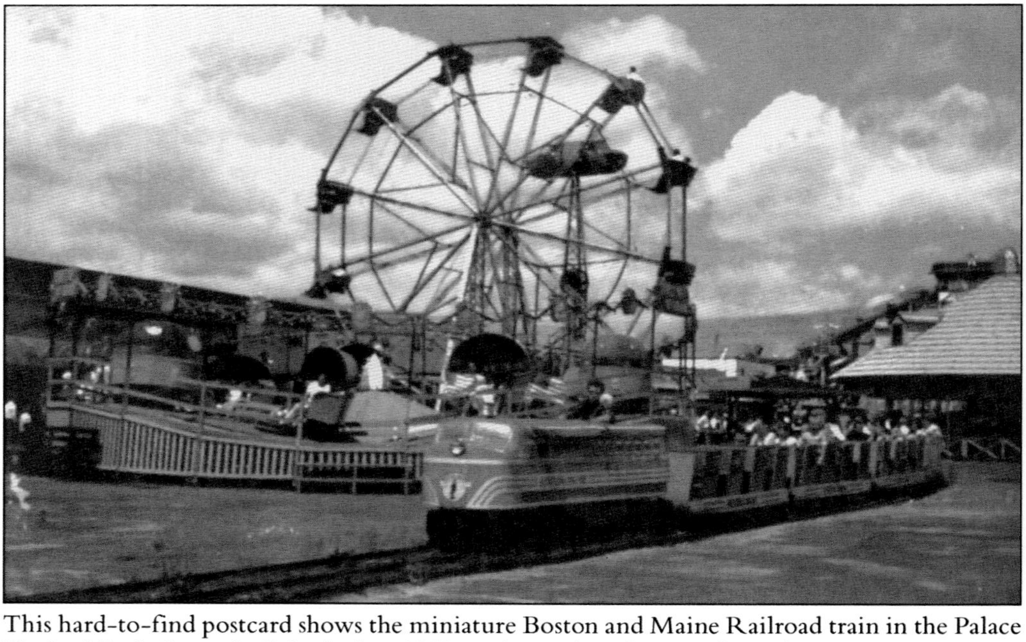

This hard-to-find postcard shows the miniature Boston and Maine Railroad train in the Palace Playland Park. It was built in the late 1950s and was phased out in the early 1960s. Many young and old enjoyed this ride around the beachfront park.

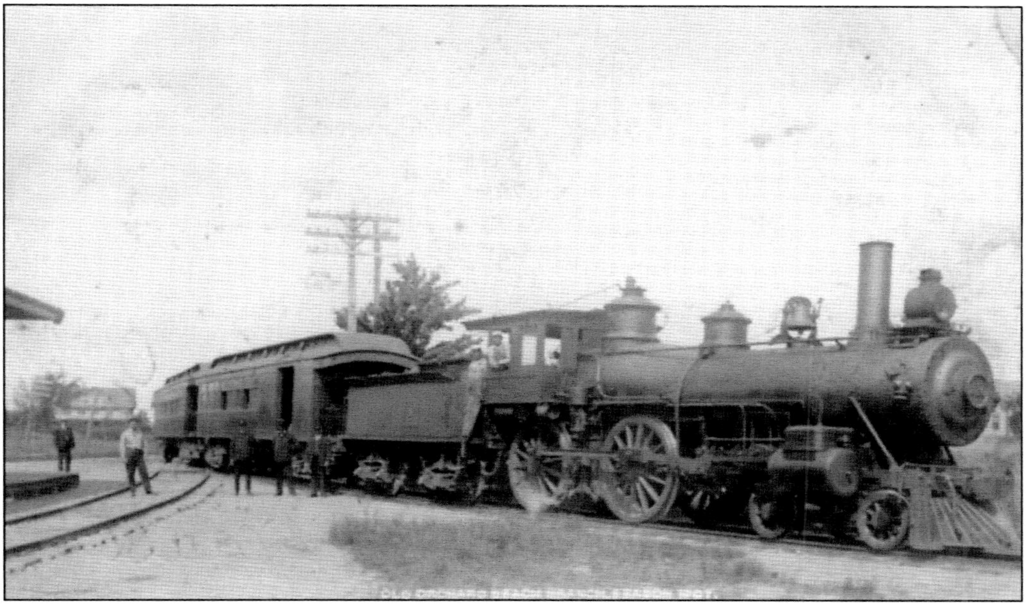

This rare real-photo postcard shows the Dummy train, branching off at Union Avenue, on its way to the Saco River. The roof of the Campground Station (1873–1924) can be seen on the left. The large building on the left is the Vermont House, formerly located at 16 Atlantic Avenue.

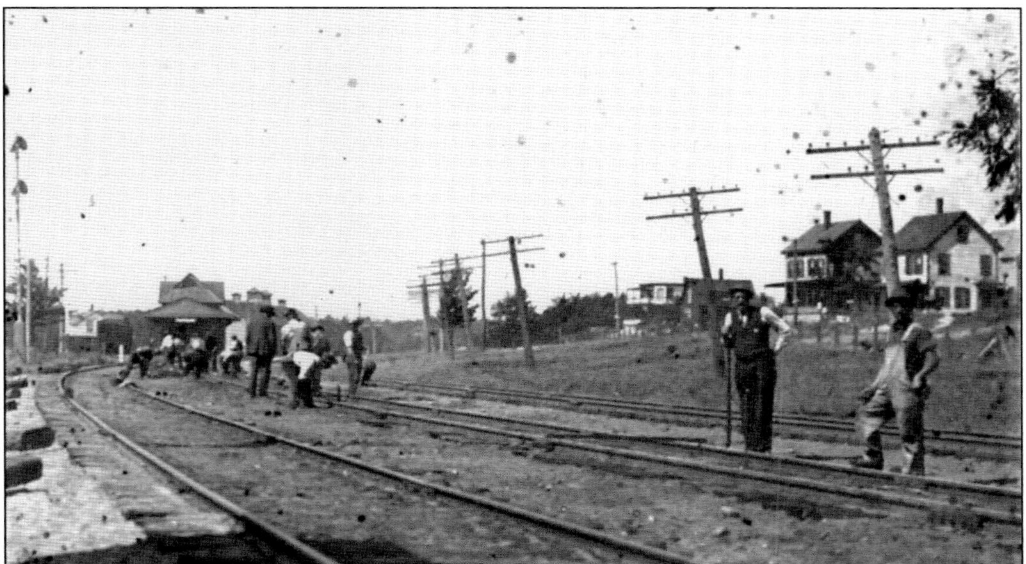

The section crew is working the rails along First Street in this *c.* 1910 real-photo postcard. The Campground Station (1873–1924) can be seen located between the tracks. It was later moved to the right, for safety reasons. The Dummy train barn can be seen to the left of the station. The two similar houses on the right, which were later connected and called Vacationland, remain standing today. (Nancy Barbano collection.)

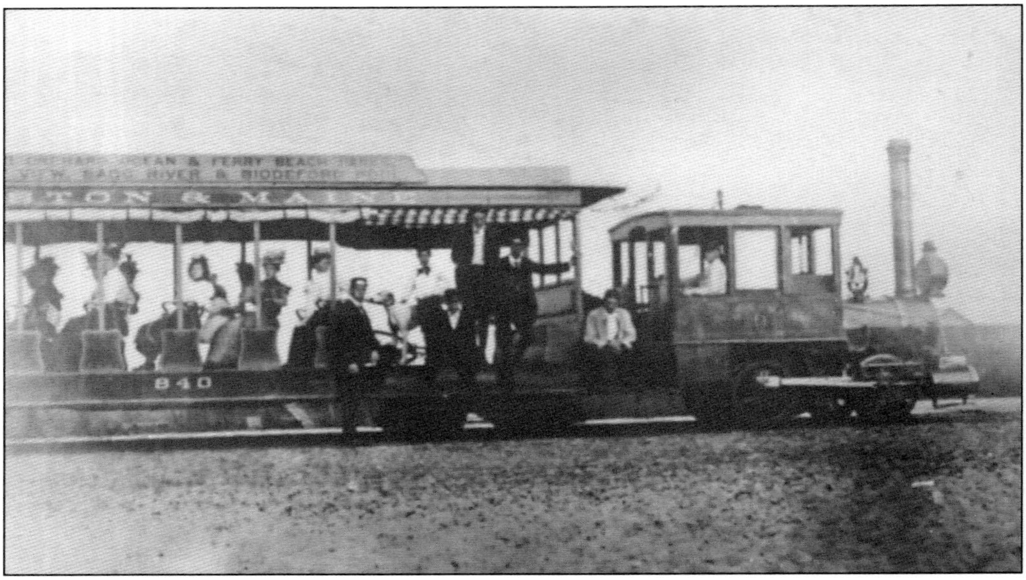


Photographer Albert Armstrong of Ocean Park took this real-photo postcard of the Old Orchard Beach branch railroad engine No. 9 heading toward Saco. The tall, skinny stack indicates that coal is being used for fuel.

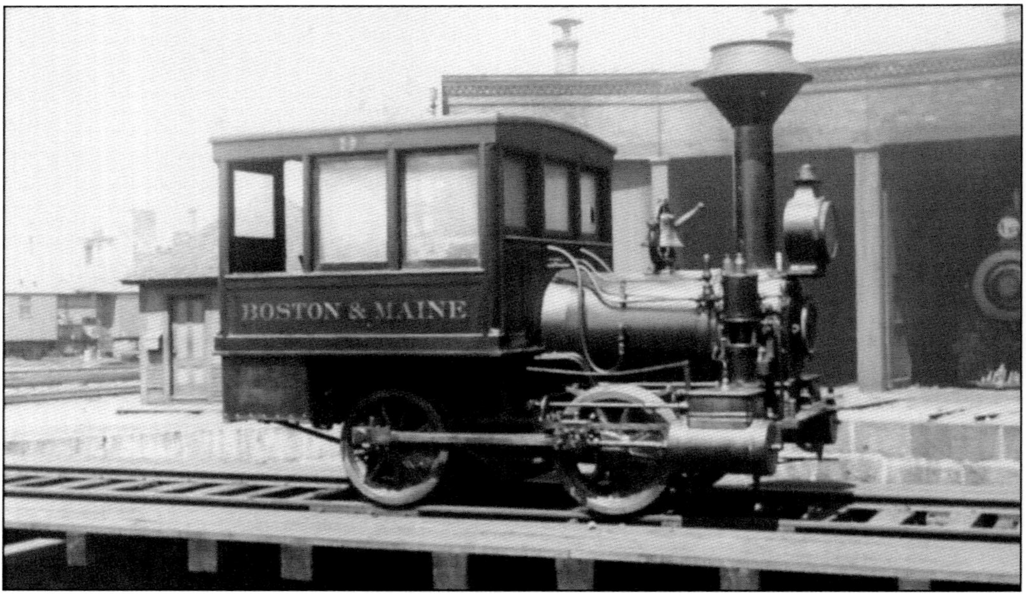


This is the official builder's photograph of engine No. 9, standing proud. This early photograph shows the fluted stack, indicating that wood was used for fuel. This engine was later converted to coal, as shown in the above postcard. This was the first engine used by the Dummy line.

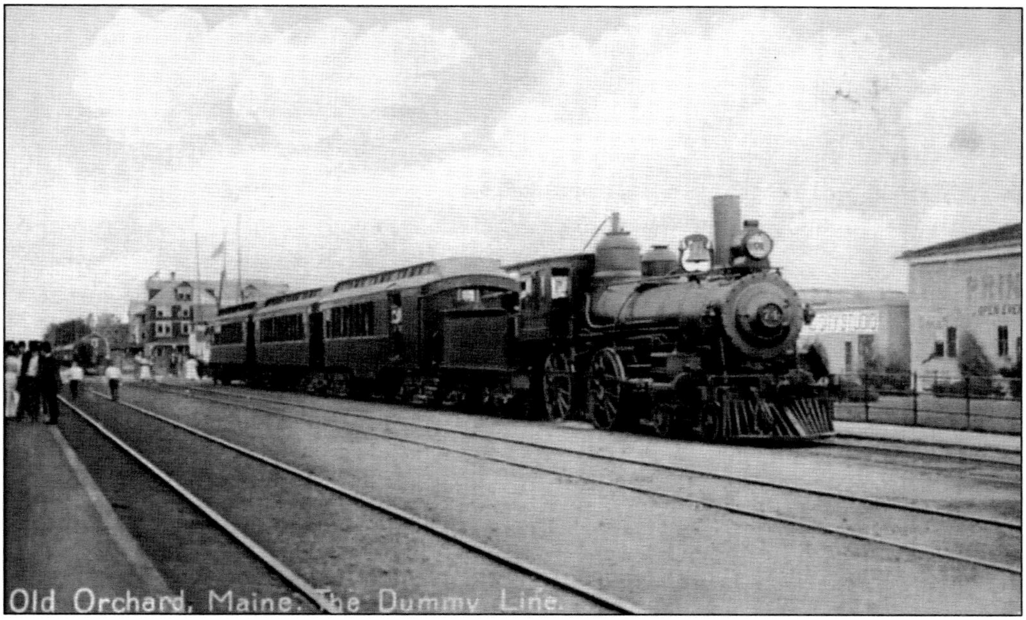


This view shows the Dummy train at the downtown station around 1904. When the original line opened in 1880, it ran from Union Avenue to the Saco River. Several years later, it was extended half a mile to the downtown station. The original Old Orchard Beach railroad was incorporated in 1876. In 1893, Boston and Maine Railroad bought the line. In 1924, the Old Orchard Beach Transportation Company bought the line and sold off the lots.

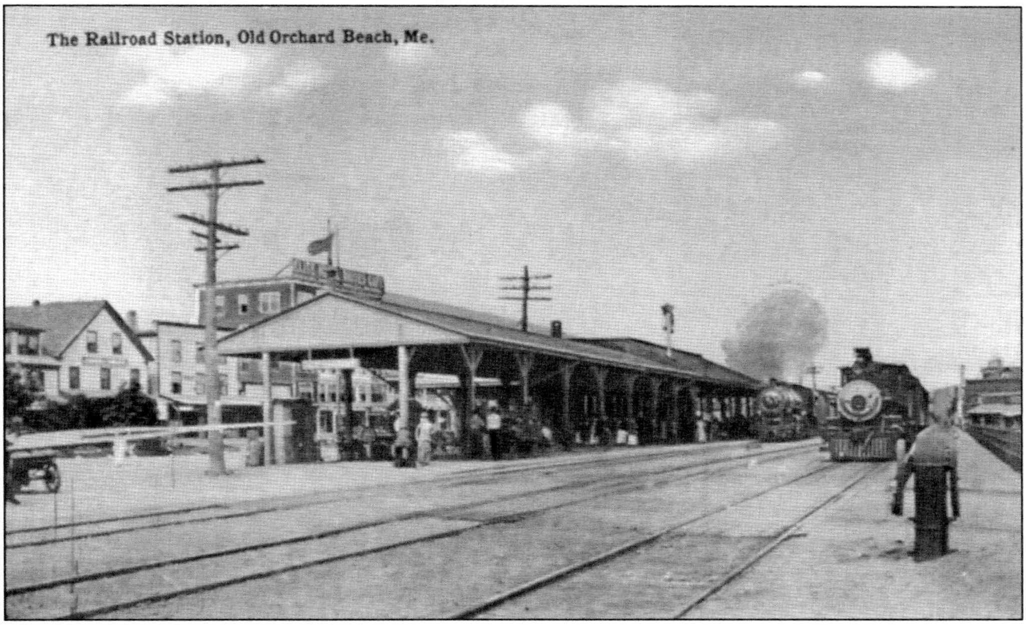


The Boston and Maine Railroad steam engine iron horse on the left is ready to roll on to Boston in this *c.* 1912 postcard. The Dummy train, on the right, is awaiting passengers before its seaside journey to Camp Ellis Station. Note the Staples Street crossing gates. Today that crossing is fenced off due to Amtrak safety concerns.

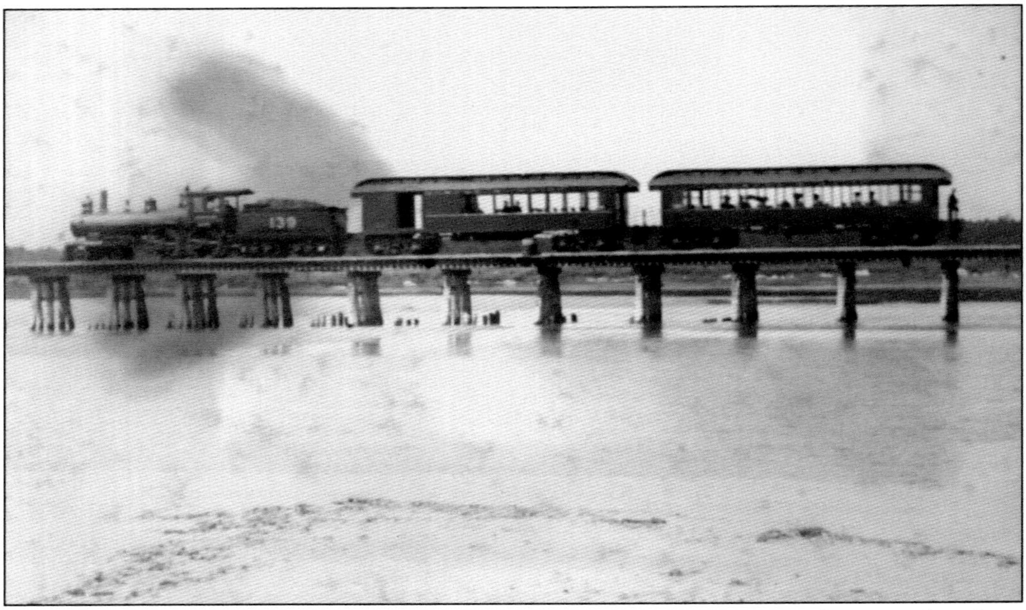

There are many photographs and postcards of the Dummy train, but very few are taken from the ocean side of the tracks. This view shows No. 139 crossing Goosefare Brook on its way to the Camp Ellis Station. The pilings can still be seen today, in the middle of Goosefare Brook.

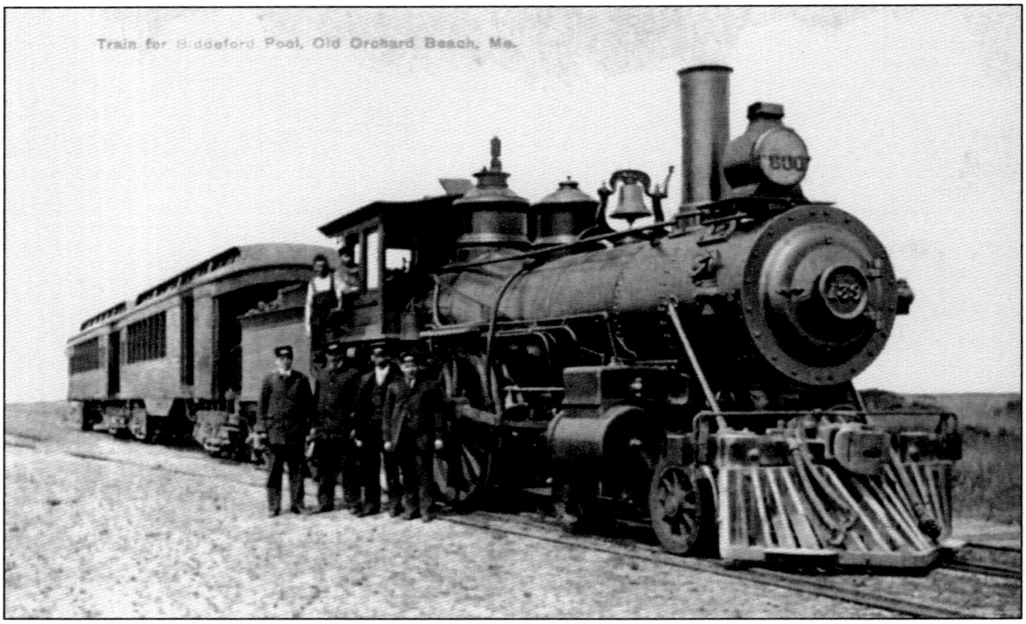


Engine No. 139 is stopped at Saco in this image. This seaside railroad opened in 1880 and was terminated in 1923, after 43 up-and-down years. The 3.24-mile branch made seven stops before it reached its terminus at the Camp Ellis pier in Saco. In 1924, the Old Orchard Transportation Company paid $10,000 to Boston and Maine Railroad for the rights.

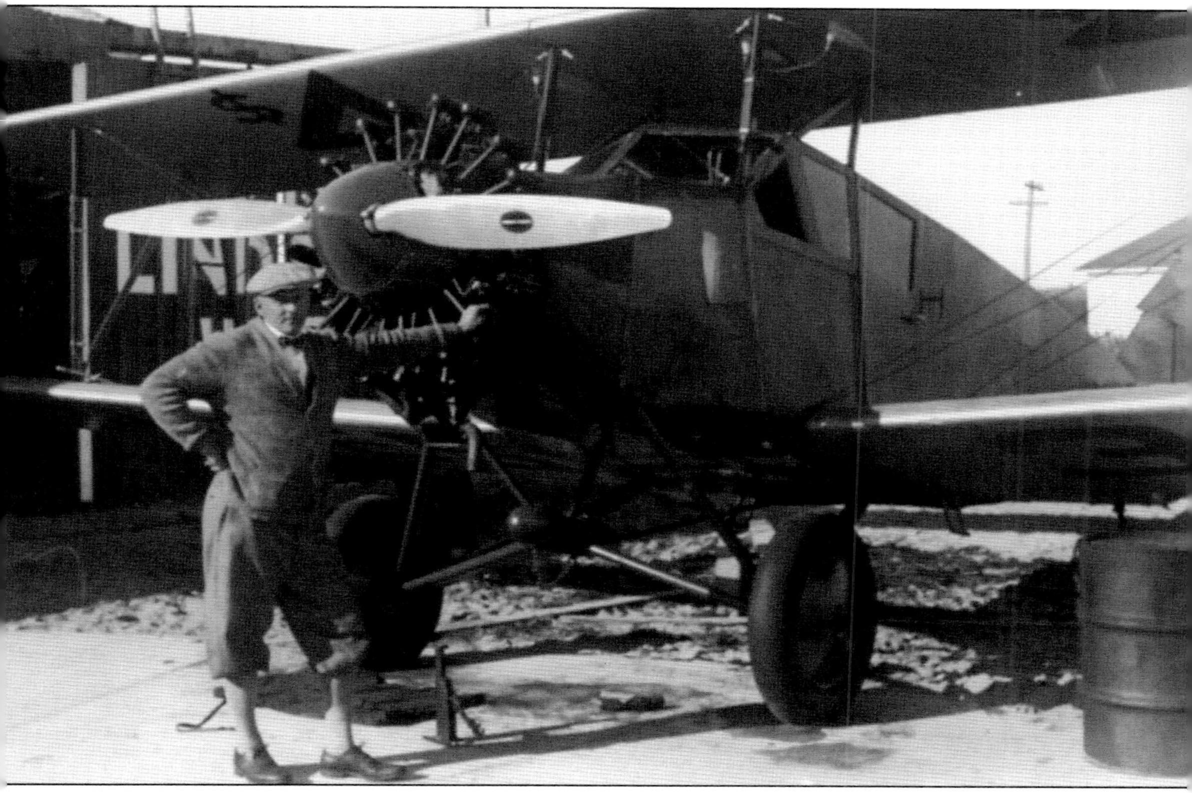

It is impossible to discuss early Maine aviation history without the name Harry Martin Jones coming to mind. Jones operated an airport in Old Orchard Beach from 1919 to 1933. Jones had many firsts in his long aviation history. In 1913, he flew over Boston and landed the first and last plane to ever land in Boston Common. He was the first experimental parcel post pilot, flying between Boston and New York. On June 14, 1919, he made the first airmail newspaper delivery in Maine, from Portland to Augusta. He left a field near the Portland Exposition building and dropped them off at a Rotary Club dinner, at Prout's Neck, in Scarborough. In his lifetime, he gave thousands of airplane rides. In fact, in 1939, he stated that he had taken up over 100,000 passengers, at $5 per ride. Jones did all right. He also gave private flying lessons. For $300, he would assure the skills needed to fly an airplane. He was so well liked in Old Orchard Beach that the board of trade made him the official and first aerial policeman in Maine. He was provided a policeman uniform, and a police badge was painted on the side of his plane. Also, a life buoy was attached to the fuselage. For $25, one could get a ride from Old Orchard Beach to Portland and back via Prouts Neck and Scarborough Beach. The round trip would take 25 minutes and take one up to 4,200 feet. In August 1971, Harry "Safety First" Jones made his last appearance in Old Orchard Beach, where he was honored by the Maine Aviation Historical Society and the Old Orchard Beach Historical Society. A memorial plaque was placed in Memorial Park, honoring Maine's earliest aviators. Jones died on April 15, 1973, in Tulsa. He was 82 years old.

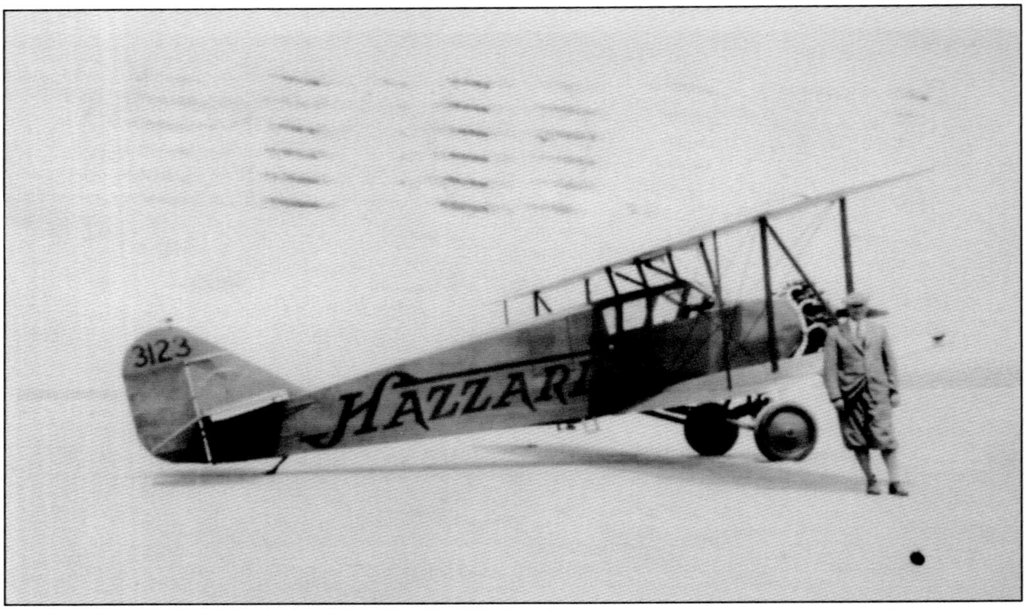


Here is Harry Jones, standing beside his biplane and promoting Hazzard shoes, fabricated by the Hazzard Shoe Company of Gardiner. Hazzard Shoe owner, Robert Hazzard, had his home near Jones's hangar on the beach. The hangar is long gone, but Hazzard's house still stands on East Grand Avenue. The house was sold to Fred Snow, of Snow's Cannery, then to Judge Nicholas Danton. It is now owned by his son, William Danton, and family.

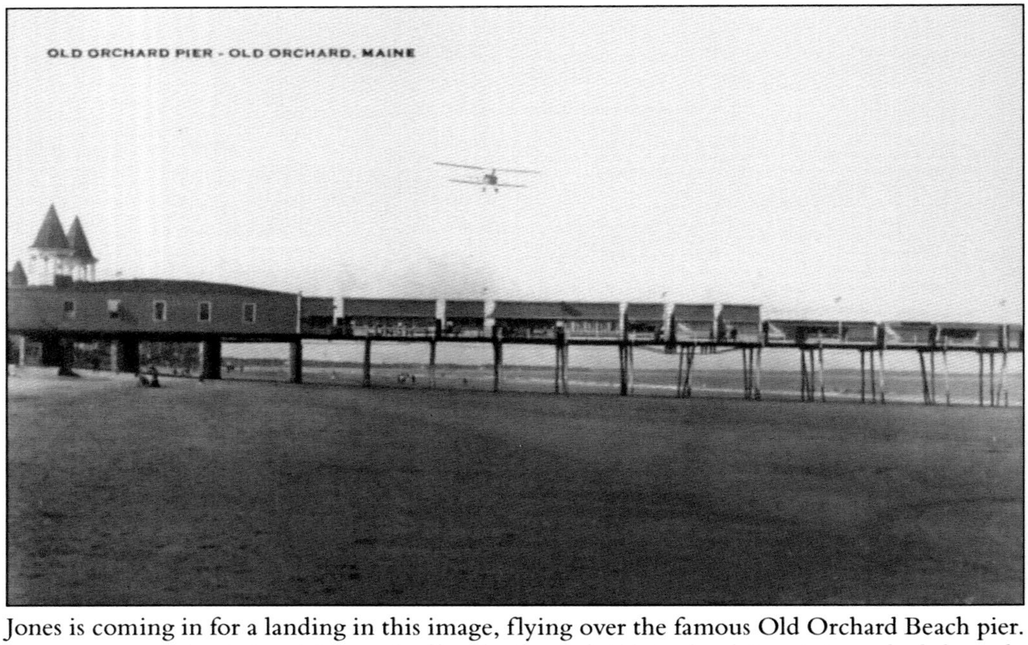


Jones is coming in for a landing in this image, flying over the famous Old Orchard Beach pier. Passengers were loaded and dropped off at the foot of Old Orchard Street. Jones had the only business in Old Orchard whose hours of operation were determined by the tides.

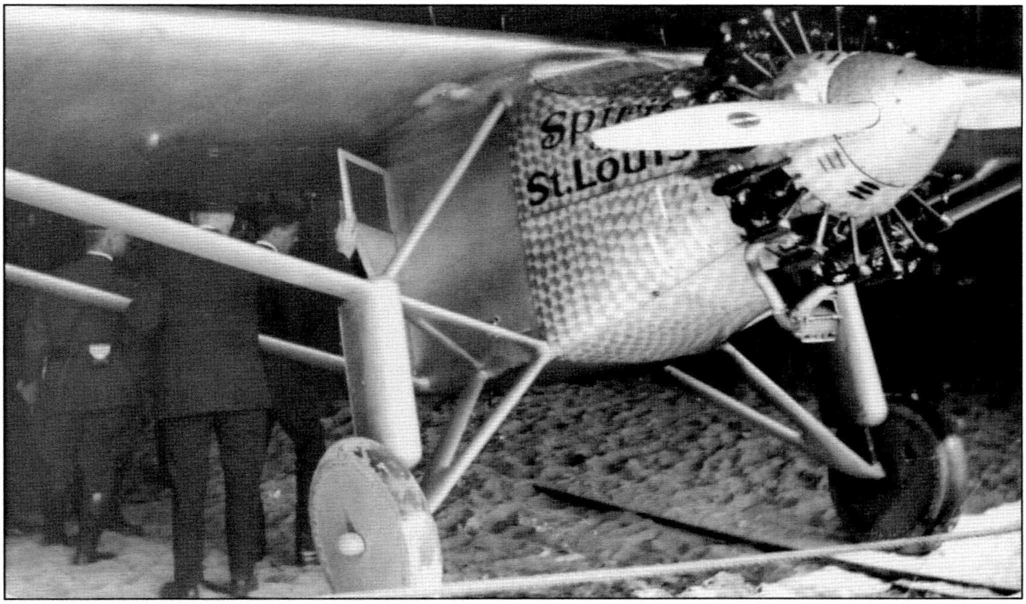

Probably the most historic aviation event in Old Orchard Beach history happened on July 24, 1927. Charles A. Lindbergh landed at Old Orchard Beach. Due to fog, his scheduled arrival at Scarborough airport was diverted to the sands of Old Orchard Beach. The first person to greet Lindbergh was the hangar mechanic Joe Snow of Scarborough. Joe said, "Greeting Lindy was the greatest surprise of my life."

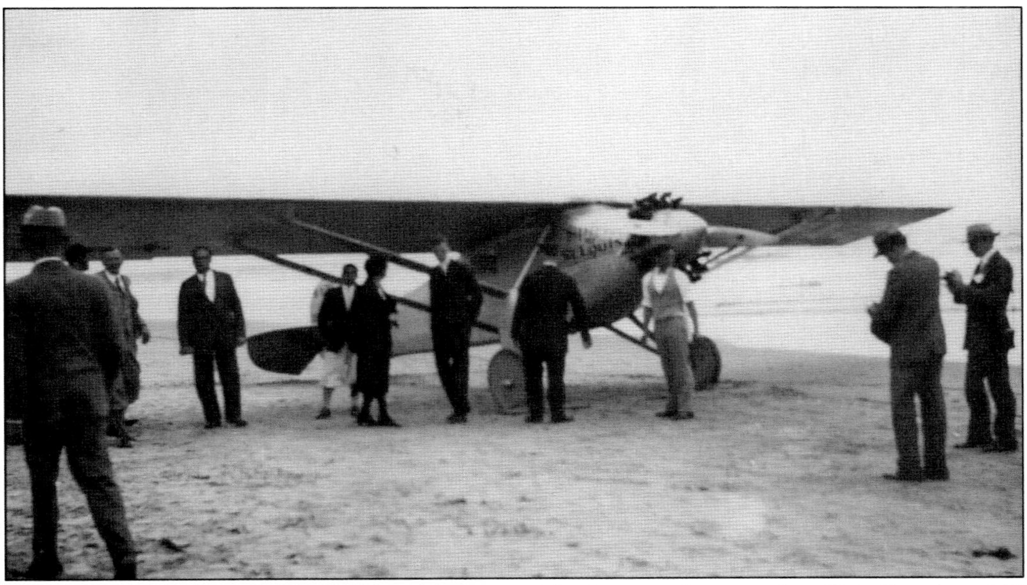

Local photographer Ethel M. Wight took most of the famous photographs of Lindbergh at Old Orchard Beach. After a brief stay, Lindbergh was rushed off to the waiting people and dignitaries in Portland. On July 19, 1977, 50 years later, the replica *Spirit of St. Louis* returned to the sands of Old Orchard. A special celebration of this historic event was held. Ann Morrow Lindbergh was invited to attend but gracefully declined. The letter she wrote to the town council is now in the Harmon Museum.

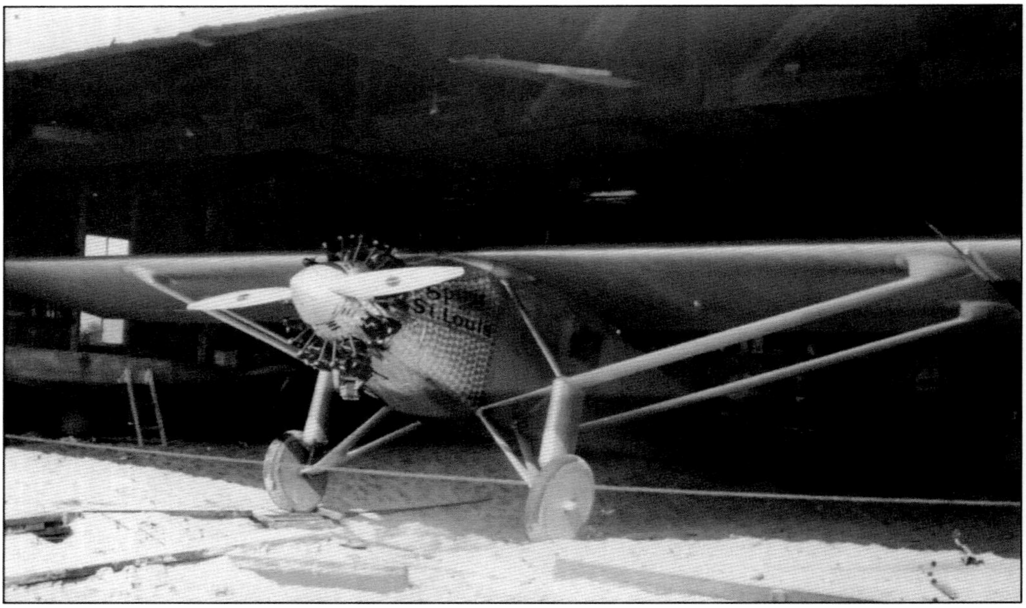

Seen here is the *Spirit of St. Louis* secured inside of Jones's hangar in Old Orchard Beach. There is much documented history about Lindbergh being fogged in and having to land on the beach. Little is written about his lead plane, however, which was piloted by Lt. Phil Love, being forced to land elsewhere. Alfred Kimball of Saco remembers seeing the escort plane at Arthur Landry's field in Dayton on that memorable day. His uncle Benjamin Goodwin was one of the trusted people left in charge to watch over the plane for the night. Lieutenant Love returned the next morning to continue on with Lindbergh's 48-state tour.

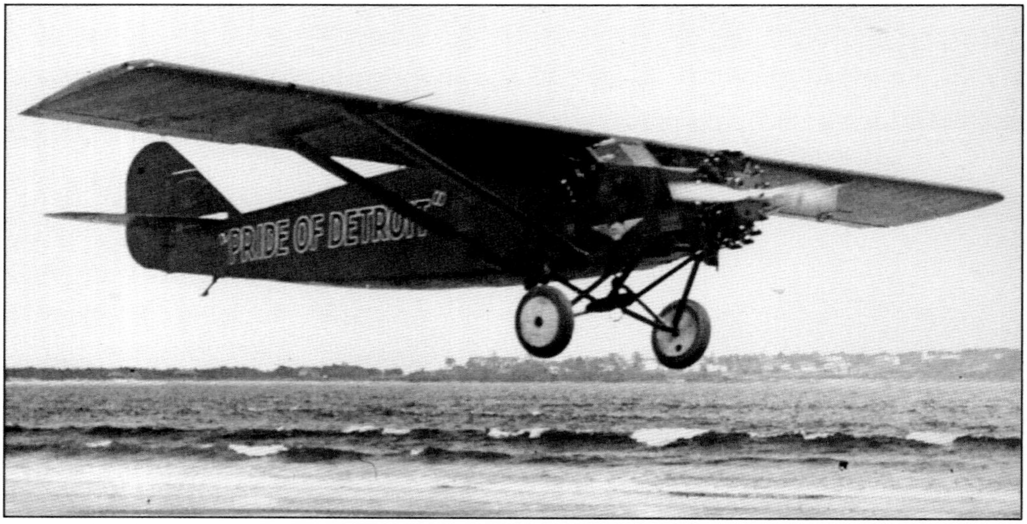

The *Pride of Detroit* was the first plane to attempt a transatlantic flight from Old Orchard Beach. Pilots William Stewart Brock (1887–1932) and Edward F. Schlee (1887–1969) left Old Orchard Beach on August 24, 1927, on their around-the-world tour. They landed in Newfoundland, then went on to England, and then aborted in Japan. The plane is now on display in the Ford Museum in Dearborn, Michigan.

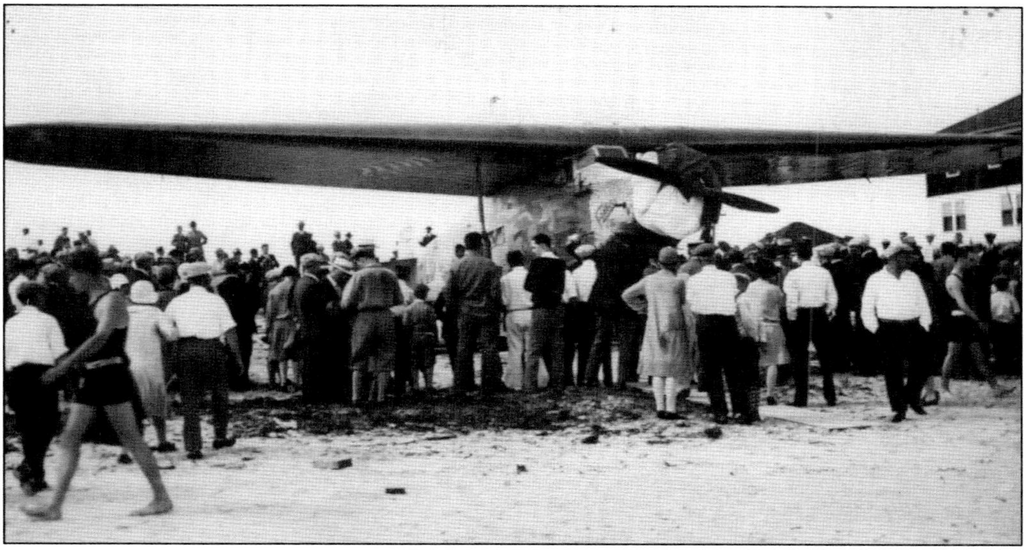

The second plane to attempt a transatlantic crossing from Old Orchard Beach was *Old Glory*. The giant Fokker monoplane departed at 1:21 p.m. on Tuesday, September 6, 1927. Onboard were pilot James D. Hill, copilot Lloyd Bertaud, and Phillip Payne, as a representative of William Randolph Hearst, grandfather of Patty Hearst, who sponsored the ill-fated flight. Part of their cargo was a message from Gov. Owen Brewster of Maine to Mussolini, several letters from three American cardinals to the pope, and a letter from Pres. Calvin Coolidge to the king of Italy. Several days later, portions of the plane were found off the coast of Newfoundland. The men were never recovered.

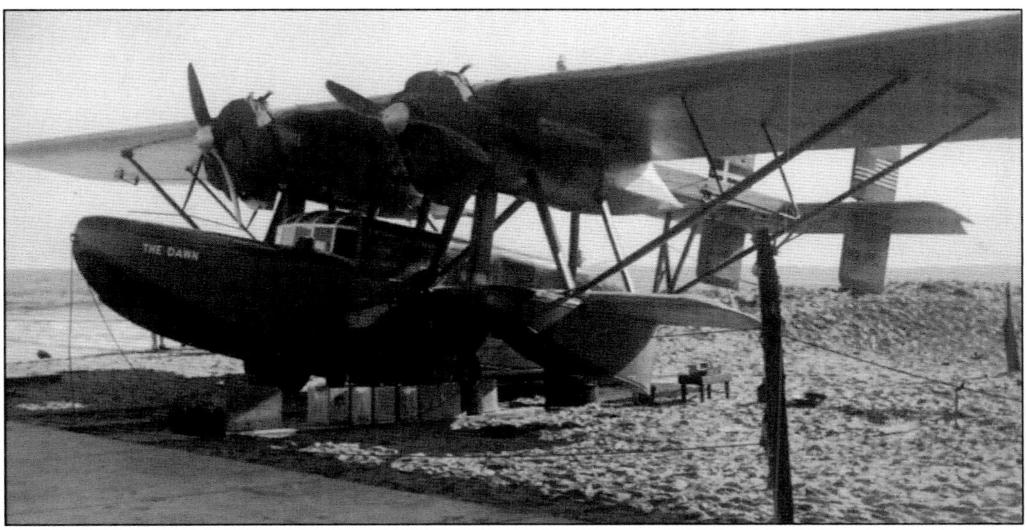


The third plane to attempt a transatlantic flight from Old Orchard Beach was the *Dawn*. Frances Wilson Grayson, niece of Pres. Woodrow Wilson, and two others were troubled by weather and mechanical problems. On October 23, 1927, they attempted their final try but turned back after 500 miles due to an engine problem. On October 30, the *Dawn* left Old Orchard Beach for Curtis Field, New York. On Christmas Eve, the multimillionaire realtor and three others finally departed Roosevelt Field, New York, for Copenhagen, Denmark. They were never seen again.

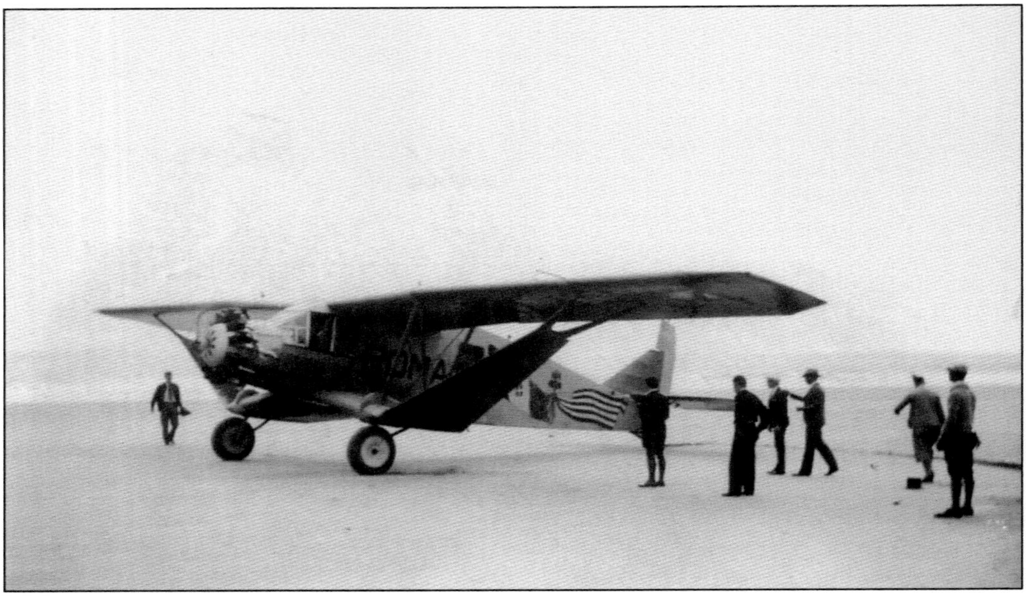

The fourth plane to attempt the transatlantic flight from Old Orchard Beach was the *Roma*. After the takeoff was delayed by wind the day before, the *Roma* took off on Wednesday, September 19, 1928. Developing engine problems, the plane returned to Old Orchard Beach. Eventually the flight, after much delay, was called off and never materialized again.

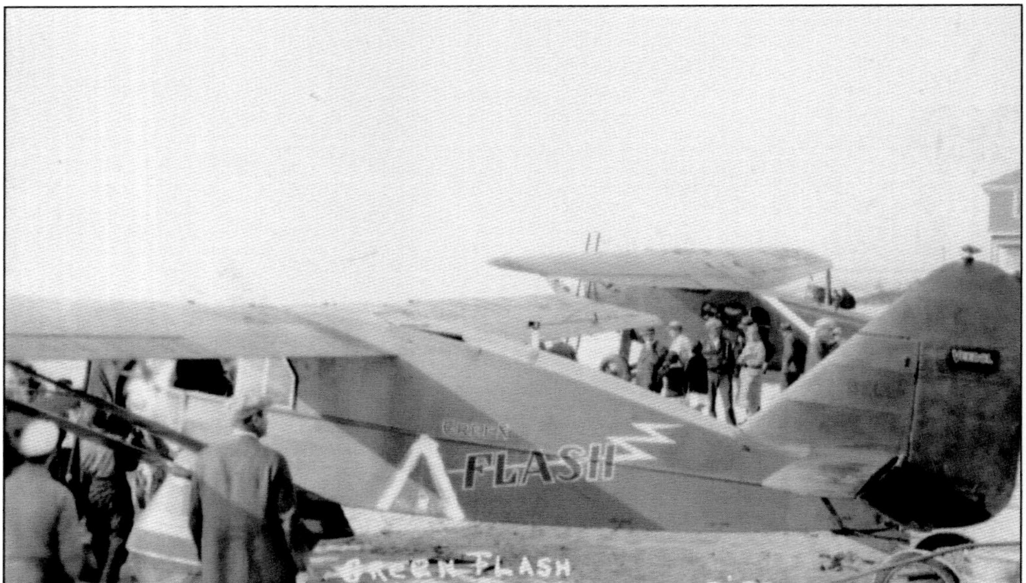


The big race is on in this image. The American Bellanca monoplane *Green Flash*, with pilot Roger Q. Williams and navigator Lewis Yancey, prepares to attempt the 4,400-mile race to Rome, against the French giant monoplane *Yellowbird*.

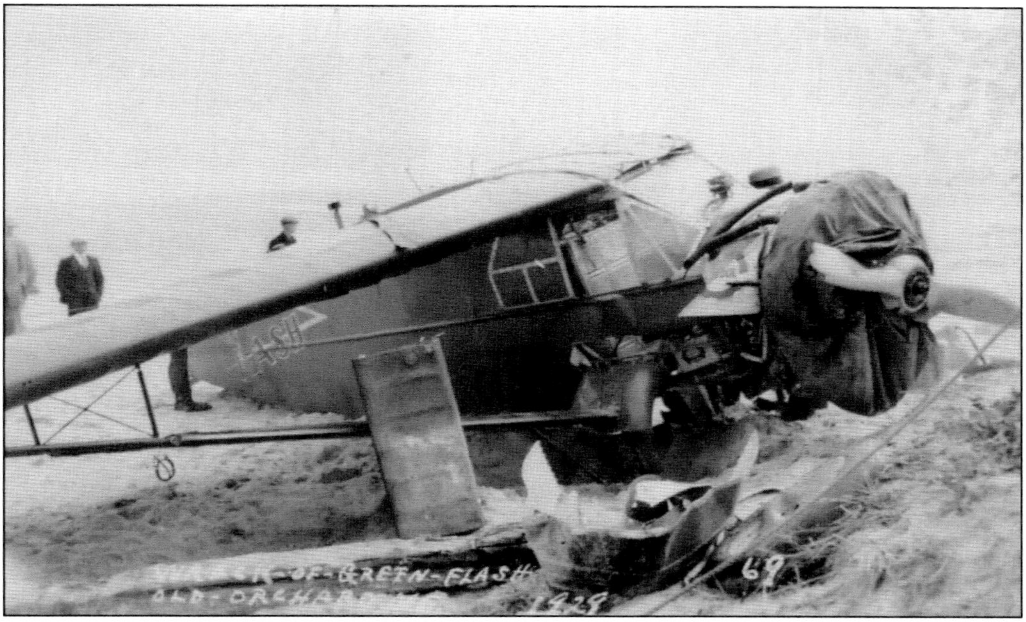

After weeks of planning and preparation, the flight of the *Green Flash* was quickly over. While speeding down the beach for takeoff, one wheel hit a soft spot in the sand, causing a ground loop and a nosedive, snapping the propeller and damaging one wing, thus ending the Americans' hope of beating the French crew.

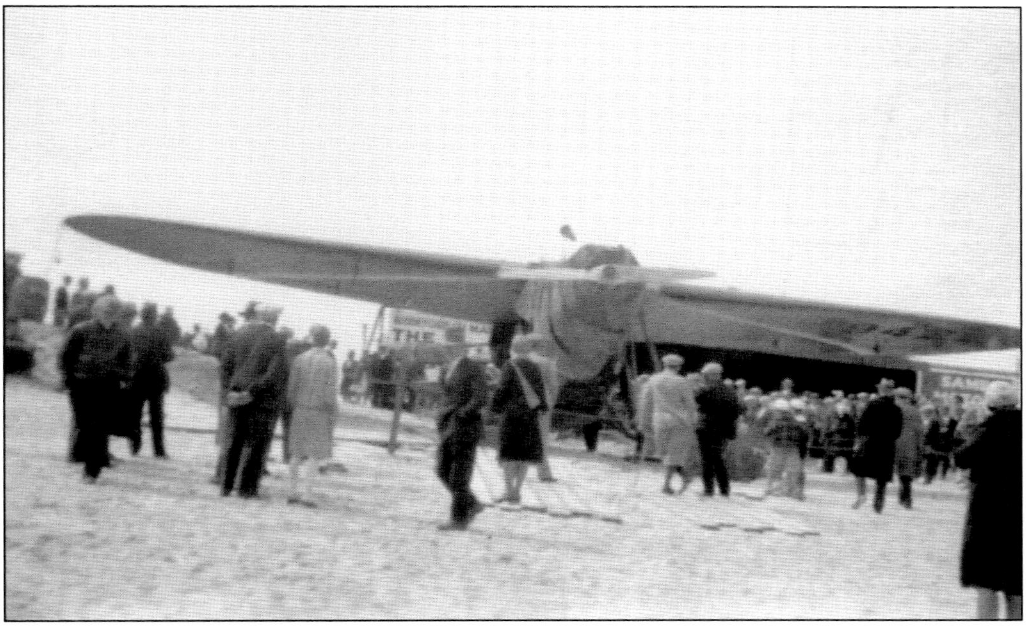

Leaving the Americans behind, the French plane *Yellowbird* flew on to Santander, Spain. Shortly after takeoff, the crew discovered that they were not alone. A young boy from Portland, Maine, named Arthur Schrieber walked forward and announced his presence, to the dismay of the crew, who had some thoughts about throwing him overboard. They decided to allow Schrieber to stay, and thus the world's first transatlantic stowaway made aviation history.

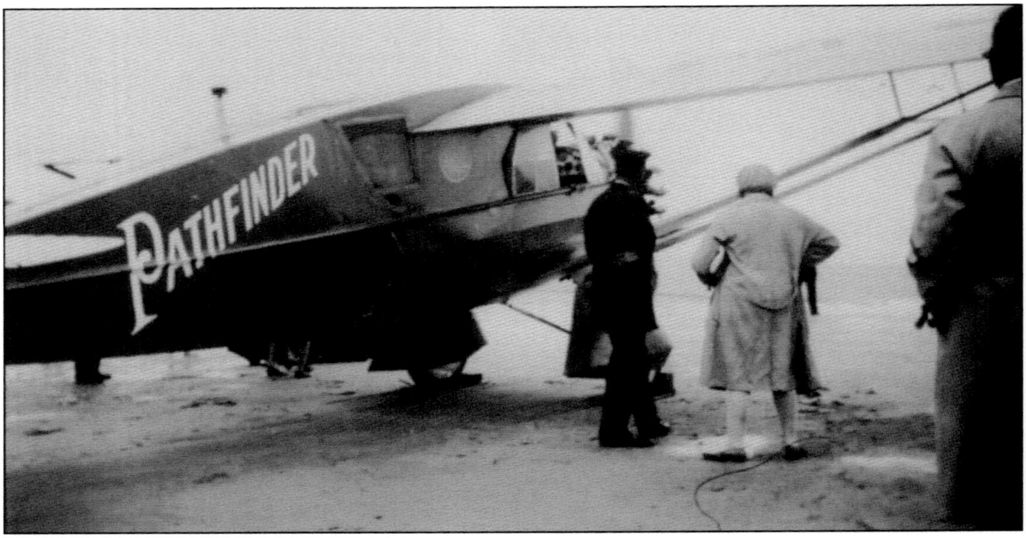


On July 8, 1929, just 25 days after their first failed attempt, the crew of *Green Flash* procured another plane, the *Pathfinder.* Pilot Roger Q. Williams and navigator Lewis Yancey were the crew. This time it was a successful transatlantic crossing to Santander, Spain. This was the last plane from Old Orchard Beach to make the crossing. There were two more attempts in later years, but both were unsuccessful.

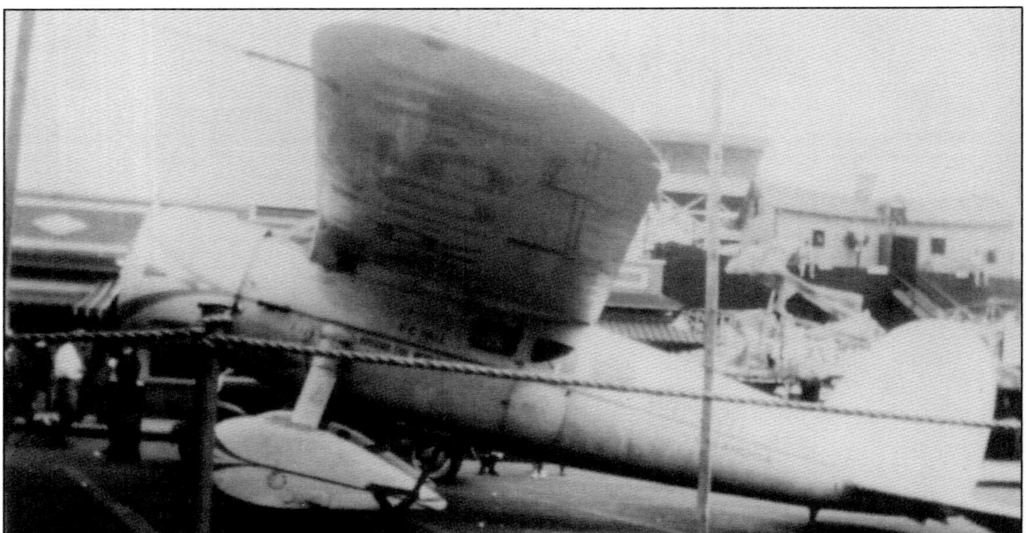

Seen here is Wiley Post's Lockheed 5B *Winnie Mae*, nicknamed "Around the World," at Old Orchard Beach. Post and Harold Gatty, navigator, bent their propeller attempting takeoff on August 16, 1931. They were delayed one day, until a new propeller arrived from Boston. For 25¢, the public was allowed to sign their names on the fuselage.

# *Two*

# Houses and Hotels

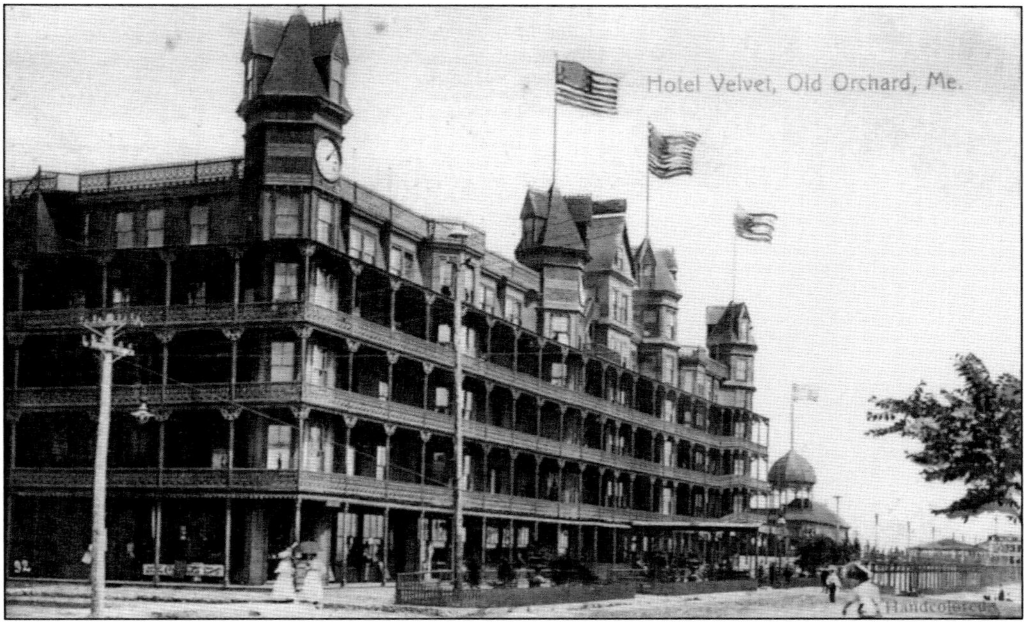


The grandest hotel in Old Orchard Beach was the Velvet Hotel. The Velvet Hotel was moved to the above location in 1899. It was formerly located on East Grand Avenue, behind the present-day Whitehall building. The Velvet Hotel was moved on skids, by placing a windlass on lower Old Orchard Street and using a team of 18 oxen. Its new location is where the present-day Grand Victorian Hotel/Motel complex is being built. In 1907, fire consumed this hotel and many others during the worst conflagration in Old Orchard Beach history.

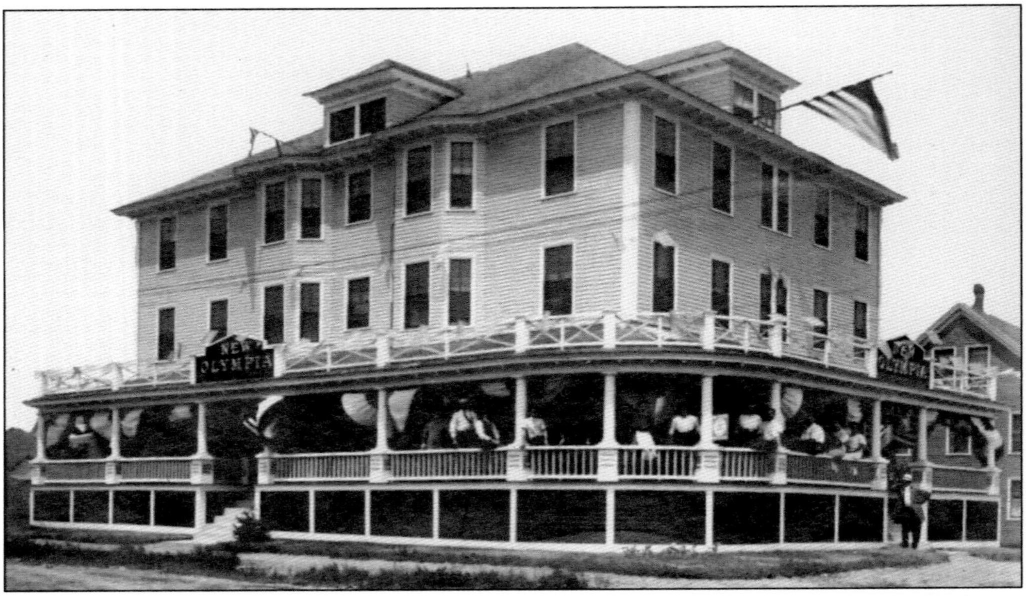


The New Olympia Hotel was built on the same site as the original Olympia House, which was destroyed in the big fire of 1907. The hotel was built in 1911 by the former owner, Emma Jordan of Epping, New Hampshire. This hotel, located at 10 Milliken Street on the corner of Imperial Street, received its final blow on April 16, 1982. The building was totally destroyed during a midnight blaze. It is currently used as a parking lot, and plans for a high-rise condominium are in the air.

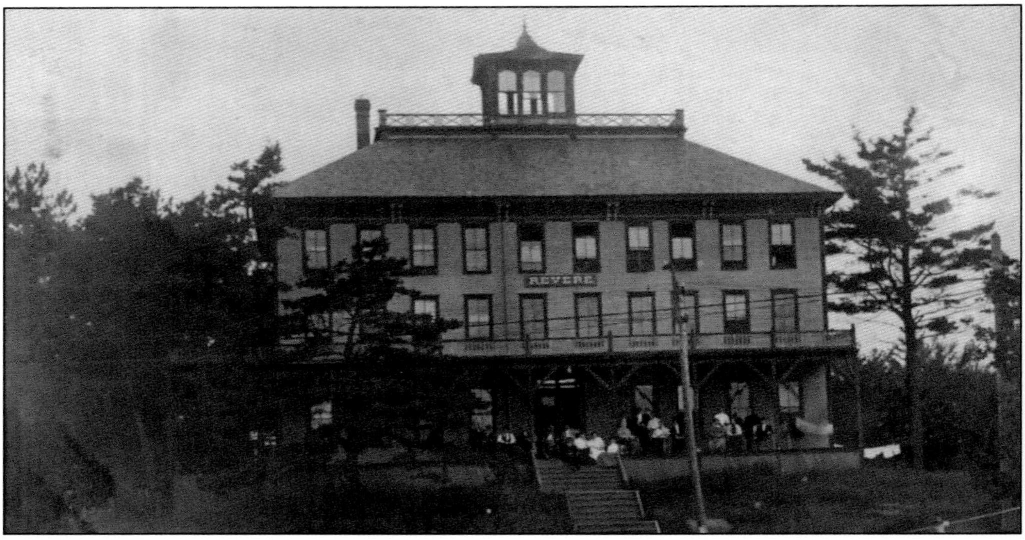


Construction of the Revere House commenced in 1881, and it opened in June 1882. It was located at 46 Saco Avenue, where the present-day Atlantic Breeze Motel is. It was built by Lovey A. Pillsbury. The 63-by-42-foot, three-story hotel with an 80-foot ell had 60 rooms and was topped off with an observation platform and cupola giving a panoramic view of Old Orchard Beach. In 1930, the name was changed to the Lookout. It was razed in 1964, and the Swiss Colony Motel was built. In the late 1980s, the property was sold to John and Kim Verreault and the name changed to the present-day Atlantic Breeze.

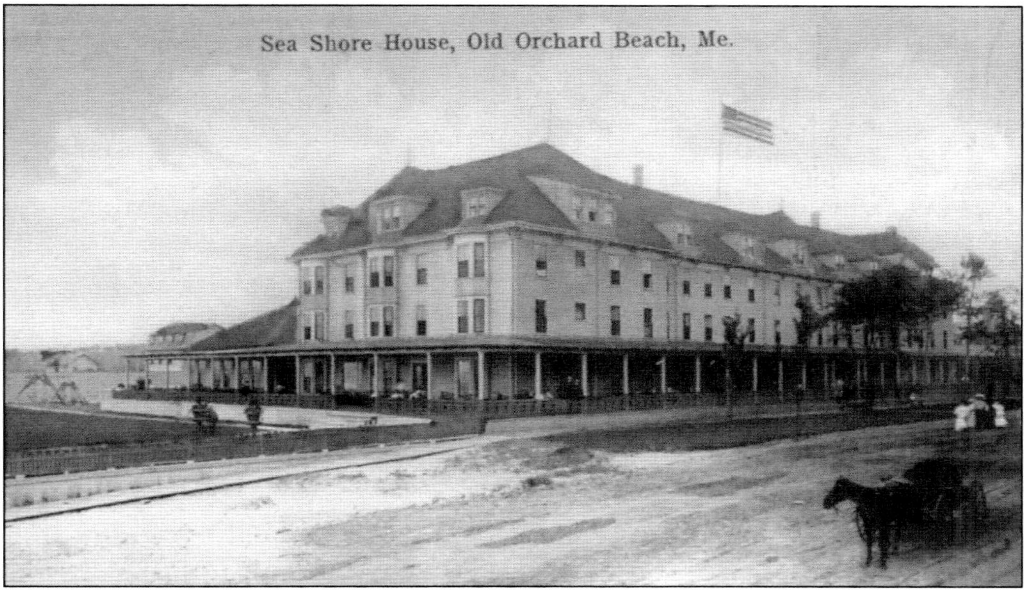


The Sea Shore House, 1873–1907, was built, owned, and operated by Frank G. Staples. The contractor was George H. Herring, who also built the 1873 railroad station, the Ocean Park railroad station, and the Old Orchard House, among others. In 1879, the addition of two stories increased the size to accommodate 300 guests. The fire of August 15, 1907, destroyed this fine hotel.

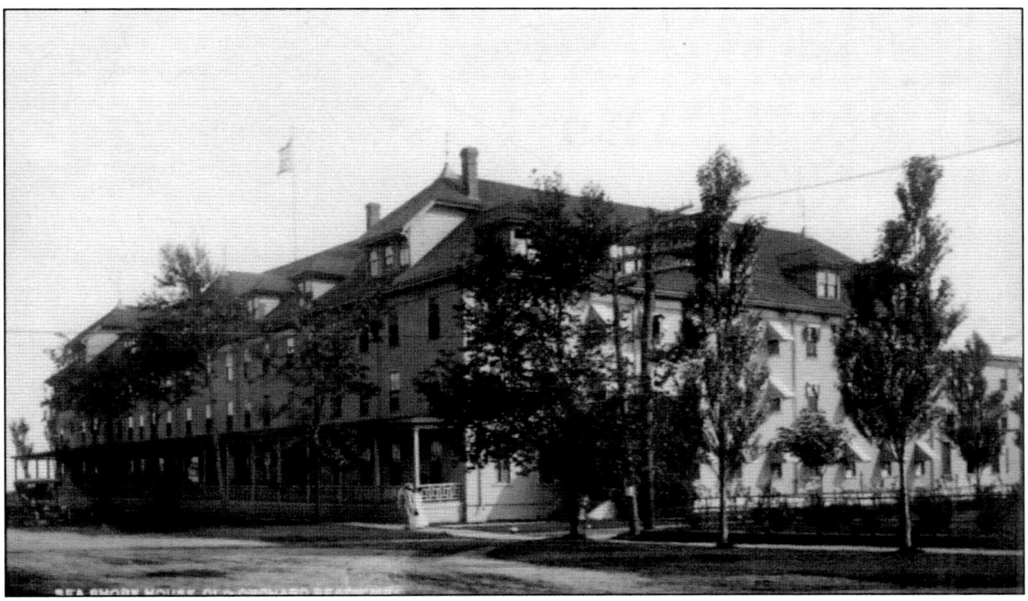

The Sea Shore House was located where the present-day Palace Playland amusement center is. In 1916, the Staples family sold the old Sea Shore House lot to Charles W. Usen and Joseph Balster of Boston for $60,000. This attraction became the Coney Island of the North, becoming the largest amusement center in New England.

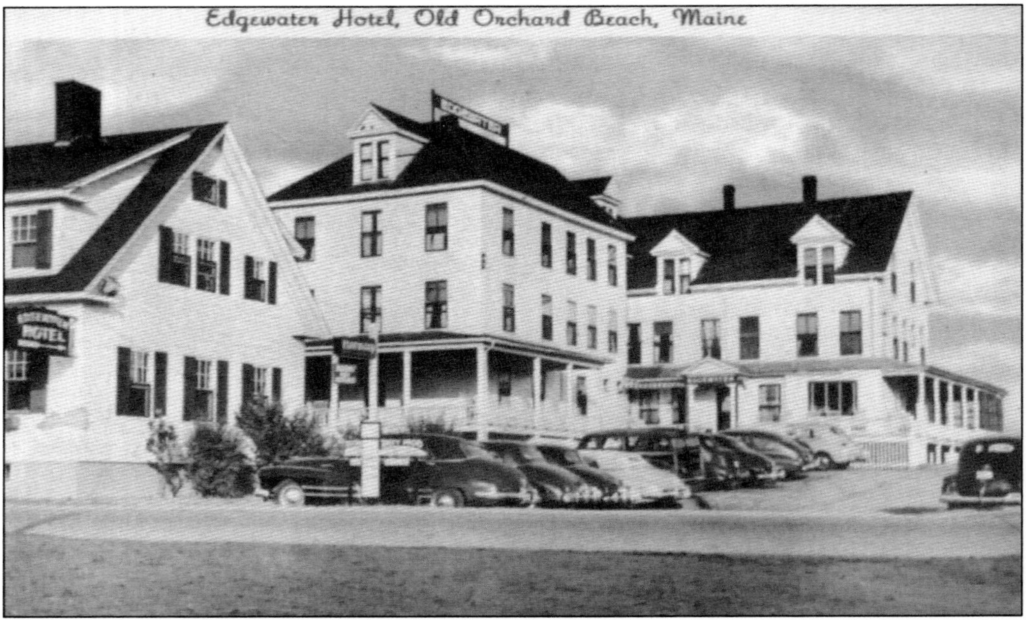


The Edgewater Hotel was originally built in 1899 by the Abbott sisters and had 32 rooms, which was later expanded to 50 rooms. The Abbott house name was changed to the Edgewater in 1945. In 1959, the house on the left was moved to Odena Avenue and is currently owned by the Garon family. In 1965, the large hotel was razed, and a two-story, 25-unit motel was built, adding to the previous 10-unit motel, making the present-day motel, 35 units, owned by the Janelle family.

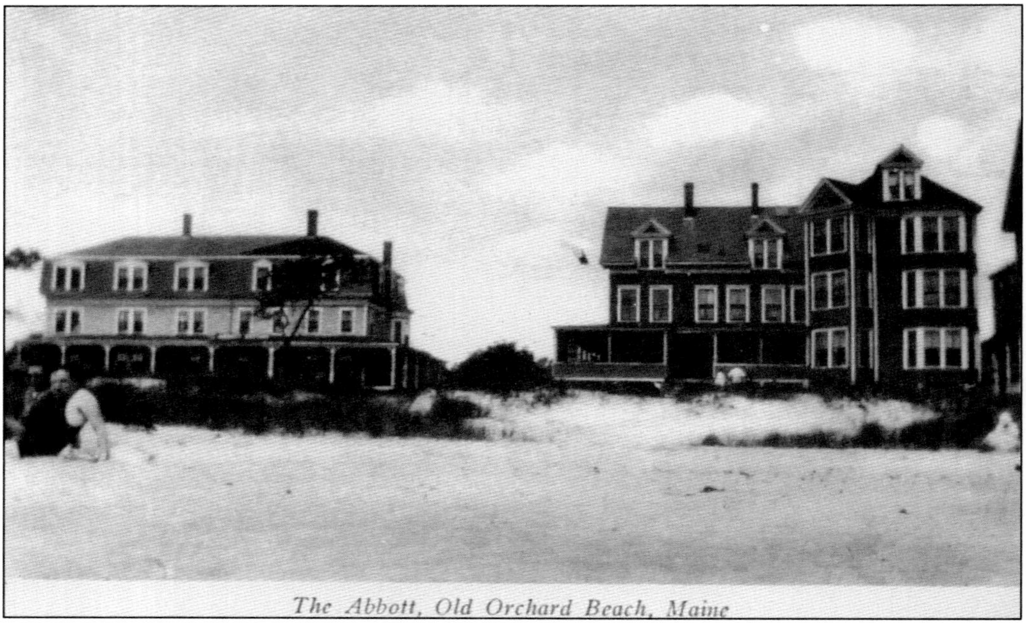


The mansard-style hotel on the left in this postcard is the Abbott Cottage. It was built in 1895 and later expanded to 20 rooms. In 1967, it was converted into the Old Colonial Motel and is currently owned by the Davis family.

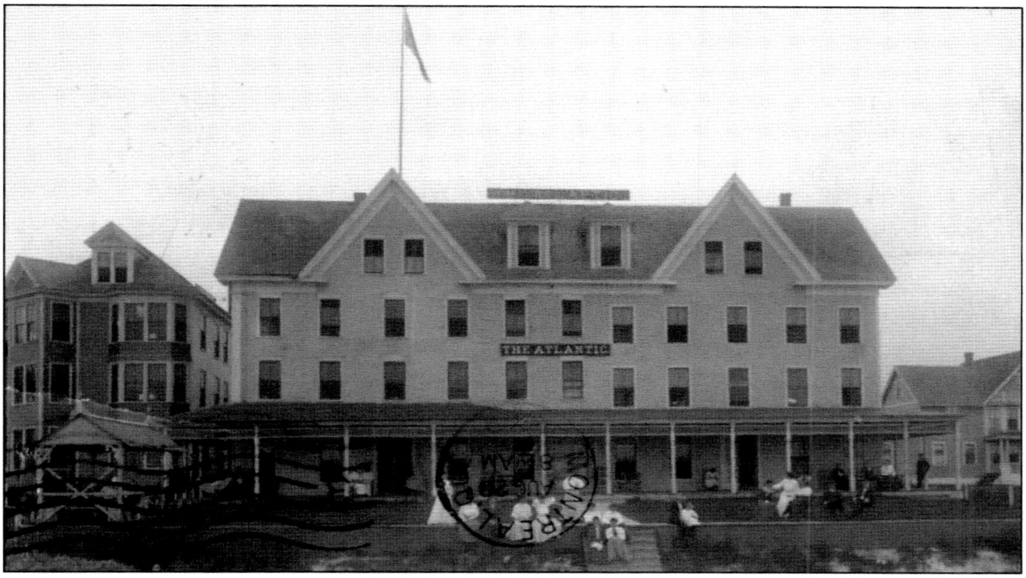


The original Atlantic House was destroyed by fire on January 15, 1876. The above hotel was built in 1880 and opened on July 10, 1880, on the same site as the previous hotel. It was built on the 56-by-151-foot lot and had 30 rooms. In 1884, it was sold. In 1886, Sarah D. Moulton purchased the hotel. It was again sold in 1899 to Perley Stevens. At the beginning of the 20th century, the Atlantic and Hatch Houses were merged to greatly enlarge the size. In 1965, it was razed and the present-day Joseph's by the Sea restaurant was built at 55 West Grand Avenue.

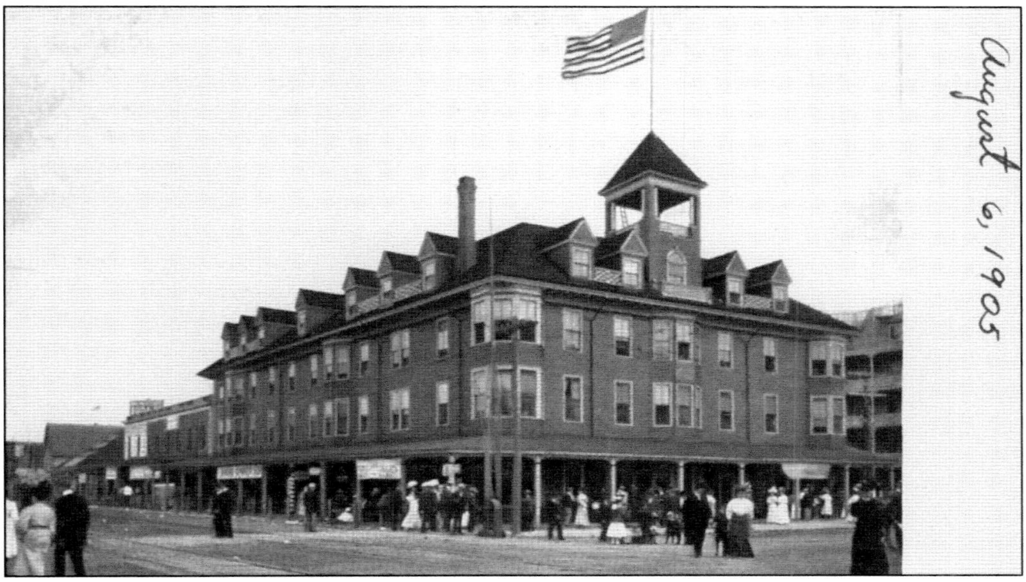


The Alberta, 1898–1907, was built where the present-day Whitehall building is located. William L. Alden of Portland was the owner. Construction began in November 1897. The Alberta was situated on the former site of the old Gorham House, which was moved in sections to several locations around town. J. F. Lombard had the contract for the foundation. The Alberta was 125 feet by 75 feet and four stories high. The hotel's name was derived from the hotel owner's sister's name, Alberta Parsons. This hotel, along with 17 others, came to an end on August 15, 1907.

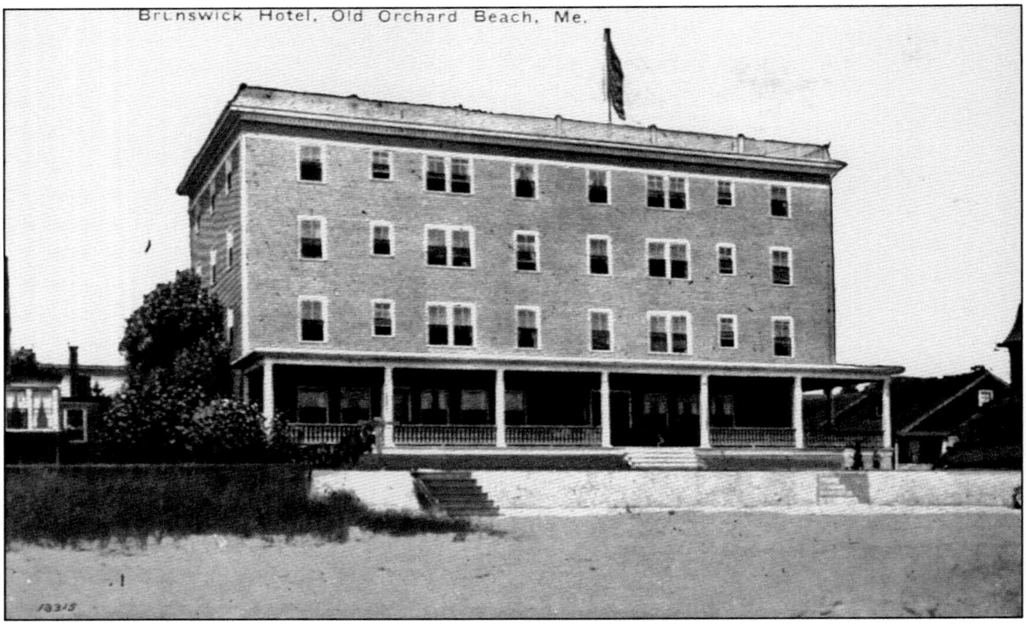


The Brunswick Hotel was built in 1912 by John Felch Hutchinson on the same site of the former Brunswick, which burned in 1882. Hutchinson worked at the Sea Shore House as a porter for Frank Staples until 1907, when the great fire of 1907 destroyed the Sea Shore House. The Hutchinson family ran the hotel until April 16, 1945.

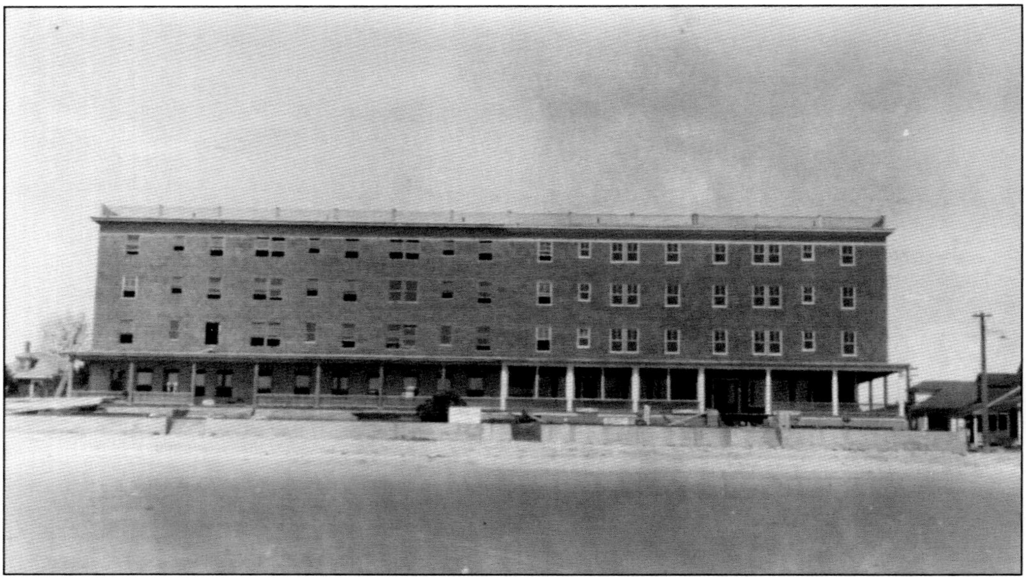

The above postcard shows the enlarged Brunswick in 1928 under construction. The family home to the left of the old Brunswick Hotel was moved around the corner to 4 Fourth Street to allow for the addition. In 1983, the hotel was raised two stories for a total of six floors and converted into 27 condominium units. Later part of the first floor was converted into a restaurant, a cocktail lounge, and seven motel units. It was during this 1928 enlargement that the hotel was increased to 93 rooms.

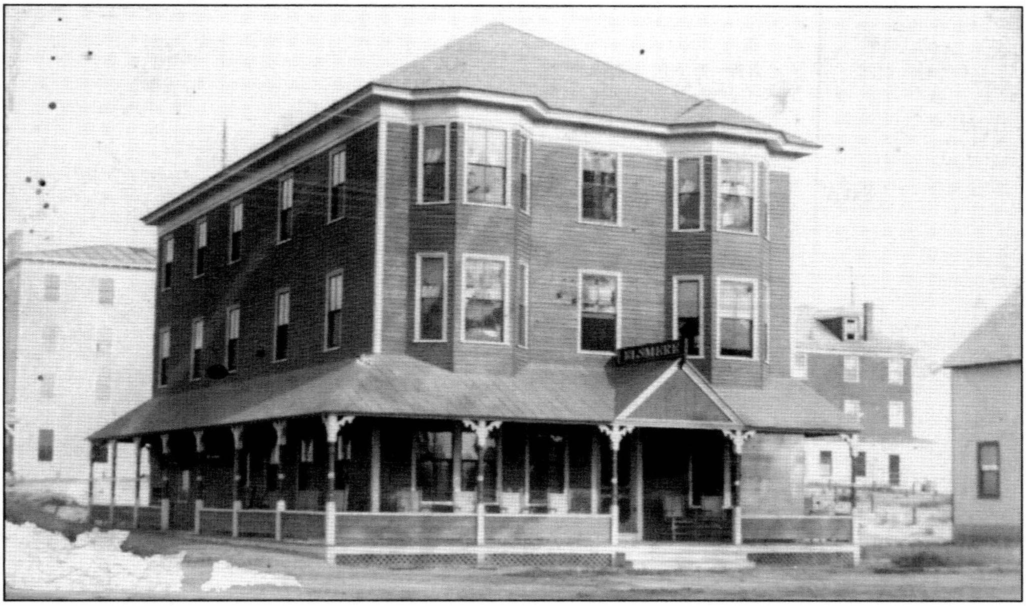


The Elsmere was built in 1908 by T. B. McKeering. In 1920, the Elsmere was physically moved and connected to the Linwood Hotel and called the New Linwood. In 1984, the New Linwood, the Vesper, and the Elsmere were razed, and the new 55-unit, eight-level condominium Linwood Arms was constructed.

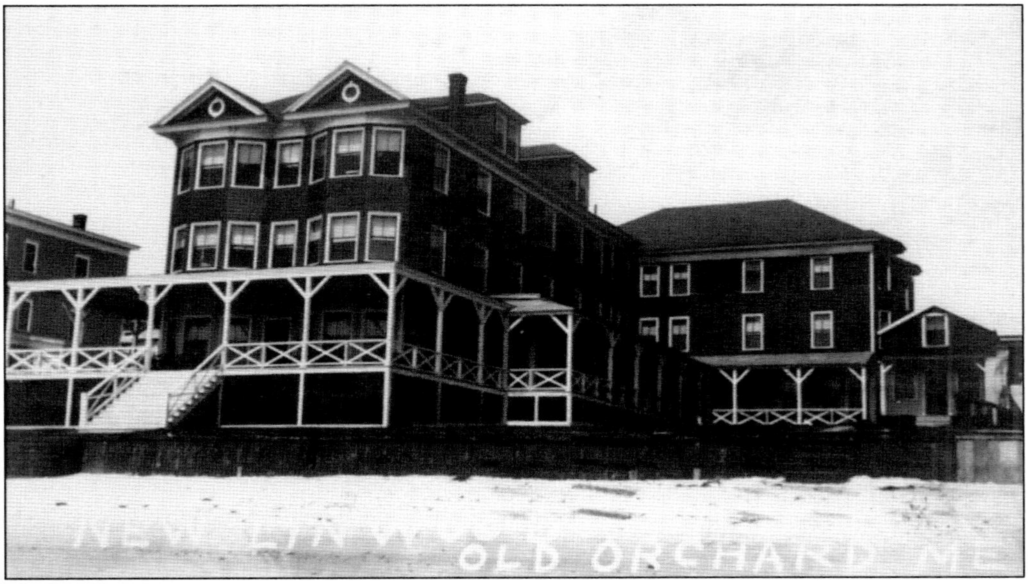

The above real-photo postcard shows the two hotels melded together. The New Linwood and the Elsmere hotels were located at the original site of the previous Linwood, which burned on August 15, 1907. Today the entire block, East Grand Avenue, East Surf Street, Aldine Terrace Street, and Dube Street encompass this lot.

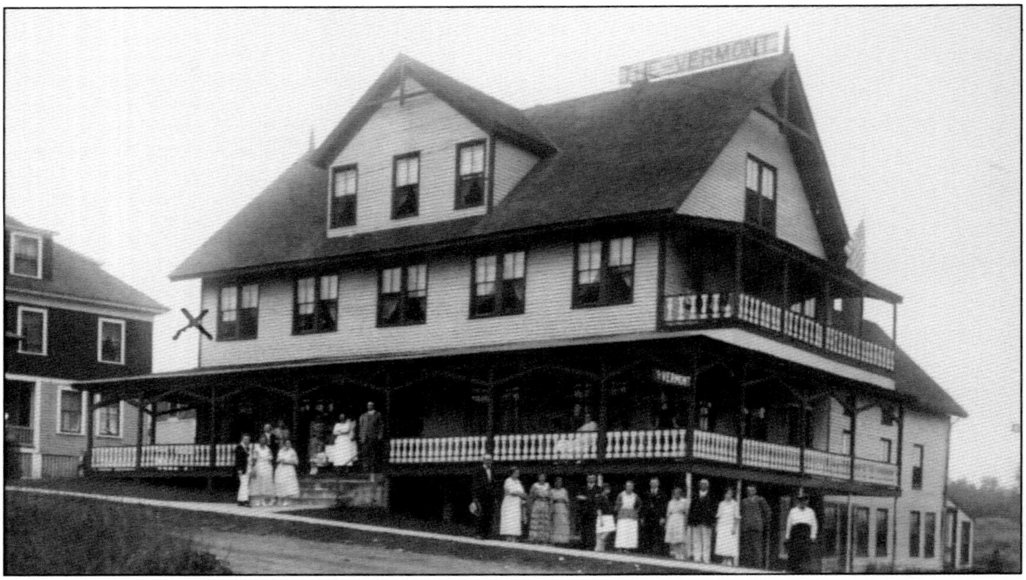


The Vermont House was originally called the Lowell House when it was built in 1889. In 1899, Dr. Charles A. Eastman purchased it and changed the name to Eastman's Women Sanitarium. Rooms in 1889 were $7–$10 per week. In 1904, Dr. Eastman was charged and convicted of manslaughter in the death of a young girl named Edith McIntire, who died during an illegal abortion that he performed. Eventually he was sentenced to one year in jail. The name was later changed to the Vermont House, and it was razed in 1969. A single-family home was built on this lot located at present-day 90 First Street.

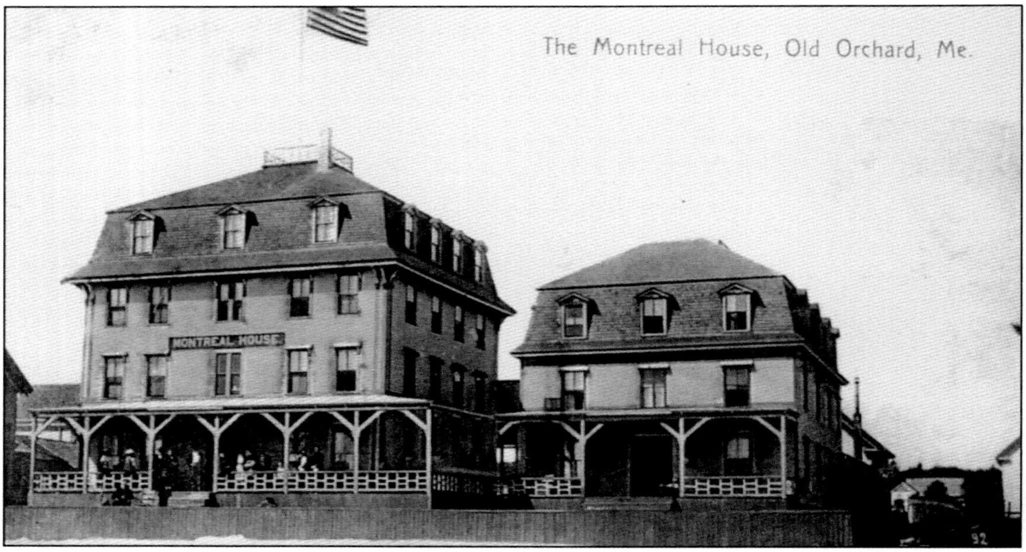


The Montreal House was built in 1874, just after the arrival of the train at its doorstep. The two earlier buildings were enlarged in 1898. Longtime owner Frank W. Blanchard died five days after he sold it in 1919. The name changed to the Beachwood Hotel in 1945. The carriage house was converted into five motel units in 1951. In 1952, more motel units were added. In 1975, fire destroyed the original houses. Currently the Beachwood Hotel is owned by the Cloutier family and contains 44 beachfront units.

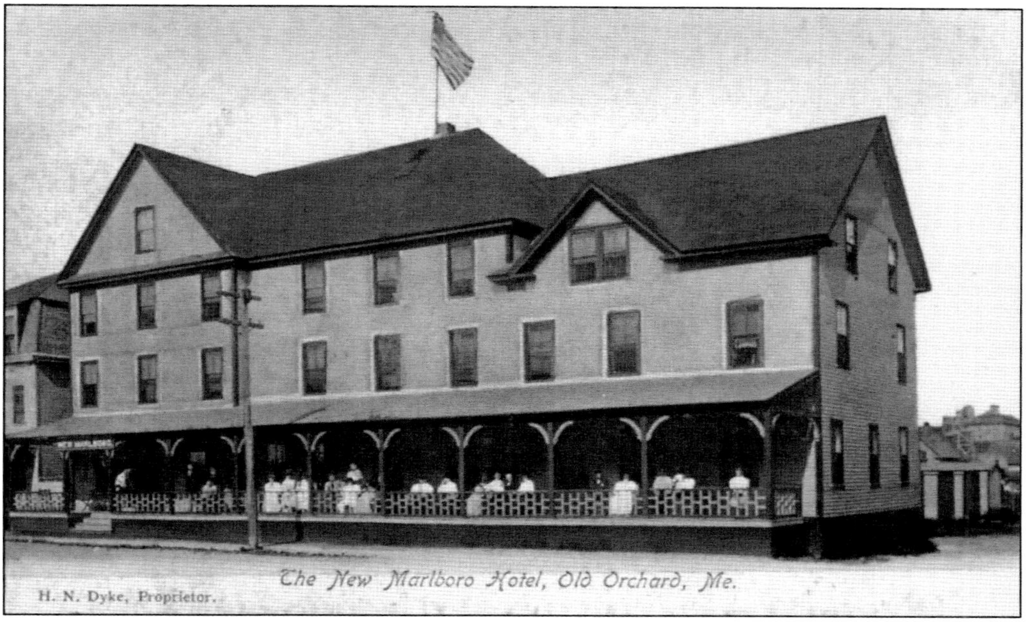


The New Marlboro Hotel was owned by H. N. Dyke and later by John Dyke. Not much is known about this 3.5-story hotel. The construction date remains unknown. However, on August 15, 1907, the end came for this fine-looking hotel. This is the only known postcard to exist of this hotel. It was listed as a $20,000 loss after the 1907 fire. It was located on East Grand Avenue.

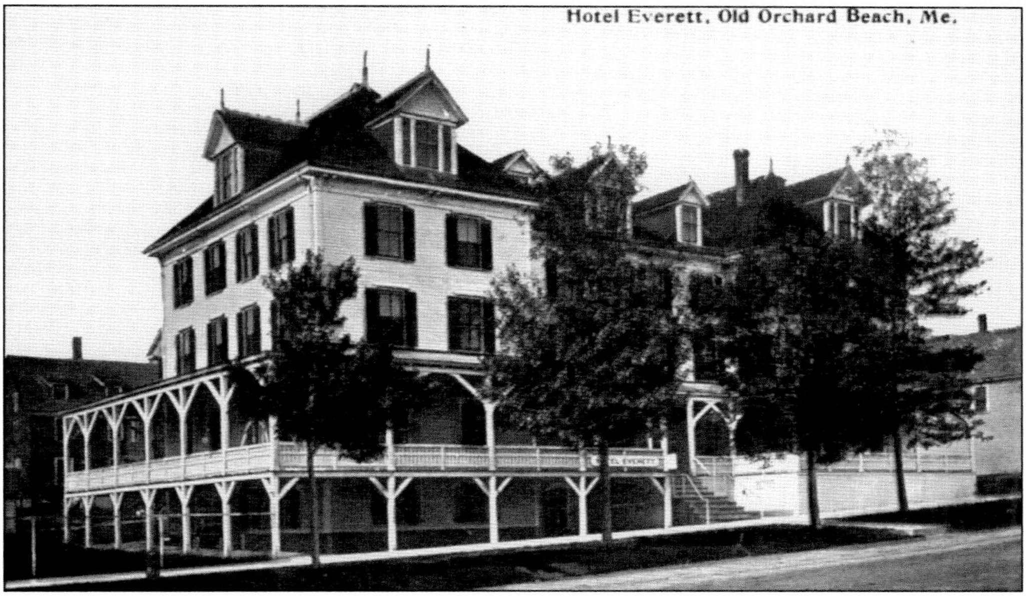


The Everett Hotel cost $3,500 when it was first constructed at 33 Old Orchard Street. The name changed to the Old Orchard House in 1946, after the larger Old Orchard House was razed. The hotel opened in 1884 under the proprietorship of Marie F. Libby. The hotel accommodated 150 guests. Rooms in 1884 were $2 and $3 per day and $12–$20 per week. Bedchambers were lighted by gas and connected with the office by means of electric bells. The hotel was destroyed by fire on October 17, 1976, and is now a parking lot.

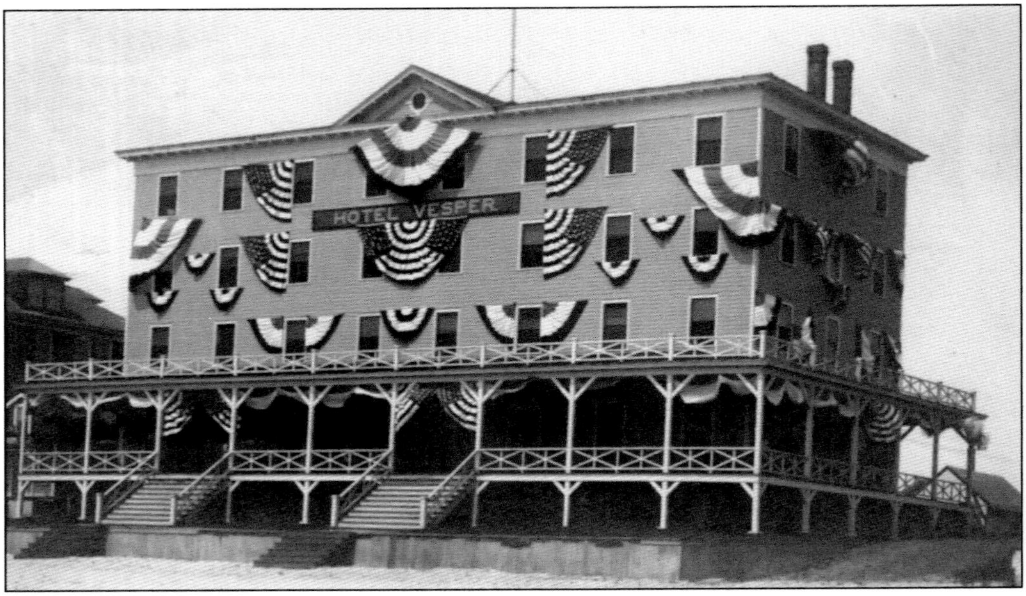


The Hotel Vesper was located on the seawall, on the corner of Aldine Terrace. It was built in 1907 by Charles H. Campbell and run by he and his wife, Kate. It was under several owners until Roger Dube sold it in 1984. This lot, along with the New Linwood Hotel, was razed in the spring of 1984, and the condominium Linwood Arms was completed in 1985 on this site.

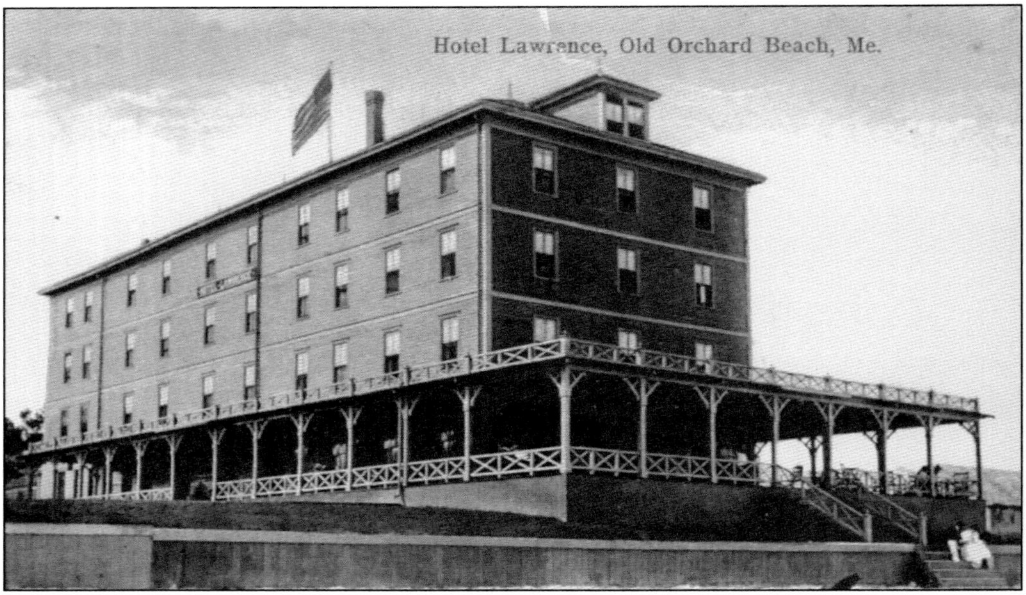


The Lawrence Hotel (1882–1907) was built on the former site of the Lawrence House, which burnt in 1881. The contractor was H. Dick, of Massachusetts, for E. W. Barton. The hotel was 100 feet by 40 feet and could hold 150 guests. Many dress hops (dances) were held at this hotel. The hotel takes its name from Barton's hometown of Lawrence, Massachusetts. The hotel also had gas lighting and electric bells connected to the front office. The Lawrence House was another victim of the great fire of 1907. Today the Casablanca condominium occupies this site.

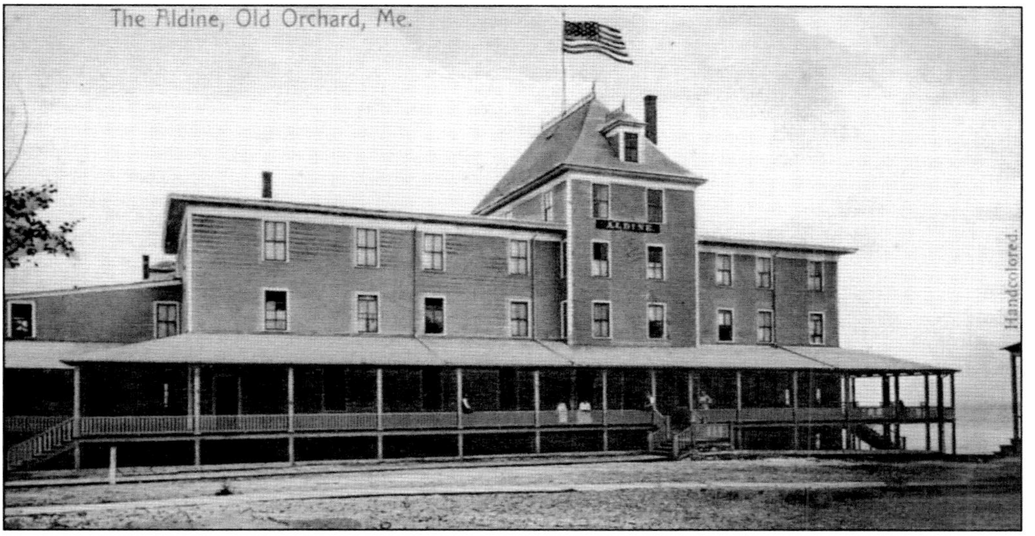


The Aldine Hotel (1883–1907) was built on the oceanfront by Samuel Haines, who owned the original Aldine Hotel (1880–1881). The old Aldine Hotel was located farther up the street. Haines sold the old lot for $1,200 in 1882 to Samuel Day of Lewiston. Haines used this money to build the new hotel on the seawall. Each room had speaking tubes. The broad piazza was 300 feet with four main floors above and two more in the central part. Construction commenced in March 1882 and was ready for the 1883 season. Each room was furnished with the finest hair mattresses available. The hotel was extensively remodeled in 1904, with every room having an ocean view. Again the fire of 1907 destroyed this once-beautiful hotel.

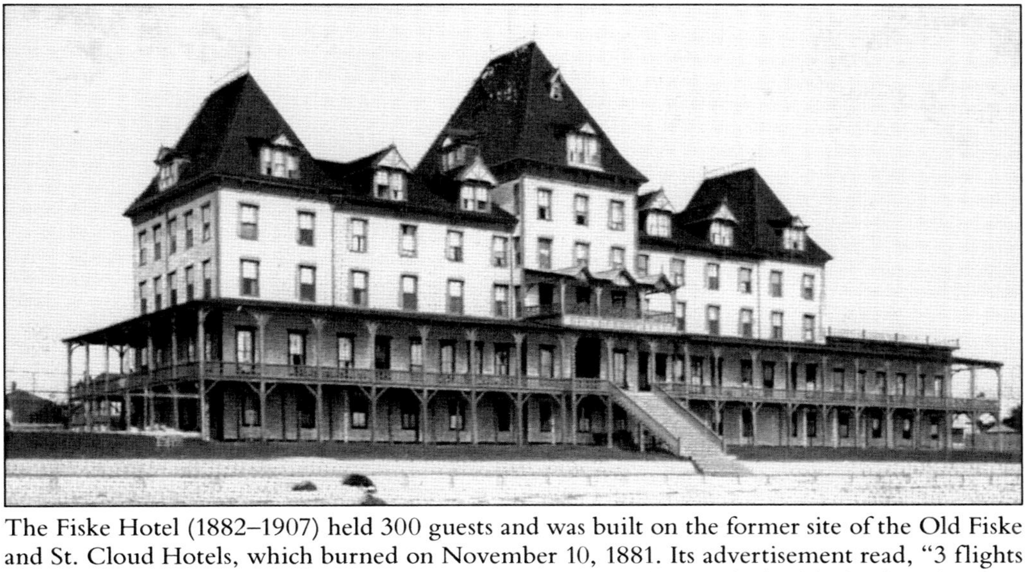

The Fiske Hotel (1882–1907) held 300 guests and was built on the former site of the Old Fiske and St. Cloud Hotels, which burned on November 10, 1881. Its advertisement read, "3 flights of stairs on every floor, fire escape from every room, hot salt water baths, black ash and walnut furniture." It had its own telegraph office, telephones, first-class laundry, fine orchestra, billiard hall, bowling alley, 135 rooms, and six floors. The rates in 1898 were $18–$30 weekly. The Fiske Hotel also had its own baseball team. The two previous Fiske Hotels were destroyed by fire. This hotel, the last, opened on July 1, 1882. It was 206 feet by 40 feet with a 116-foot ell. As with many others, the fire of 1907 destroyed this elegant hotel.

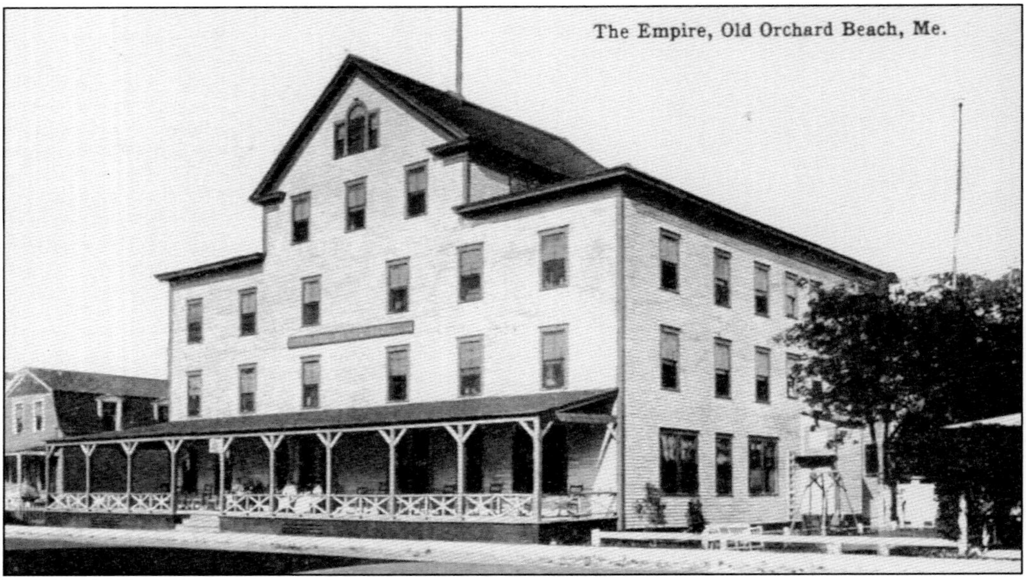


The Miller Hotel was built in 1909 by the Kassell Miller family of Brookline, Massachusetts. The name was changed to the Empire in 1910. The original location was on East Grand Avenue, as shown above. It was moved in 1917 to the oceanfront. It was one of the old-time kosher hotels in town. The contractors who built the hotel were the Beaudette brothers, Henry and George, who also built the Jack and Jill Slide, Noah's Ark, and the Coal Mine. It was razed in 1963, and the Skylark Motel was built in its place.

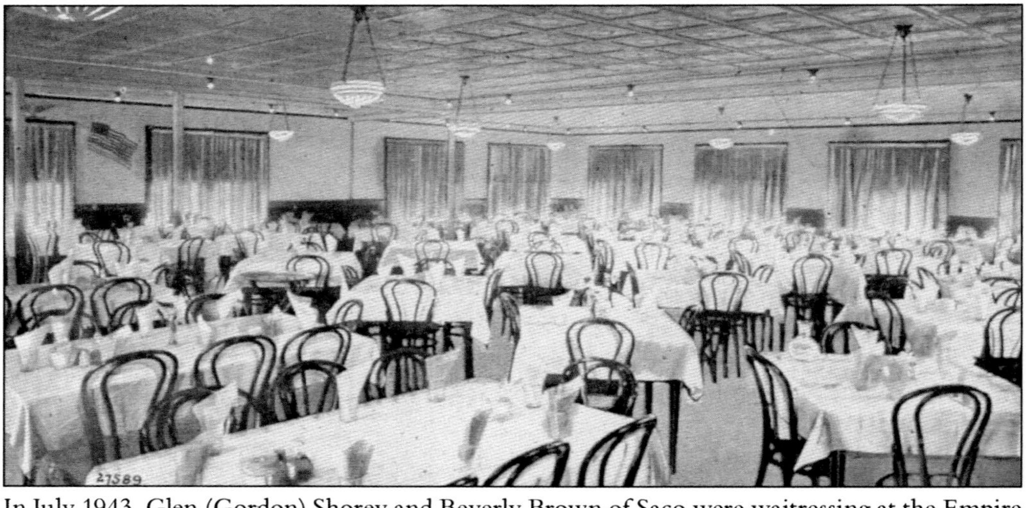


In July 1943, Glen (Gordon) Shorey and Beverly Brown of Saco were waitressing at the Empire dining room, along with friends Evie Bell, Elsa, and Ingrid from Lewiston. They decided to give the owners, Maurice and Otto Miller, an ultimatum; they wanted $75 cash plus $25 cash instead of $75 cash and a $25 savings bond for their summers pay or they were going to walk out. Otto told them to walk. Before they exited, however, they were called back and told that they would agree to the girls' terms. Glen Shorey remembers getting a $25 tip from one family for one week of waitressing. She also recollects the dining room had potted palm trees, white tablecloths, and a beautiful metal ceiling. She recalls the dining room was a very busy place and a great summer job.

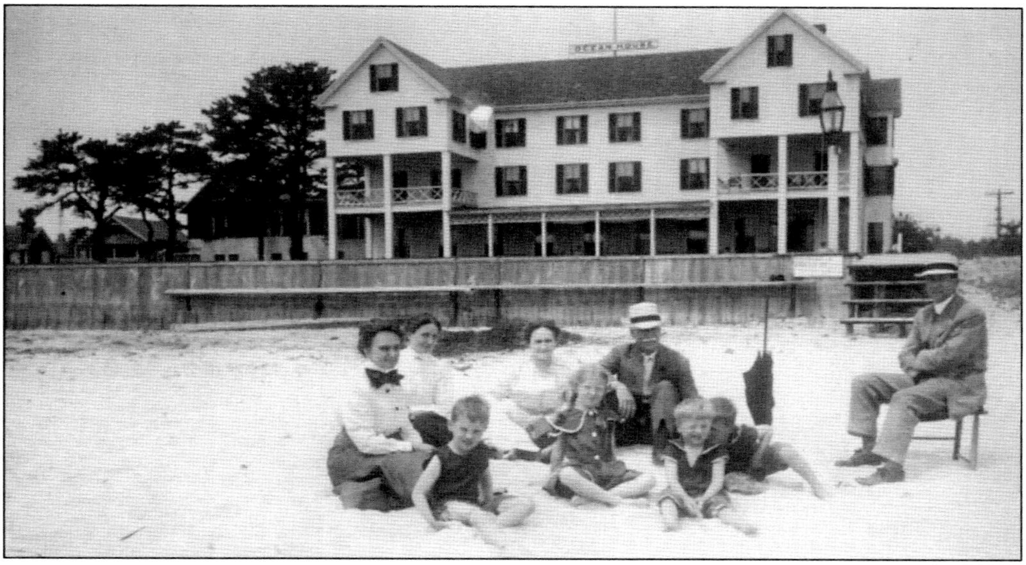

The Ocean House is the oldest standing oceanfront hotel remaining in Old Orchard Beach. It was built in 1904 by John C. Pierce. A 1905 advertisement mentions tennis courts, a barbershop, table tennis, and croquet. In 1940, Bill Clark bought the hotel for $9,500. In 1945, Roland Sylvestre purchased the Ocean House for $40,000. Today the Ocean House is owned by the Pouravelis family. The real-photo postcard shows the Ocean House not long after it was built.

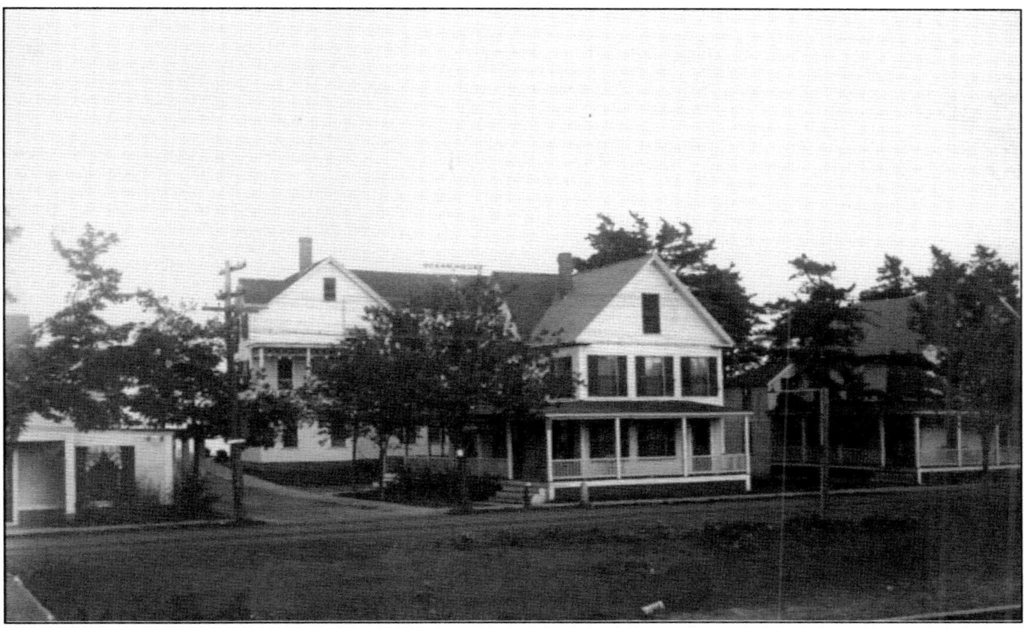

There are many views of the front of the Ocean House. This *c.* 1915 real-photo postcard shows a rare rear view of the hotel and cottages. The photograph shows the corner of Pierce Street and West Grand Avenue. Note the railroad tracks in the lower right-hand corner, with no buildings on this side of West Grand Avenue. The postcard is dated 1915.

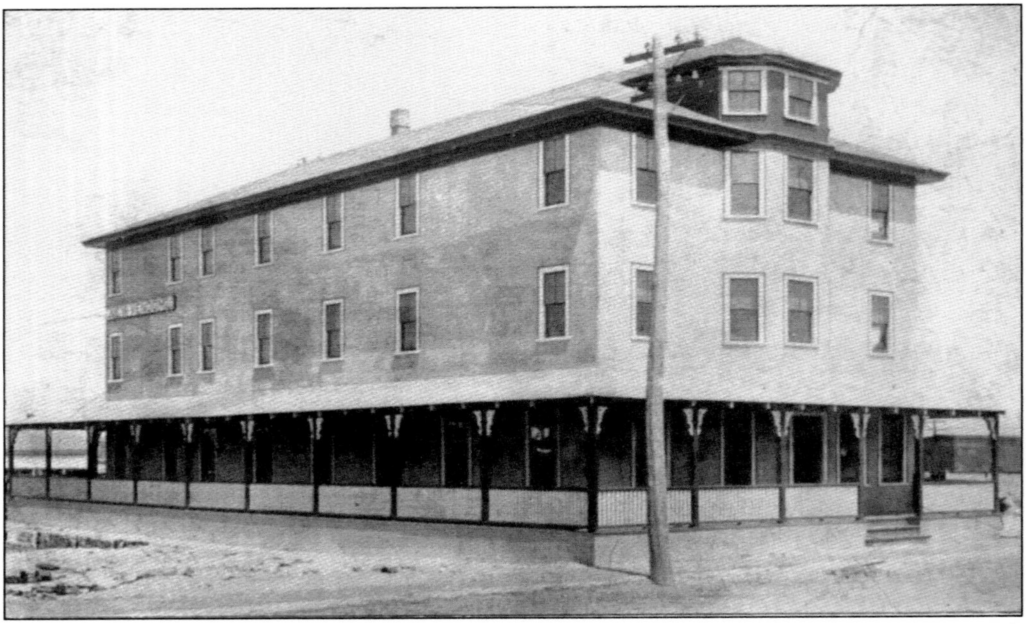

The New Vendome Hotel was built on the same site as the original (1902) Vendome Hotel, which burned in 1907. The New Vendome Hotel was rebuilt in 1908 by George Bunce and had 32 rooms. On November 17, 1958, the New Vendome Hotel was completely destroyed by yet another fire. This hotel was located on East Grand Avenue where present-day Vorias' parking lot is.

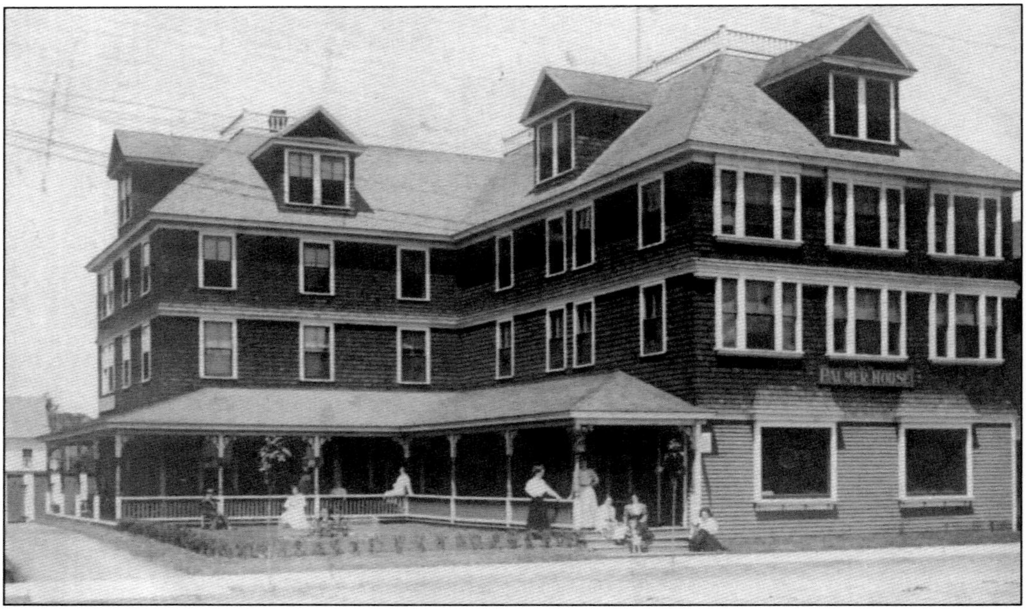


The New Palmer House (1908–1958) was also built on the same site as the original Palmer House, which was destroyed in the August 1907 conflagration. Rebuilt and opened in 1908 by Archie L. Jacques, the new 47-room hotel was destroyed on November 17, 1958, along with the Vendome and a private home. Today a parking lot at 12–20 East Grand Avenue occupies the site.

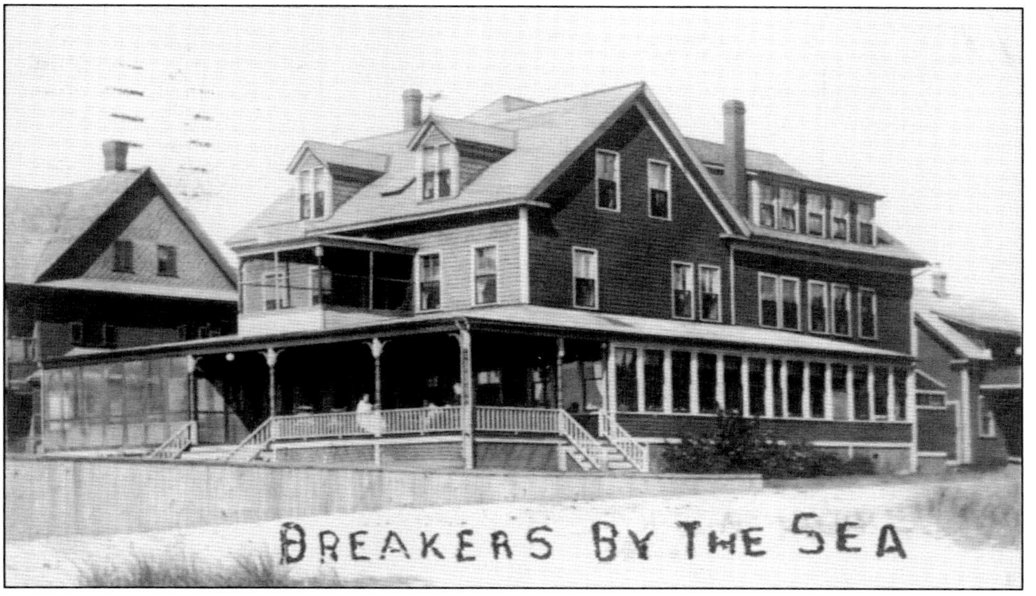


The Breakers by the Sea (1914–1986) was located on the seawall on the south side of Ocean Avenue. It was built in 1914 and operated by George D. Sears. It was sold to S. L. Brown in 1929, upon the death of Garret D. Sears. It was eventually sold to the Armstrong family, which ran the Breakers by the Sea for many years. In 1968, James and Jacqueline Nadeau purchased it from Robert Armstrong for $25,000.

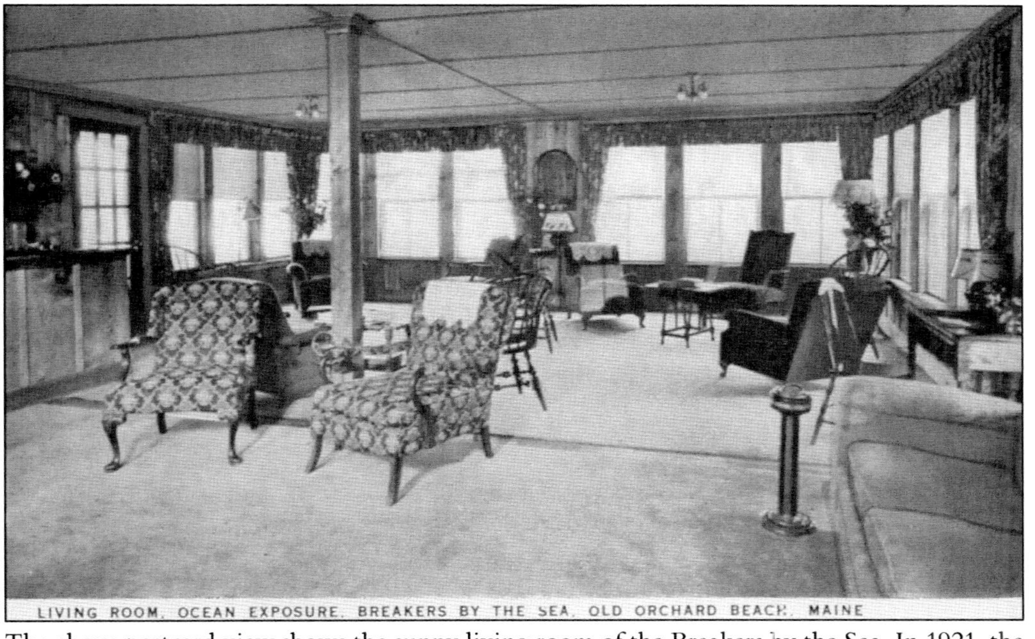


The above postcard view shows the sunny living room of the Breakers by the Sea. In 1921, the hotel was completely remodeled. In 1986, the hotel was sold and razed. In its place, a new 18-unit condominium called the Breakers was built. In 1987, the selling price ranged from $109,000 to $189,000 per unit.

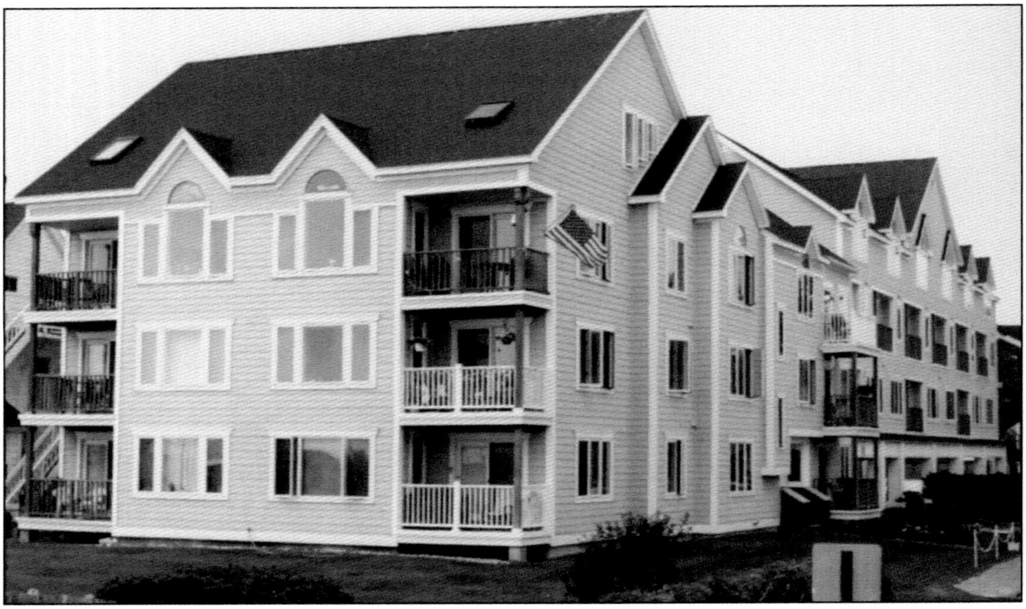

The photograph above shows the Breakers condominiums in August 2006. The developer was Bob Wellman. In 1987, the number of condominium units in Old Orchard Beach had exceeded 1,000. Today that number continues to climb. Presently units at the Breakers sell for upwards of $300,000.

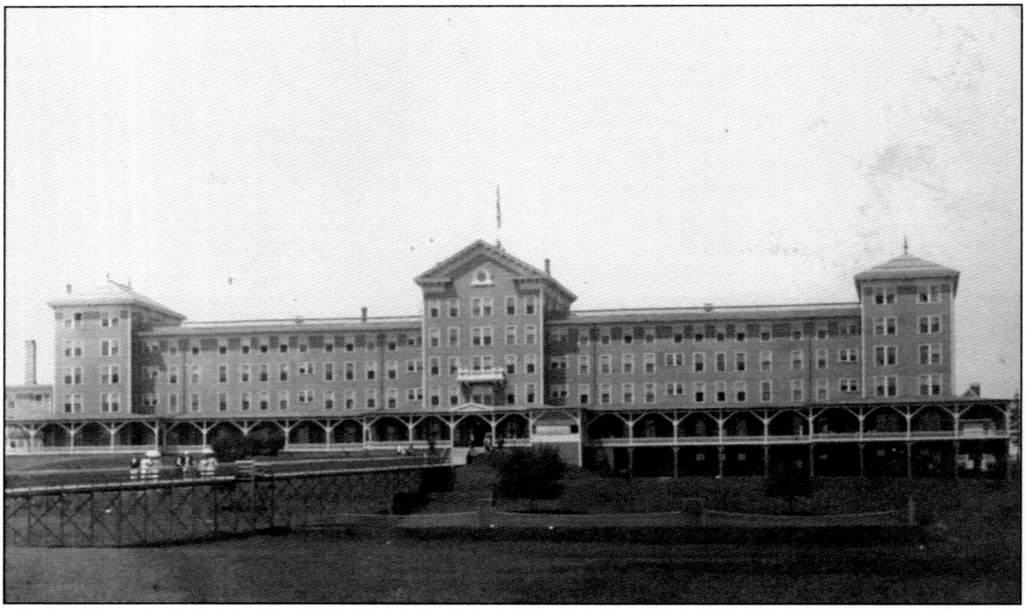

Old Orchard's largest hotel was the Old Orchard House. It was built in 1876 for Ebenezer Staples by contractor George W. Herring. Herring also built three train depots in Old Orchard and Ocean Park. It is said that the money from the sale of the wooden snow scoops, patented by Henry Staples, son of Ebenezer, paid for the construction costs. Spires of Portland and Mount Washington could be seen from the roof of the hotel. The long walkway to the railroad was built in 1899.

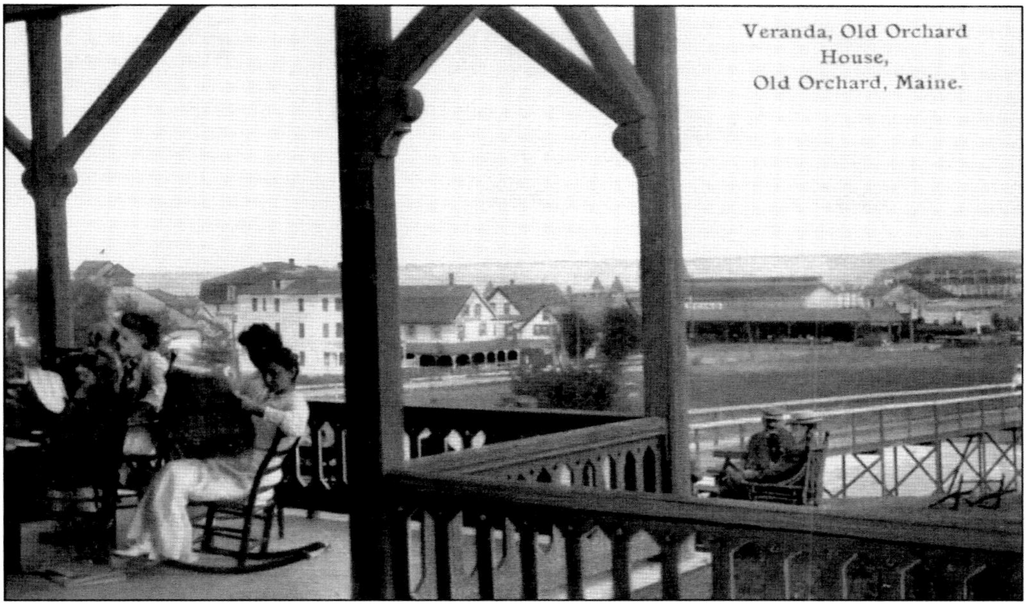


In April 1876, during a late snowstorm, the framing of the hotel collapsed and had to be rebuilt. The hotel was known for its all-female bands. There were 250 rooms that accommodated 500 guests. According to a 1900 advertisement, average prices were $6 per day and $16–$50 per week, depending on the view. The building was razed in 1943. Currently the Rite-Aid store occupies this site.

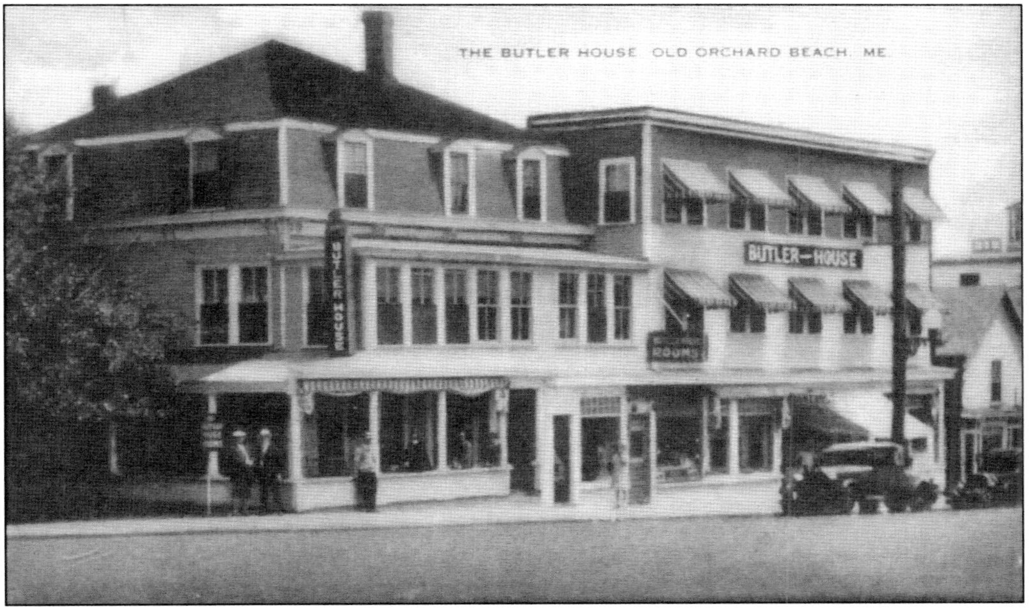


The Butler House was built around 1889 at 30 Old Orchard Street. It was truly an old-fashioned rooming house until October 29, 1975, when it was destroyed by fire. Today two department stores, Hymie's and St. Tropez, occupy this site on the corner of Seavey Street and Old Orchard Street. Mrs. Charles E. Butler sold the original 16-room house to Mrs. Ernest Bauer in the 1920s, and it remained in the Bauer family until the fire.

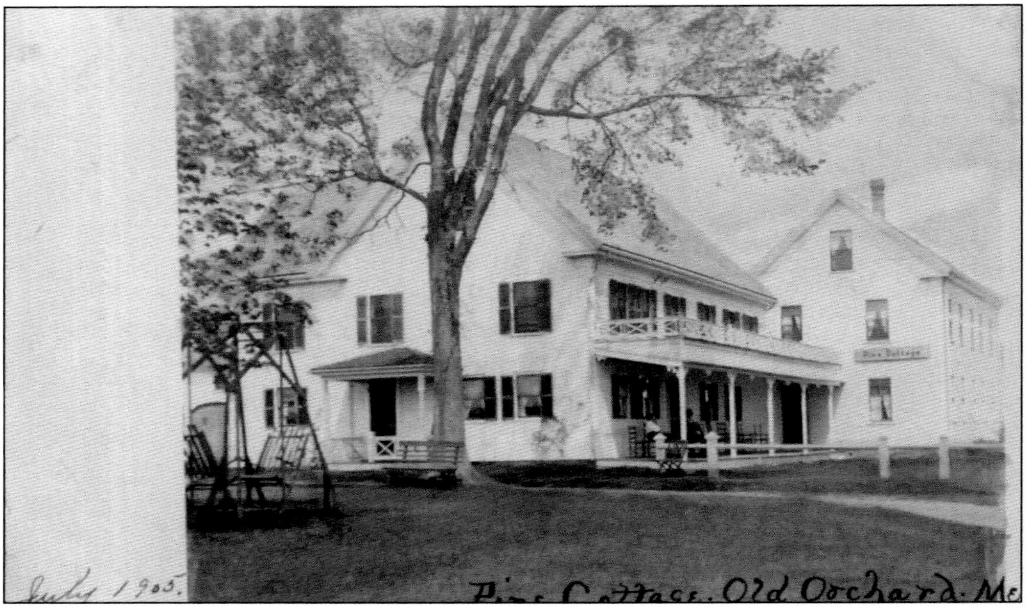


The Pine Cottage was located at 28 Portland Avenue and was built in 1873 by Alfred Milliken. A stereo view at Sabbathday Lake Shaker Village in New Gloucester shows a group of Shakers standing in front of the Pine Cottage in 1873. A 1913 brochure lists rooms daily at $2 per room and board weekly at $8.50–$14 in one of their 30 chambers.

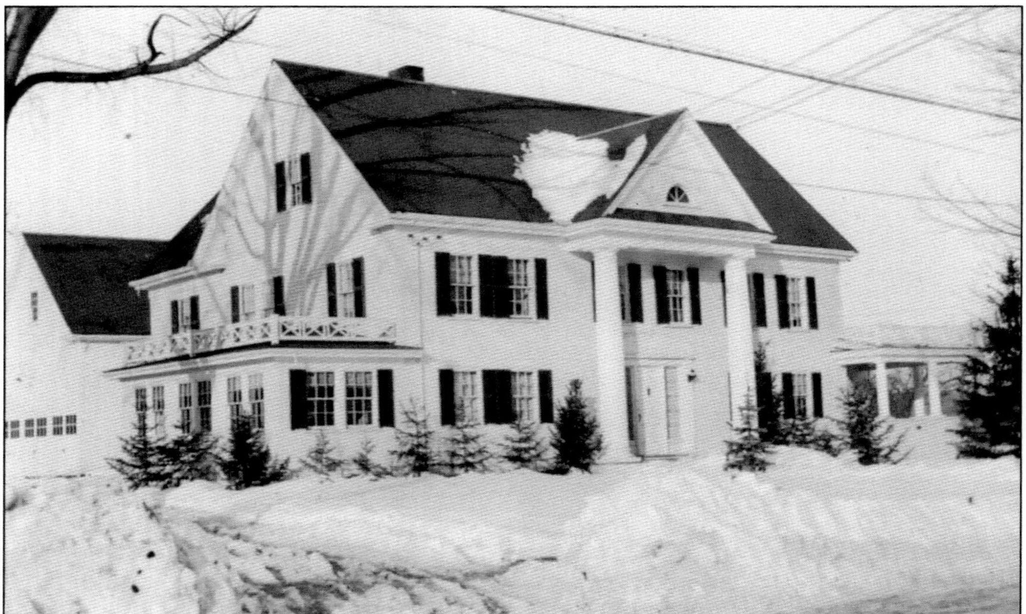

In 1943, the Elms, a tourist home, formerly the Pine Cottage, was purchased by Carl M. and Ethel M. Reed. It was sold in 1952 to Frank and Rosemary Davis and converted into a nursing home in 1959. It was later sold to the Sandy River Corporation. Today it is used as a residential treatment center.

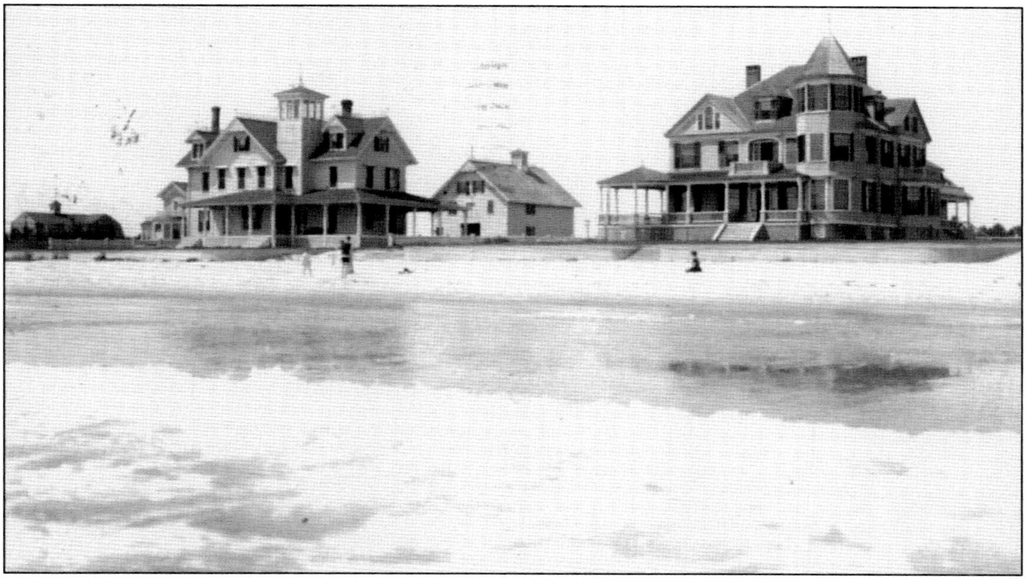

The house on the left is the Ye Rosetree Inn, the private home of Mrs. Charles Green of Baltimore, who also owned the house on the right, known as Minnie's Seaside Rest. The two houses without a doubt were the two most architecturally significant buildings ever built on the oceanfront. The Ye Rosetree Inn house was razed in the early 1960s, and a private house was built on the site. The beautiful water fountain that adorned the backyard was given to the Town of Old Orchard Beach and was placed in Memorial Park. It never operated correctly again and was later removed.

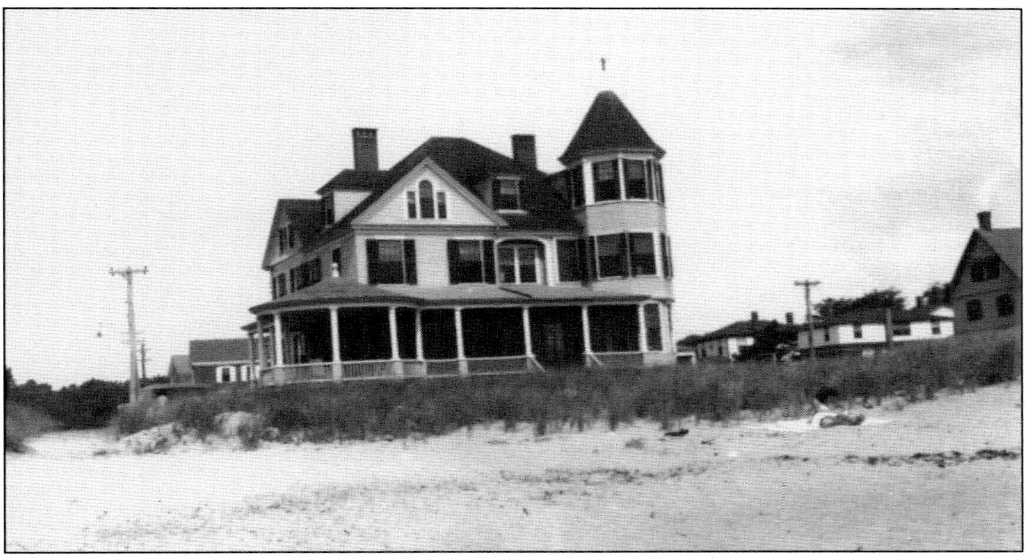

Minnie's Seaside Rest, one of the more elegant Victorians on the oceanfront, was built in 1896 by Mrs. Charles Green. The 15-room rooming house was built for the benefit of foreign missionaries seeking rest and solace. The building was purchased in 1962 by the Margarones family from the American Board of Missions of Boston. In 1984, it was sold to David Rappaport Development Company of Bangor. It was razed in 1985, and the Golden Sands high rise was built in 1986 at the 1 Sea Cliff Avenue location.

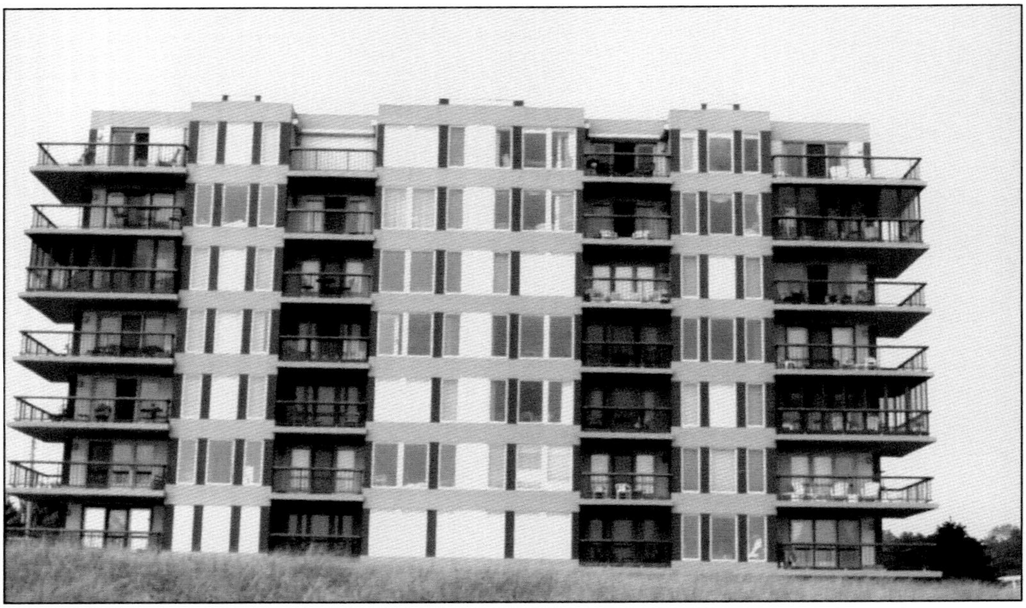

This 2006 photograph shows the present-day 27-unit, seven-floor high-rise condominium Golden Sands, which was built where Minnie's Seaside Rest once stood. Today there are nine high-rise condominiums in Old Orchard Beach. Current zoning laws prohibit erecting any building over 50 feet without special contract zoning permission. Units today at the Golden Sands condominium sell for over $400,000.

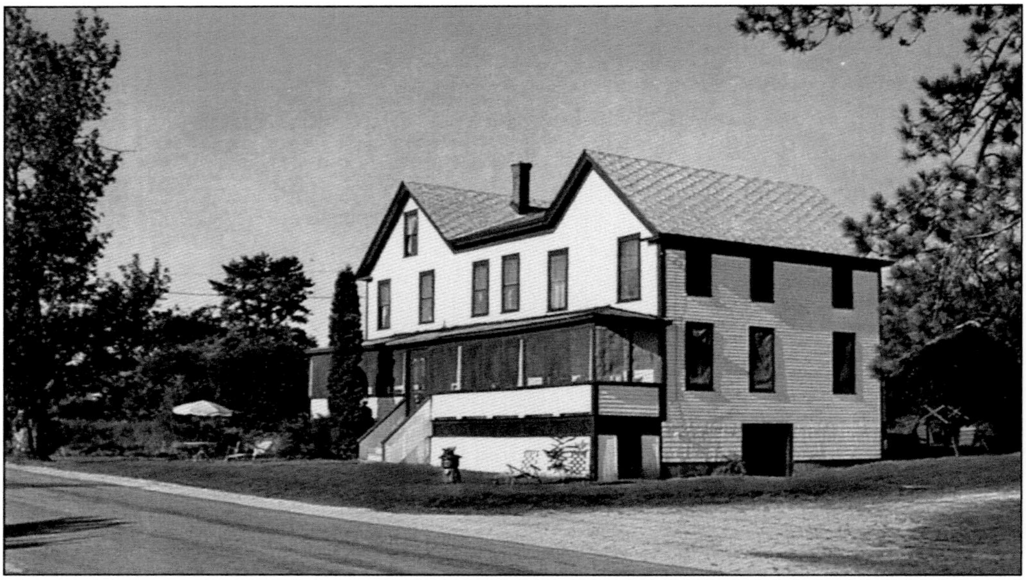

Cummings Homestead, located at 110 Portland Avenue, was purchased by Charles and Rose Cummings in 1917. In 1923, it was opened as a guesthouse and was called the House of Comfort. The Cummings family ran the boardinghouse, catering to African Americans, as other boardinghouses did not allow such. Duke Ellington, Lionel Hampton, and Louis Armstrong were among the many guests that stayed here. The house is now on the Maine Historic Preservation Commissions List of Historic Homes of Maine.

# *Three*

# Chapter and Verse

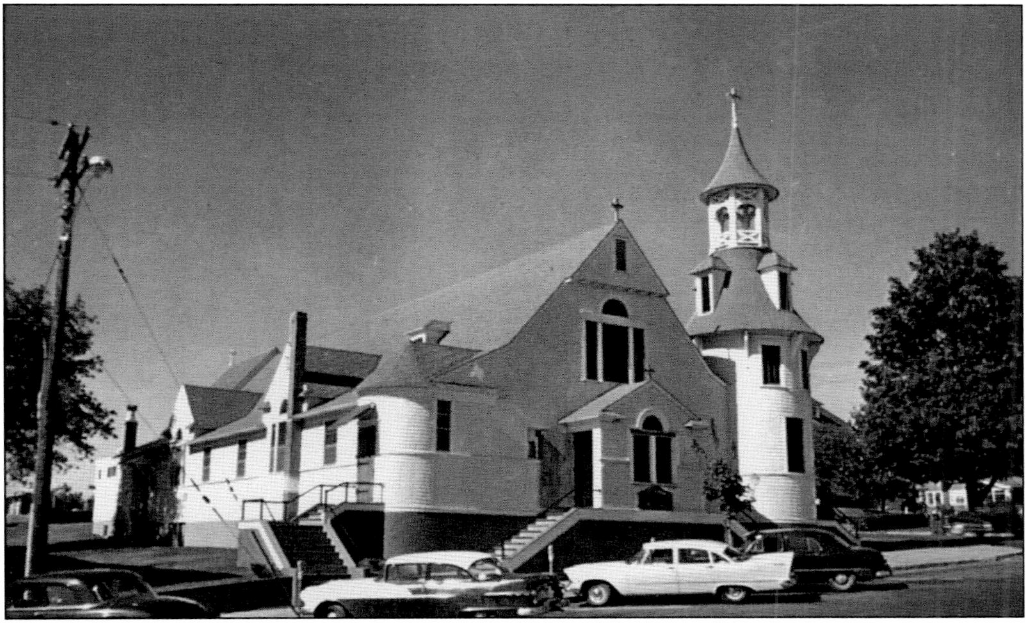

St. Margaret's Church was erected in 1895 by parishioners of St. Mary's Church in Biddeford. In January 1926, the bishop of the Catholic diocese of Portland established St. Margaret's Church as a parish with Rev. James J. Mullen as its first resident pastor. St. Margaret's Church has a year-round membership of 1,900 parishioners.

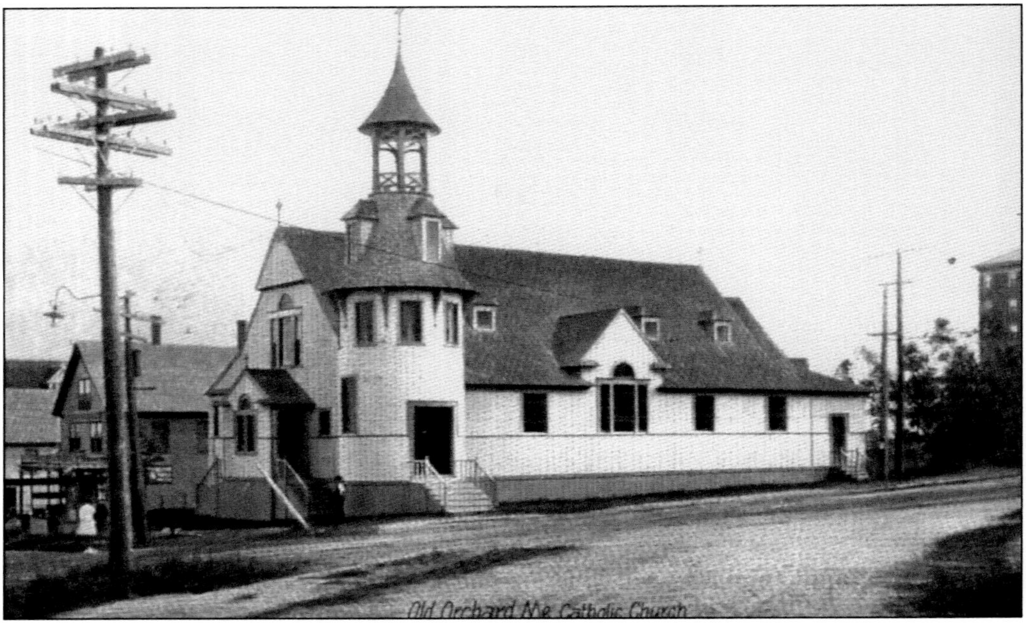


In 1915, the rear portion of the church was moved toward Staples Street. The middle section was filled in as shown in the postcard view below, doubling the existing size of the church.

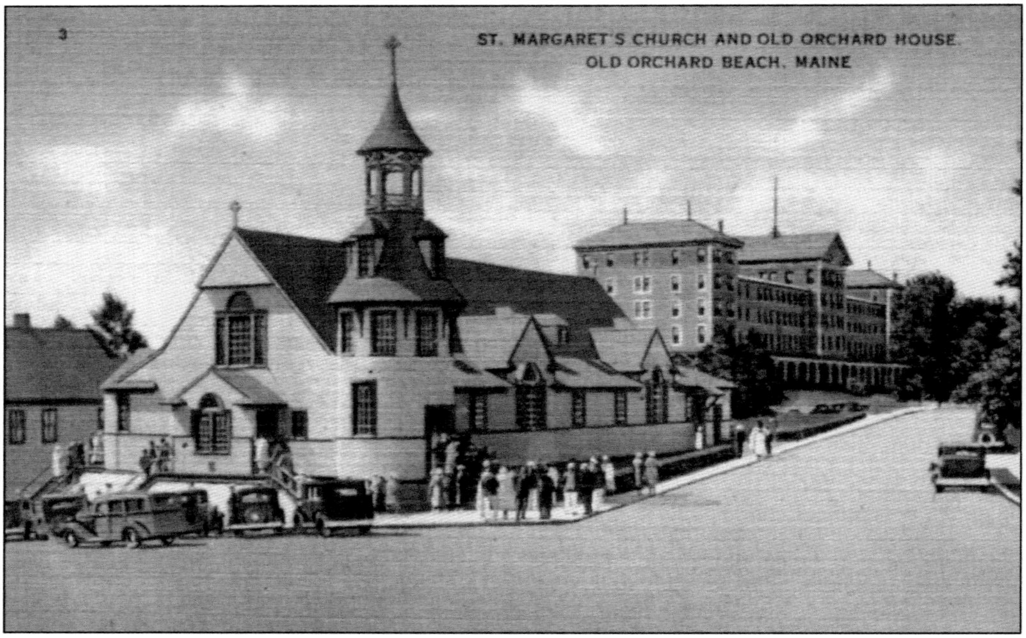


The original interior of the church was frescoed by Edwin H. Witten, who was universally recognized as one of the best decorators in the state. In June 1921, St. Margaret's Church was officially separated from St. Mary's Church of Biddeford and became a ward of the Cathedral of Portland.

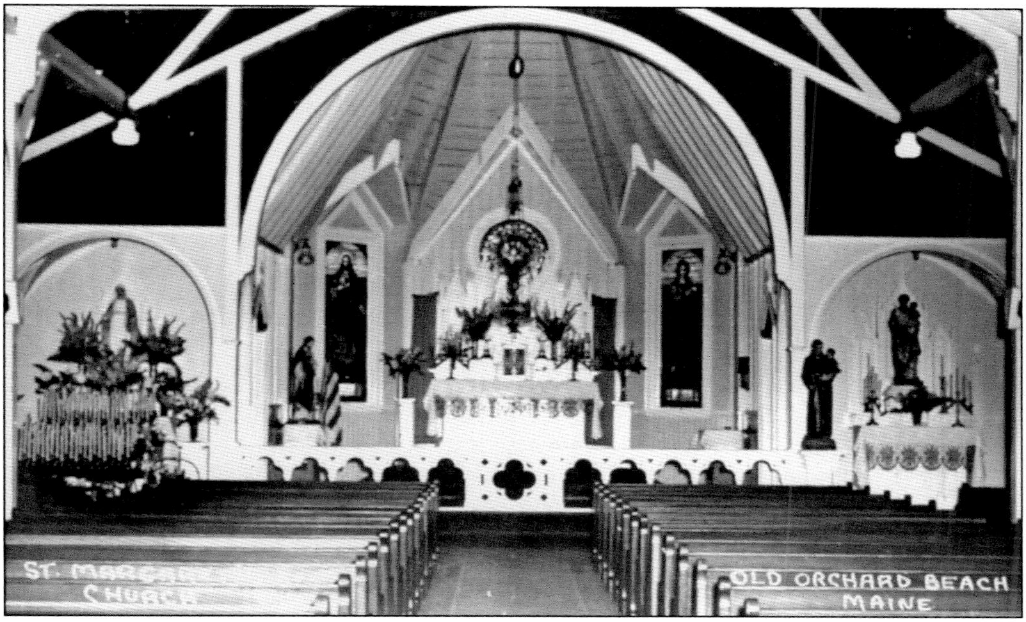


The interior view of St. Margaret's Church shows the sanctuary as it was originally built. The two windows within the sanctuary were donated by Rev. T. P. Linehan, St. Margaret's first pastor and Mrs. Henry E. Smith of Brookline in 1898.

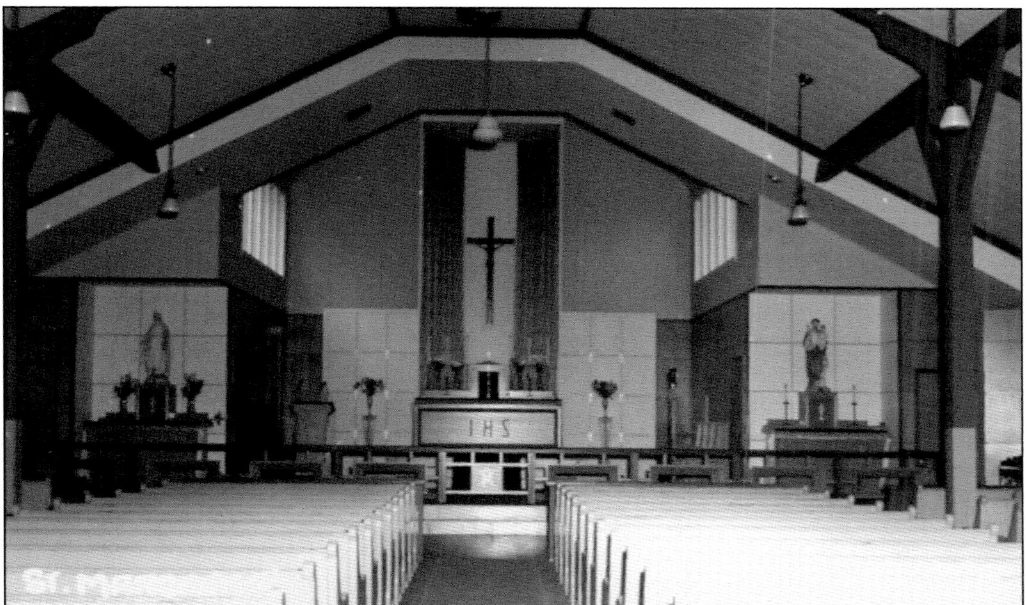

In 1969, the interior of St. Margaret's Church underwent extensive renovations. The 74-year-old edifice now has red wool carpeting stretching from wall to wall and new Vermont-grown red oak pews in a modern design. The confessionals were rebuilt and were enclosed with gold velvet drapes. The organ and choir grouping has been transferred to the front of the church, according to a 1969 *Biddeford Daily Journal* article.

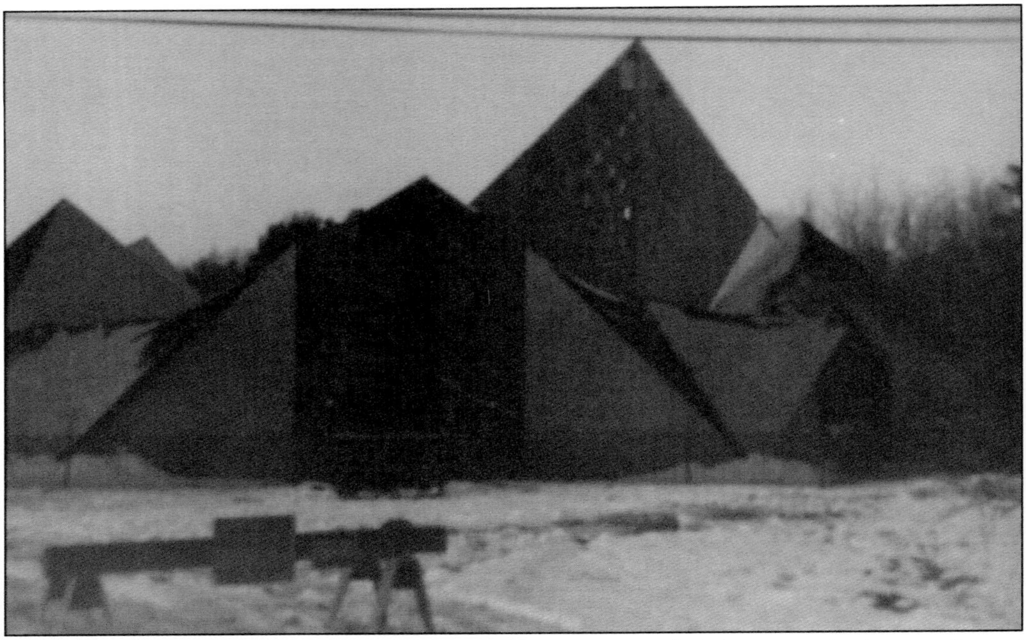

St. Luke's Chapel was constructed in the spring and summer of 1969 to contain the overflow of parishioners from St. Margaret's Church on Old Orchard Street. It was built on a 20-acre site, purchased in 1959. It was of octagonal design. The church was complete when on Christmas Eve a wet snow and wind storm battered the area. Two days later, around 5:30 p.m., the entire structure collapsed under the weight of the wet snow.

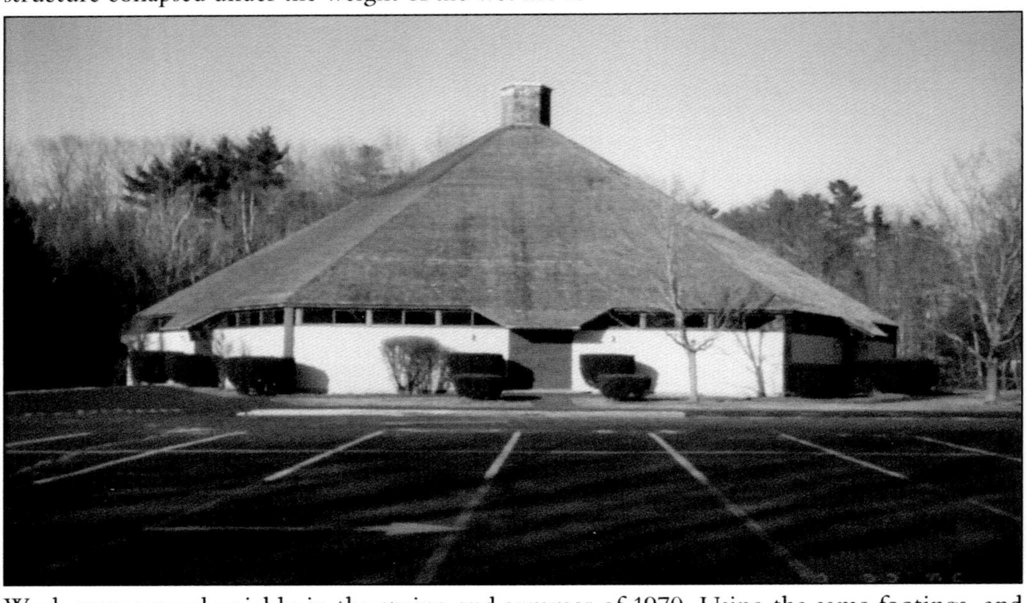

Work commenced quickly in the spring and summer of 1970. Using the same footings, and heavier, stronger beams of southern pine from North Carolina, the new St. Luke's Chapel was completed and ready for parishioners on June 24, 1971. Today the Portland diocese is considering closing St. Margaret's Church and winterizing St. Luke's Chapel for use as a year-round facility, as it provides more parking and would save money.

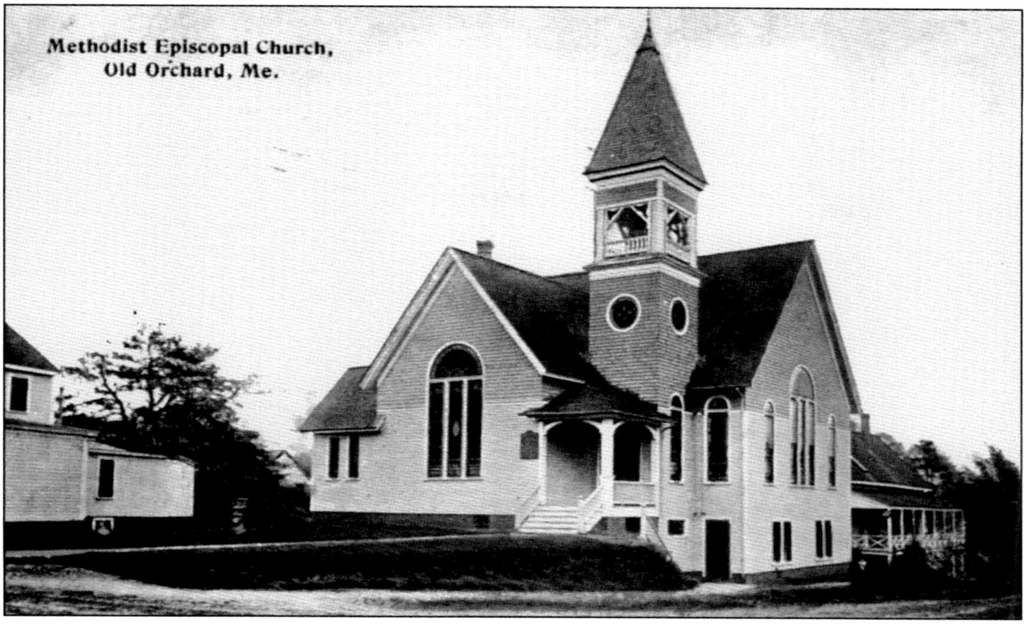


The Methodist Episcopal Church was erected in 1899 on Washington and Fountain Avenues. Previous to the completion of the church, members met in Central Hall on West Grand Avenue and in the old 1820 one-room schoolhouse. Opening services for the Methodist Episcopal Church were held on Thanksgiving Day, 1899. The official dedication was held on December 29 of that year.

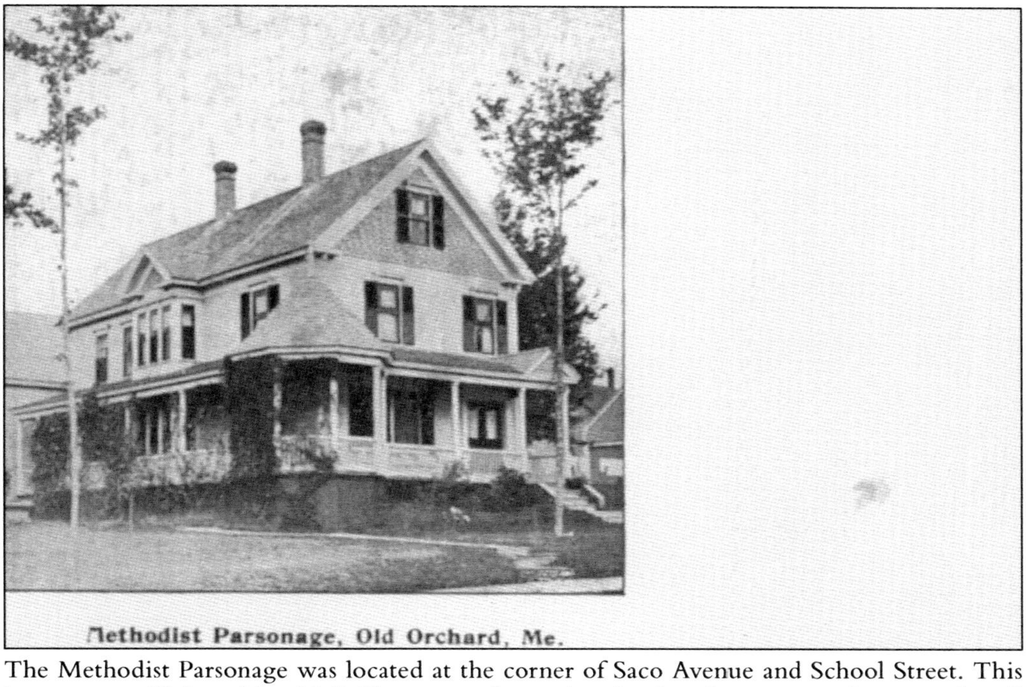


The Methodist Parsonage was located at the corner of Saco Avenue and School Street. This house was a gift from Mrs. N. S. Plummer to be used as the church parsonage. It was used until 1958, when the old 1914 brick house at 62 Cedar Avenue was purchased.

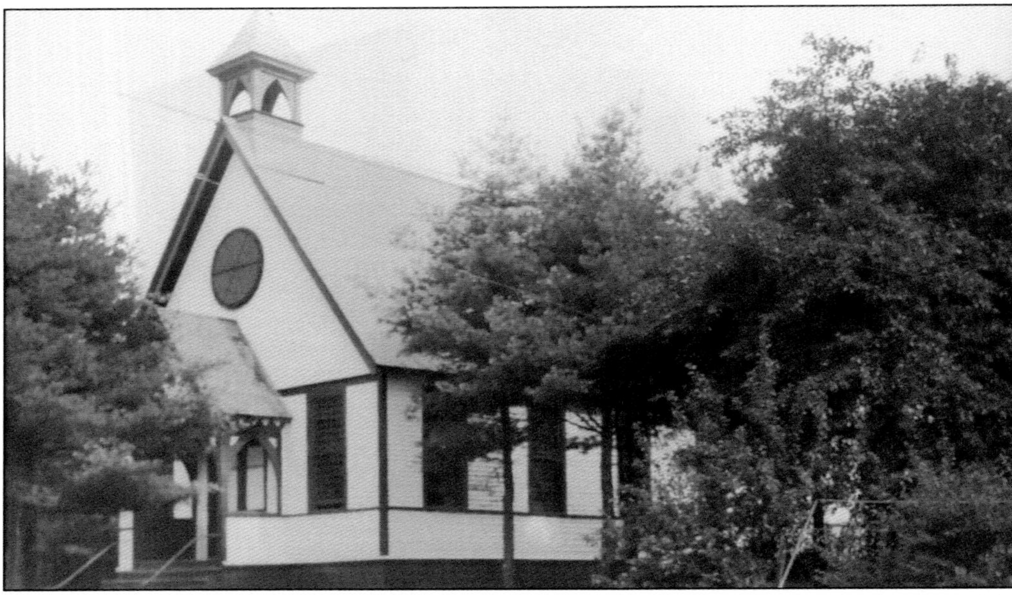

St. John's-by-the-Sea Episcopal Church is located on St. John's Street. It was designed by well-known architects John Calvin Stevens and Francis Fasset, both of Portland. The distinctive shingle-style chapel was erected in 1882 on land given to the church by the widow of T. T. Williams in 1874. Opening services were held on July 16, 1882, by Rev. E. F. Small, rector of the Trinity Church of Saco. It was used as a summer chapel only until 1938. In 1938, it was opened year round. Eventually membership declined, and the church closed. Today it stands as a vacant building.

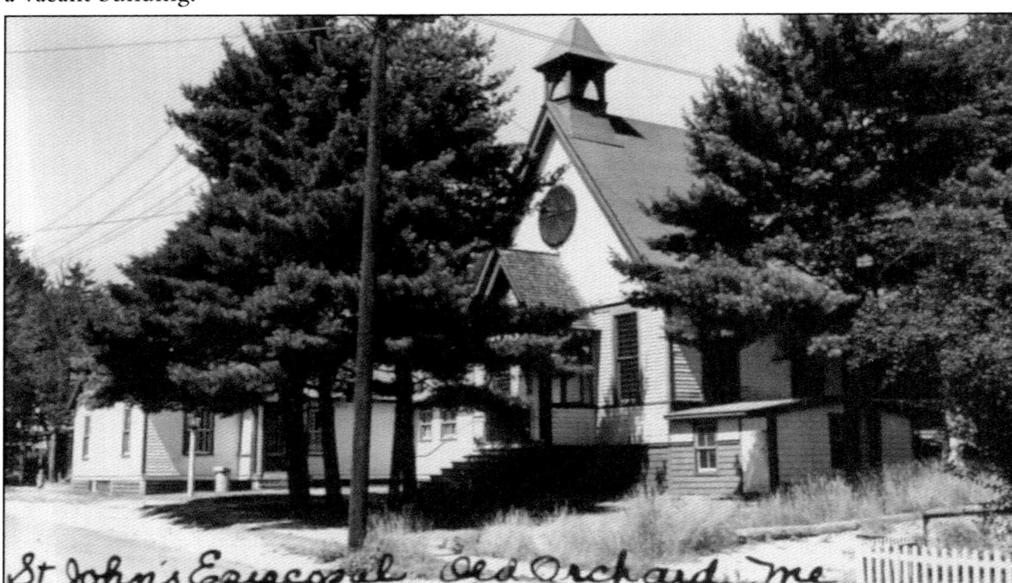


The rectory for St. John's Church was located at 4 Fern Avenue. The rectory was called the Hudson and was built in 1883 by the Reverend Hudson Sawyer, pastor of St. John's Church. The rectory was used until 1953, when it was sold to the Ellis family. St. John's Church was very active until the early 1960s. Today St. John's Church lies vacant and in need of repair.

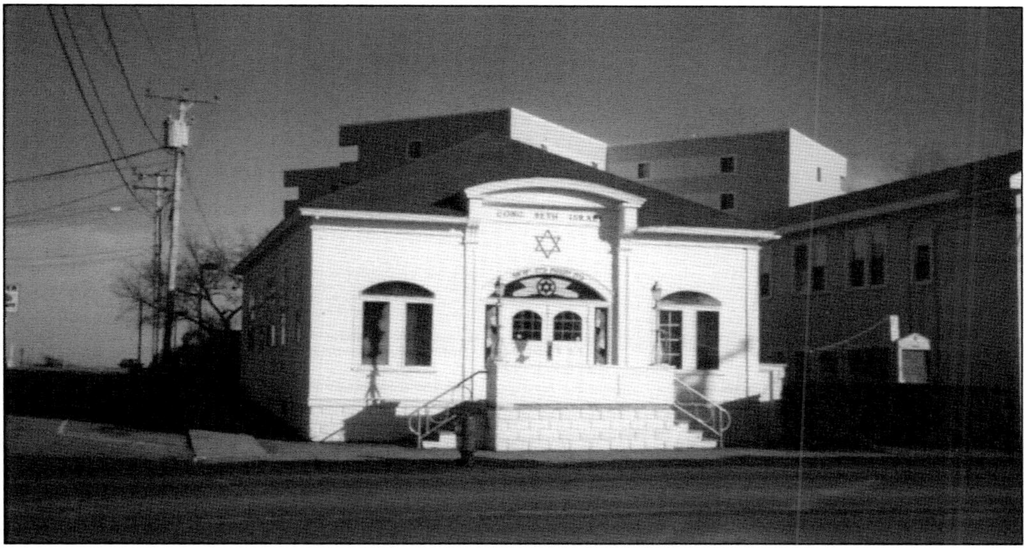

The Hebrew synagogue at the corner of Cleaves Street and East Grand Avenue was built in 1912 and opened the same year. The then green and white building with brown stained windows was built by Victor Beaudette of Biddeford. The original building had two entrances, one for men and one for women. The Beth Israel was renovated in 1946, and the separate entrances were eliminated. As shown above, two windows and one central entrance were installed.

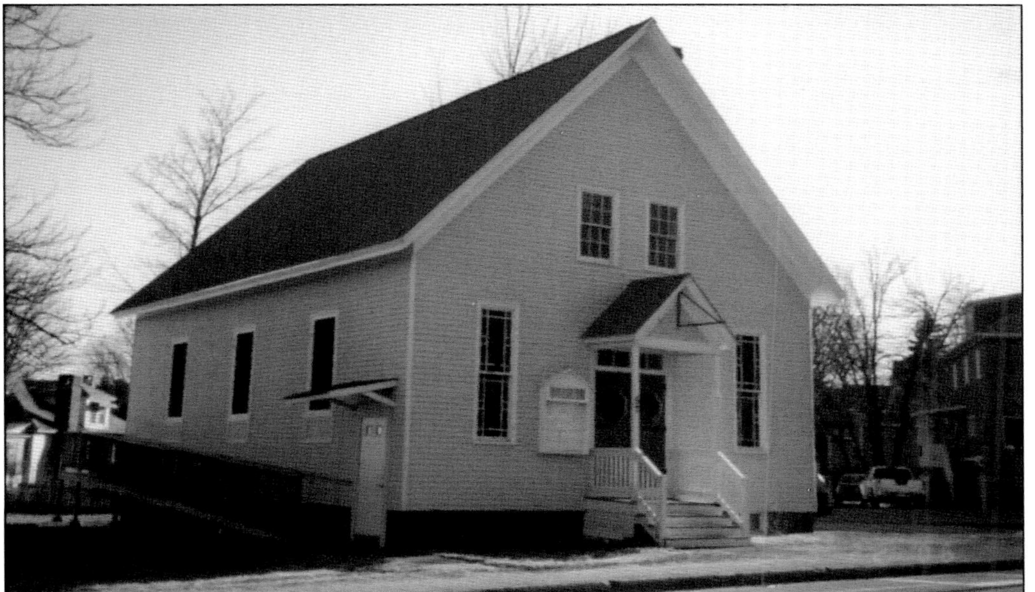

The Second Advent Church, on the corner of Carlton and Saco Avenues, was organized on May 27, 1882, and was erected in the fall of 1882. Several years later, a brick foundation was built and the church was moved 12 feet back from Saco Avenue and placed onto its new foundation. The 1911 records state that the floors were cleaned with a vacuum cleaner. Over the years, the church has been used by various groups. Several years ago, it was a dance school and the home of the Marantha Pentecostal Church, and in October 2005, Michael Roberge and Robert Magazu purchased the building and converted it into an arts, crafts, and painted furniture business.

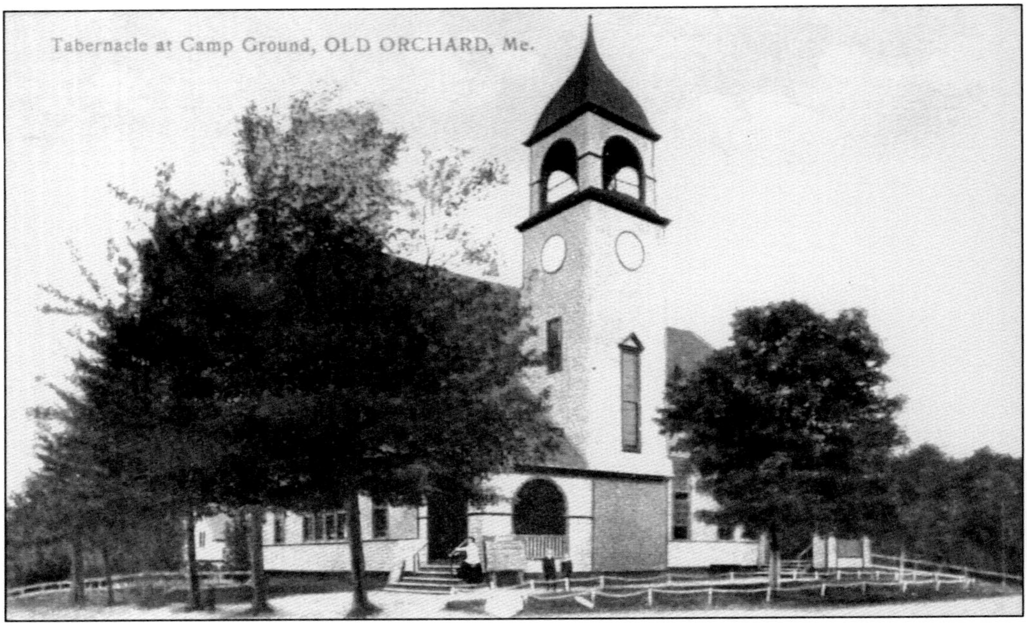


The Tabernacle is the third such structure erected on this site. The first was a tent erected in 1873. In 1879, a wooden and more weather-friendly building was constructed. In 1884, the 1879 building, which remains standing today, was enlarged and remodeled. All three structures were built by the Methodist Association. In 1899, the rear gallery was inclined to give more room for 200 more seats. The Salvation Army owns the Tabernacle today.

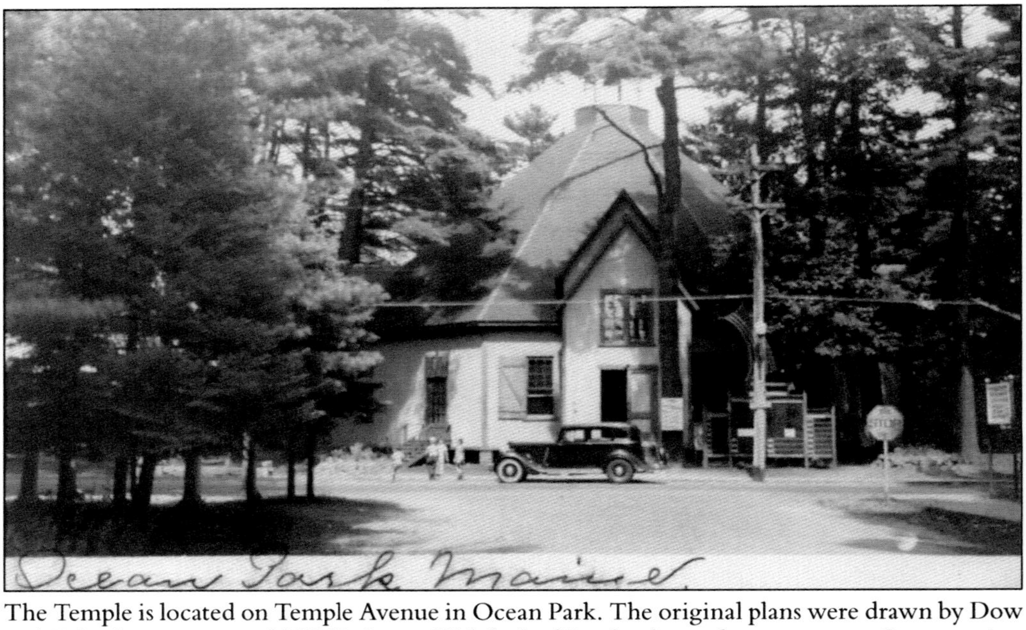


The Temple is located on Temple Avenue in Ocean Park. The original plans were drawn by Dow and Wheeler, at a cost of $27.50. James Bickford of Portland was the contractor. Construction began on June 6, 1881, and was completed on July 20 of the same year. Dedication ceremonies were held on August 2, 1881. The cost was $3,500. In 1975, the Temple was added to the National Register of Historic Places.

# *Four*

# Flames and Ashes

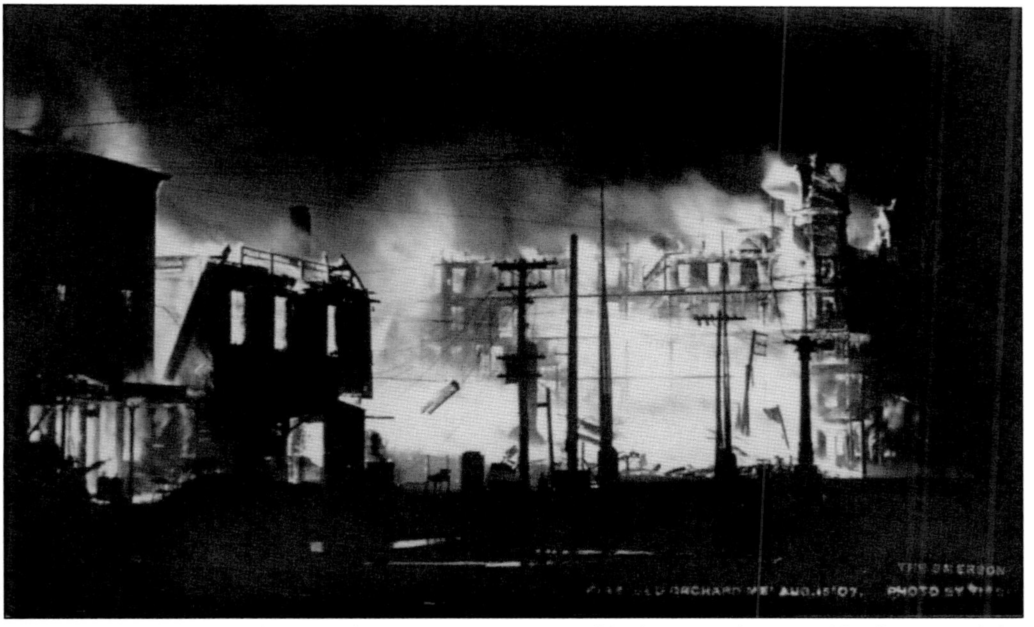

Who would have ever known that a young 31-year-old photographer would take one of the most spectacular photographs ever in Old Orchard Beach history? On Thursday evening, August 15, 1907, at approximately 9:00 p.m., local photographer Arthur L. Tisdale took the famous photograph of the Alberta Hotel (left) and the Emerson Hotel, also known as the Velvet Hotel, soon after the fire jumped over the railroad tracks. The largest fire in Old Orchard Beach history was now officially documented on glass. Nothing can compare to the destruction that occurred on that warm, summer night, in one of the town's busiest seasons to date. In six hours, several people died, several were seriously injured, 17 hotels were destroyed, 60 cottages and houses were gone, and 110 businesses were suddenly out of business. In those six dramatic hours, the face of Old Orchard Beach was altered forever, never to return to that splendor again. The next 11 pages will show this and other fires that changed Old Orchard Beach into what it is today.

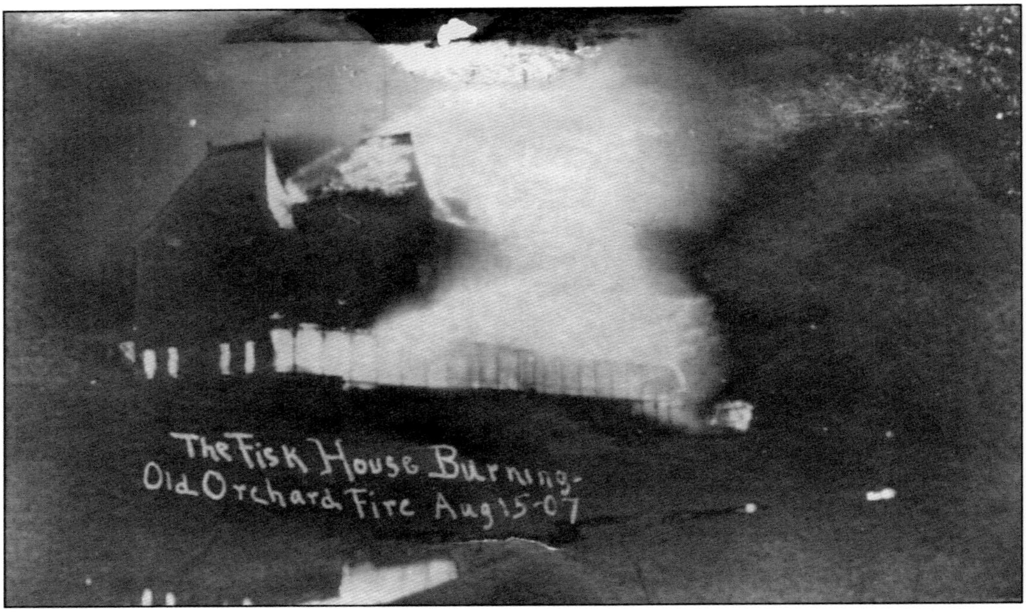


The above red color fire card shows the Fiske Hotel in its final moments. Shortly after the Emerson and Alberta Hotels were on fire, the Fiske Hotel was also ablaze. With 135 rooms and 300 guests, it was not long before the patrons were on the beach watching their possessions going up in flames. The 1882 hotel was one of 16 others that were claimed that night on August 15, 1907.

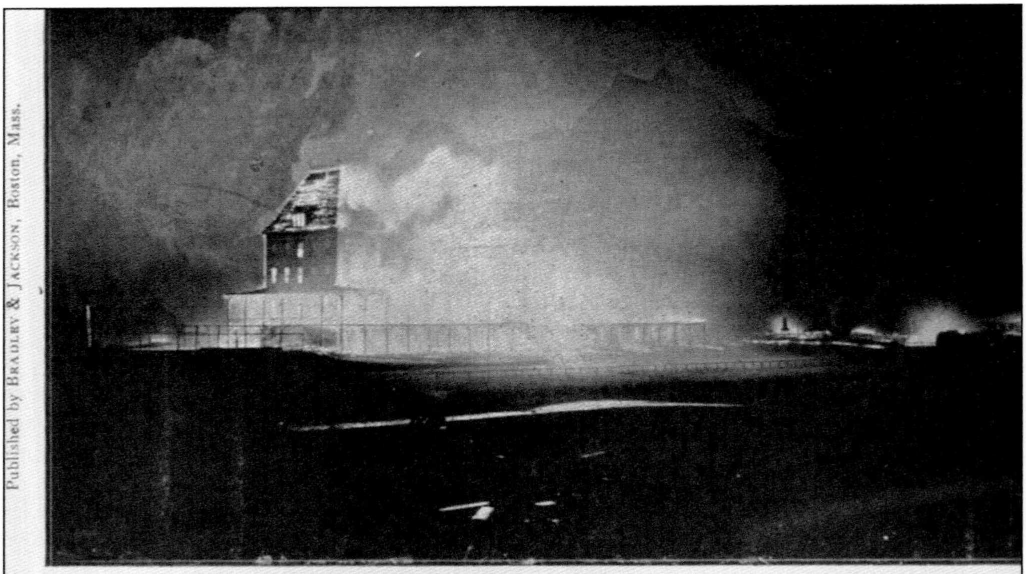


Burning of Fiske House and Surroundings at Old Orchard Beach, August 15, 1907.

It is said that no water ever touched the flames of the Fiske Hotel during the worst conflagration in Old Orchard Beach history, due to the intense heat. The many trunks and furnishings that were removed to the beach never were returned to their rightful owners. Possessions were stolen by looters as fast as they were placed on the beach. Many hotel guests were housed at St. Margaret's Church for the night, until morning when the Pullmans arrived to take them home.

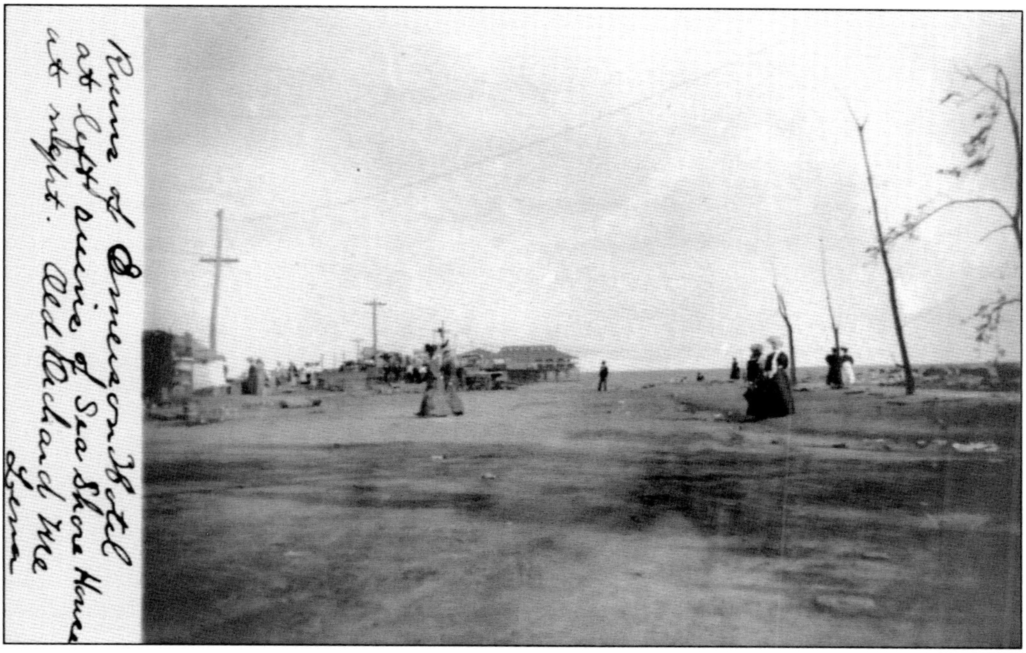

This real-photo postcard, taken shortly after the deadly fire, shows lower Old Orchard Street, called the Square; the Velvet Hotel, on the left; and the remains of the Sea Shore House, on the right. The Sea Shore House had 142 rooms and a capacity for 300 guests. The vacant lot was later sold for $3,000. Today this lot is Palace Playland Park.

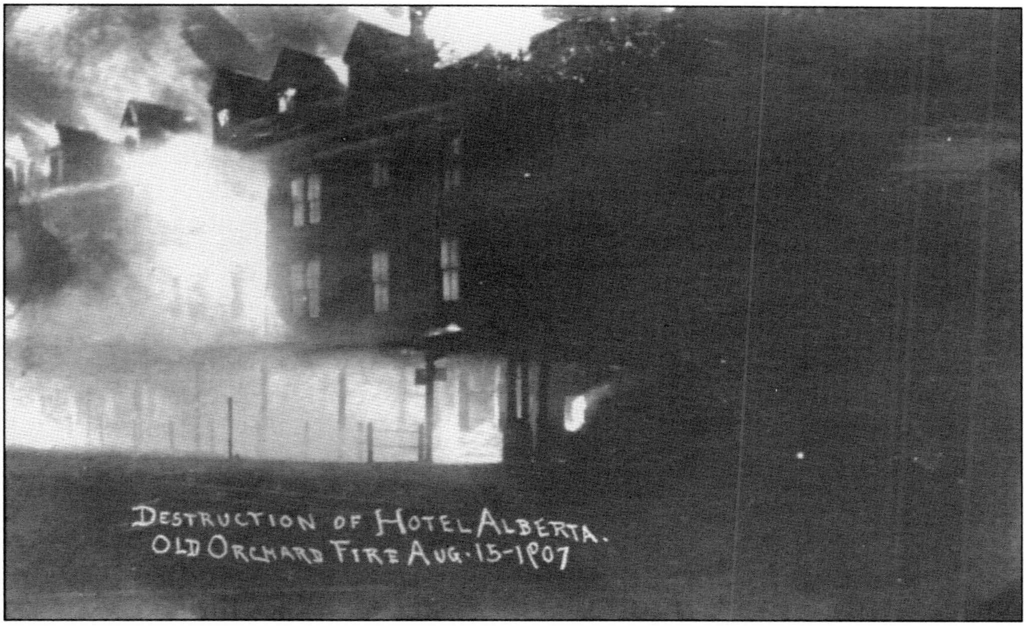


Seen here is the Alberta Hotel ablaze. This hotel was the first large hotel to catch on fire, once the flames jumped over the Boston and Maine Railroad tracks. Pier Fries and Bill's Pizza now occupy this site, in a structure known as the Whitehall Building.

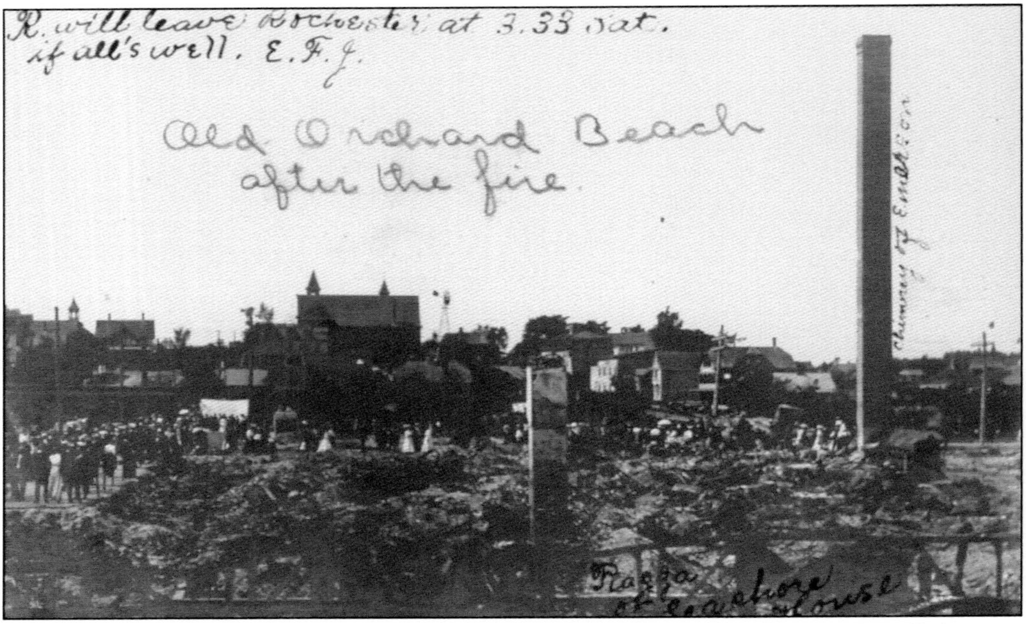


This real-photo postcard shows the destruction looking up Old Orchard Street. The tall chimney is all that remains standing of the Velvet Hotel. Today a 51-unit condominium/hotel, the Grand Victorian, occupies this site. The spires to the right are the entrance to the scenic railroad in Sea Side Park.

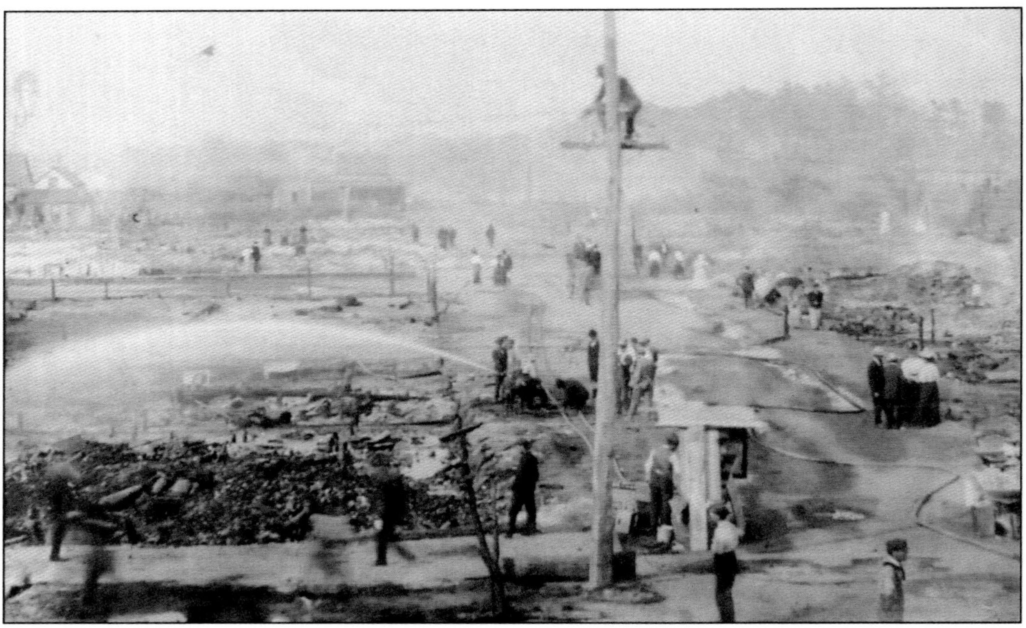

Men were still watering down the Alberta Hotel the day after the fire on August 15, 1907. This card is looking down East Grand Avenue. The local fire department was still watering down hot spots on Thanksgiving Day, four months later. Home owners at Prout's Neck were watering their roofs during the height of the fire.

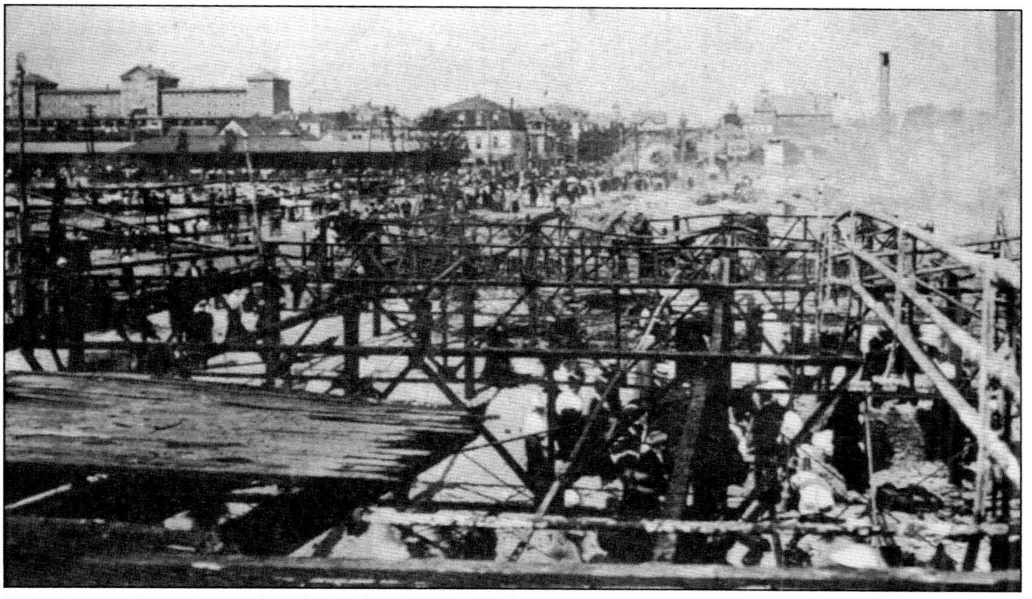

Here is another view of Old Orchard Street taken from the pier. Floorboards of the pier were pulled up to stop the fire from burning the entire pier. The twisted steel girders show the intense heat generated by the Velvet Hotel during the fire.

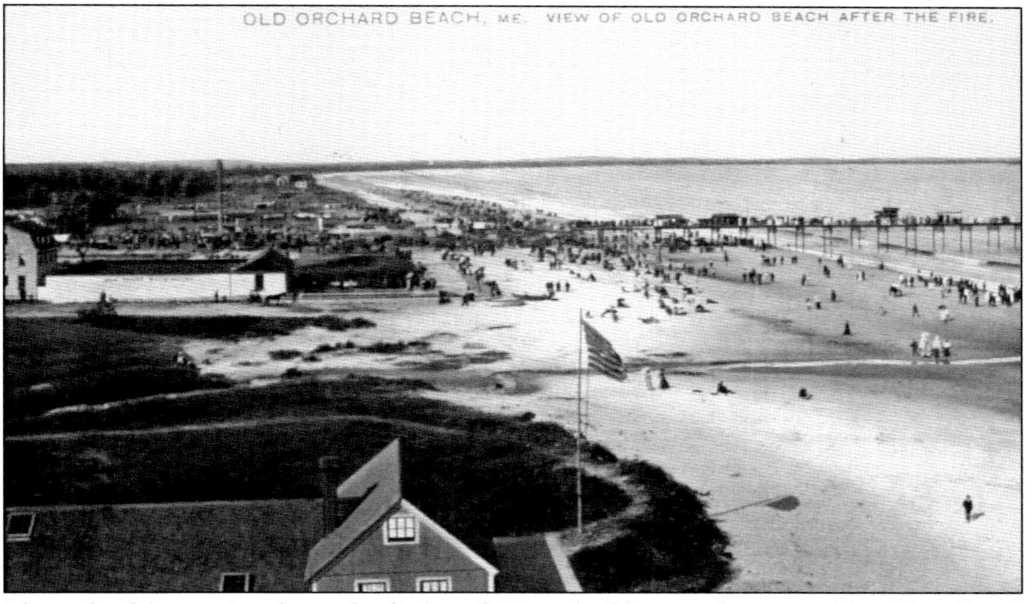


The path of destruction shows the fire's trail. Every building on the ocean side of East Grand Avenue was destroyed. The fire was finally stopped on Brisson Street. On the railroad track side of East Grand Avenue, only one building, the Boyden House, survived. Today the Executive Motel is part of that building. The brook in the foreground is Brown's Brook, which flowed down Heath Street to the ocean.

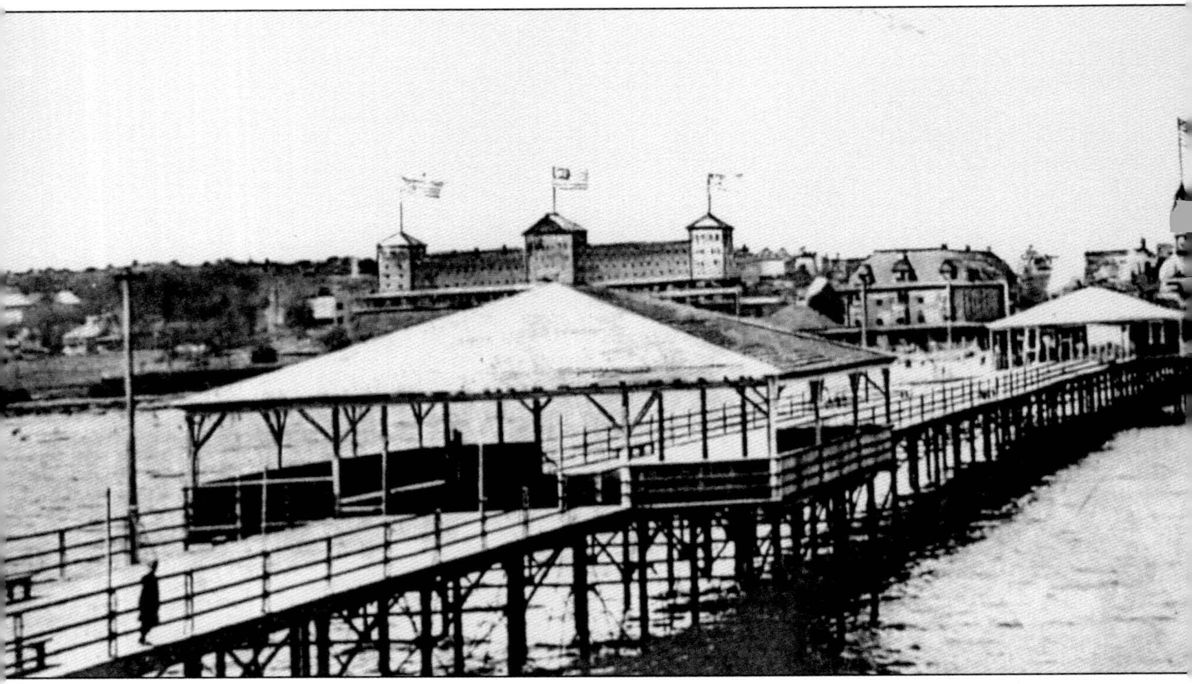

The above panorama-folding postcard shows Old Orchard Beach in all its glory. The summer of 1907 was said to be the busiest summer to date when the fire of August 15 struck. The large

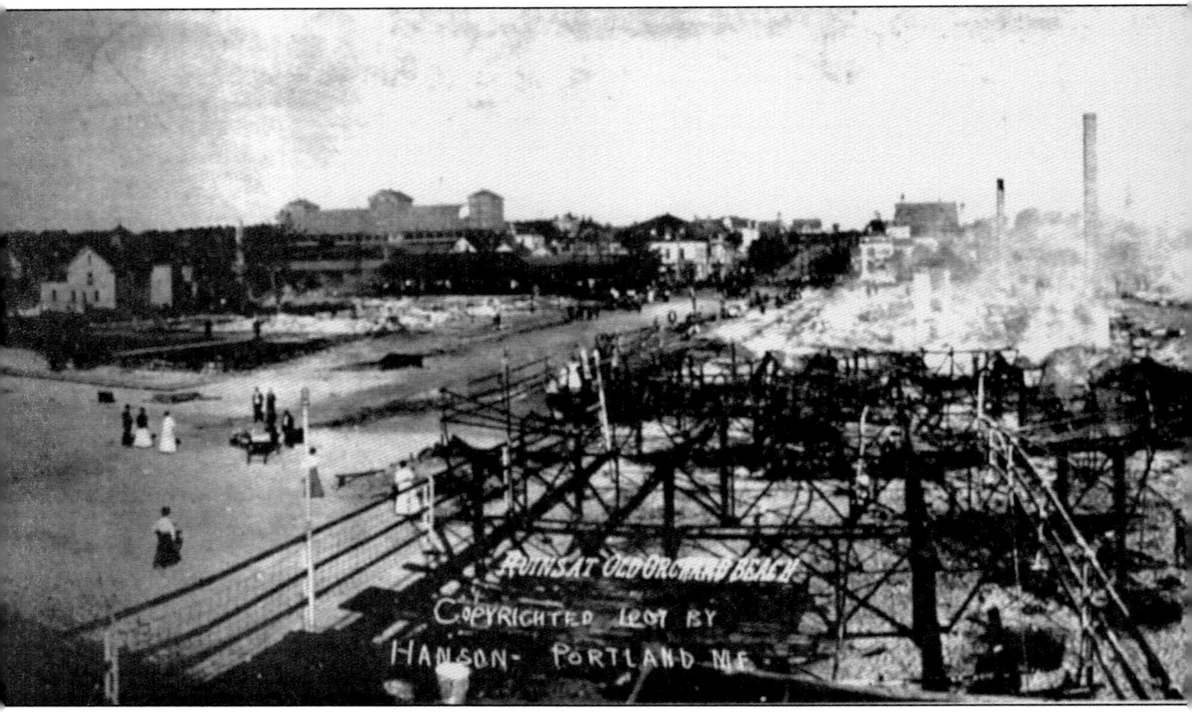


The path of destruction is apparent in the lower panoramic view, taken the following morning. Still seen on the beach is furniture from one of the hotels that survived the looters. Reports from

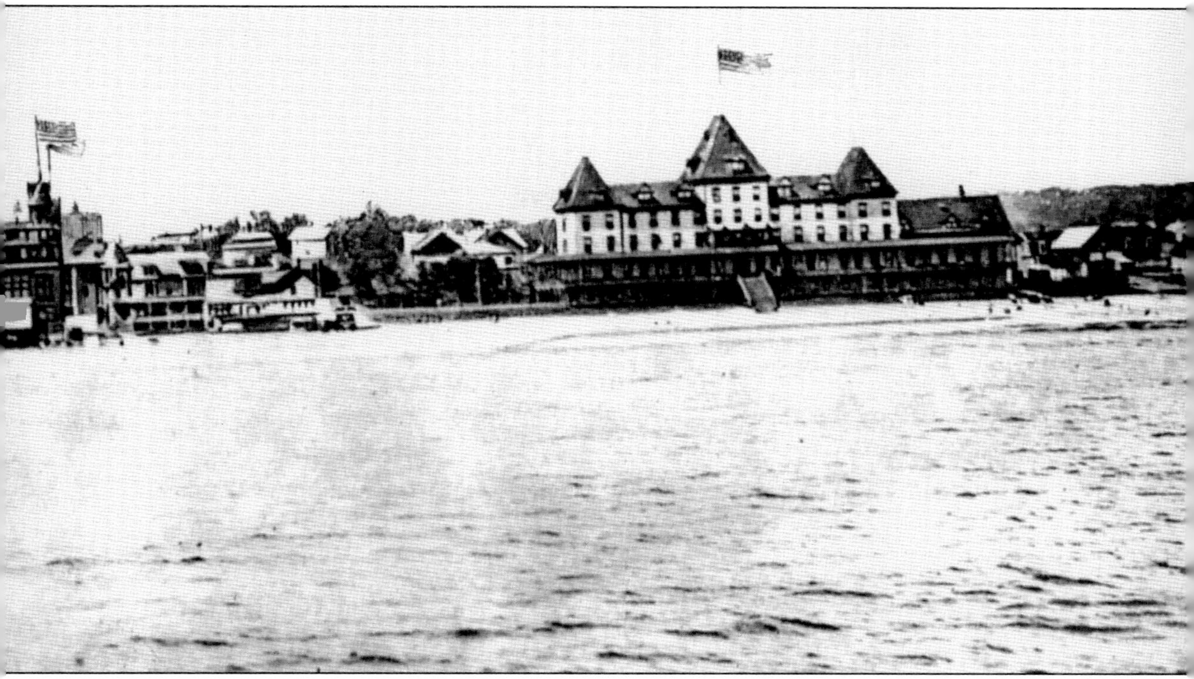

1876 Old Orchard House in the background was spared. Many displaced hotel guests were provided rooms there that evening.

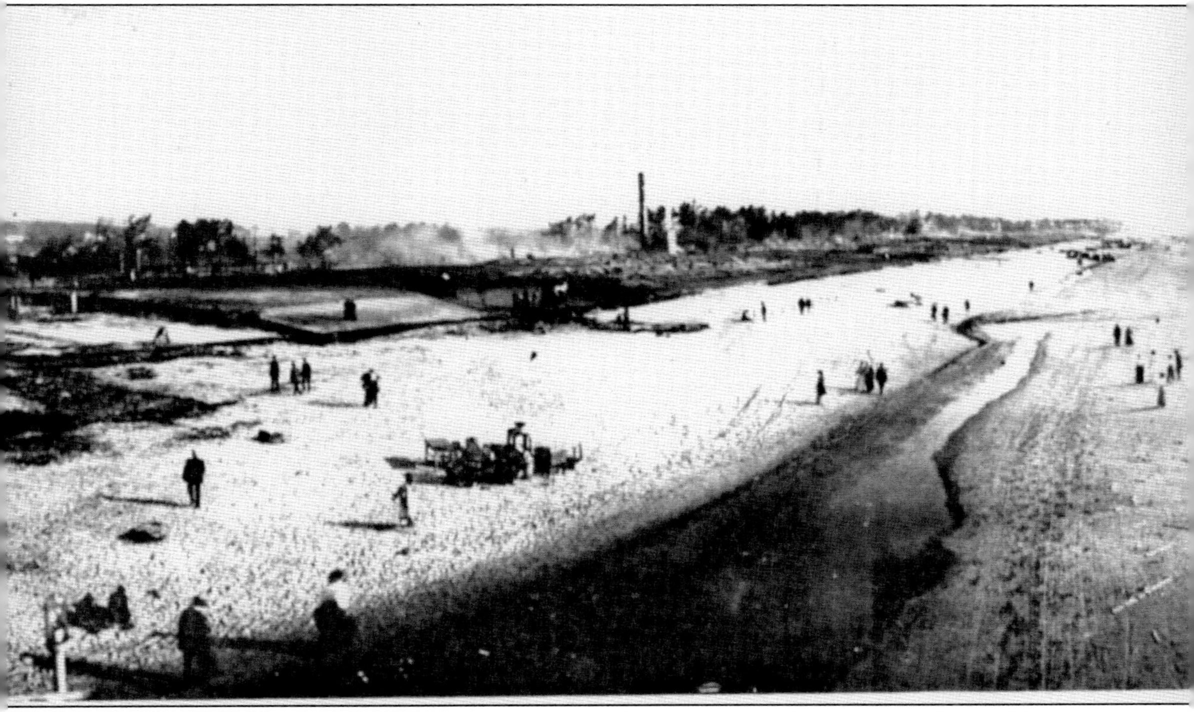

actual witnesses stated that there was not any wind that night. The fire of November 1881 was the largest in town history, until the one of August 15, 1907.

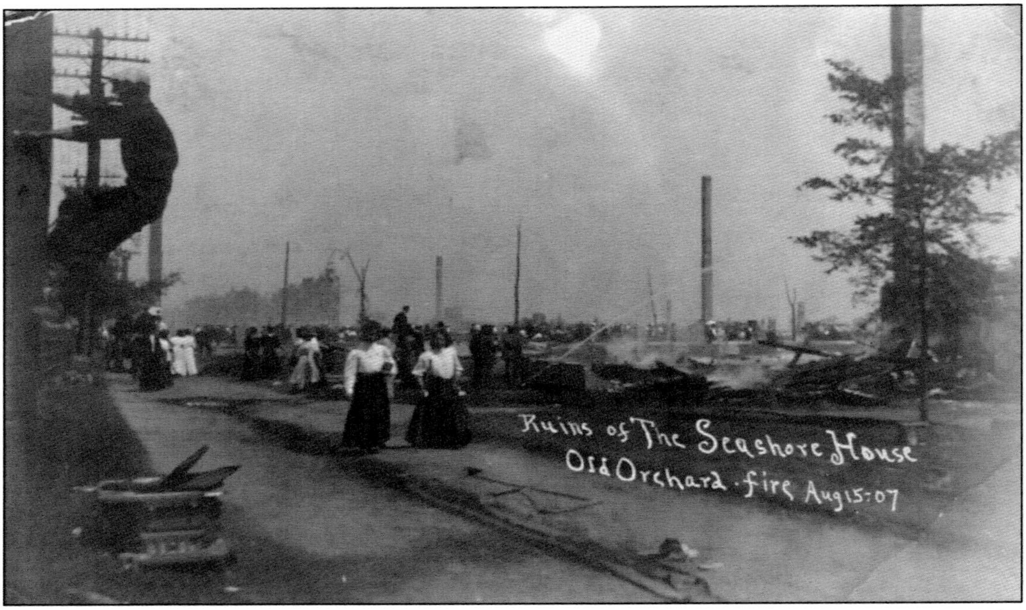


This real-photo postcard shows a lineman repairing telegraph lines on West Grand Avenue the following morning. Sightseeing train excursions were running daily from Portland. Even the steamer *Machigonne* was making trips from the Portland pier, with the American Cadet Band on board, to view the ruins from the bay.

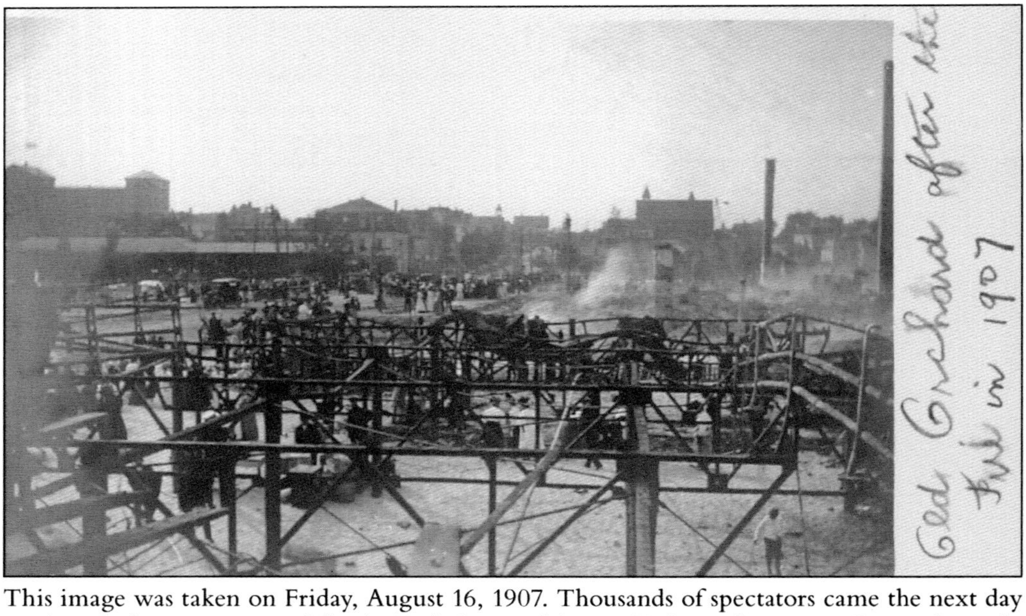


This image was taken on Friday, August 16, 1907. Thousands of spectators came the next day to view the largest structural fire in York County history. Trains as far away as Boston brought people up for the day. A total of 160 pounds of dynamite was transported to town to be used in destroying burnable buildings in the path of the fire, but the fire chief ruled this inadvisable.

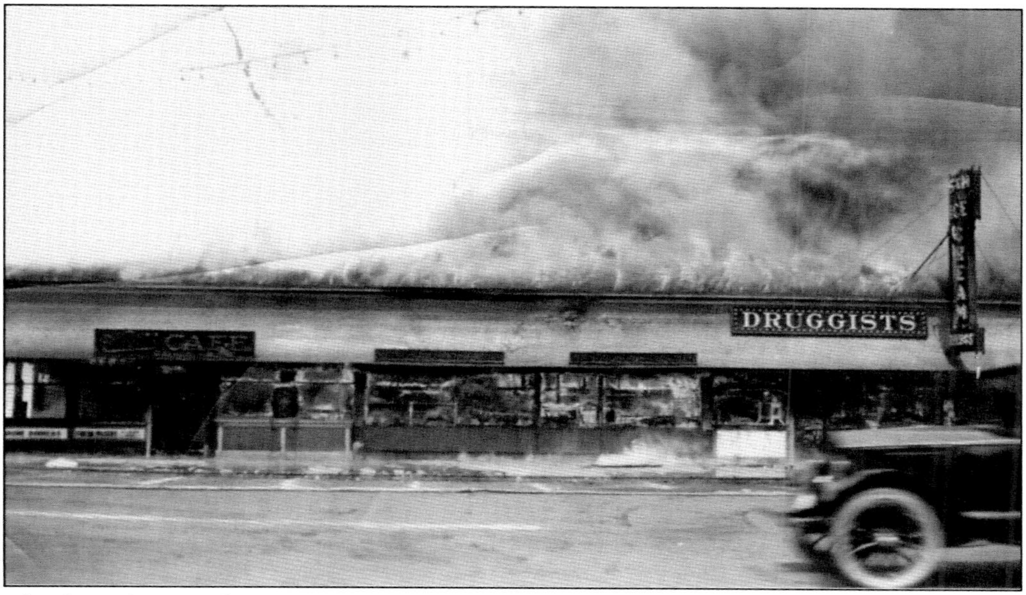


The above fire on July 2, 1922, shows Whites Café and Sears and Hinchcliffe building burning. This site had two previous fires, one on August 15, 1907, and the second on June 28, 1919. The Whitehall building, located at 12–14 Old Orchard Street, stands on the location and houses Bill's Pizza, Pier Fries, and the Dairy Queen. The building sold for $1.1 million in 2002.

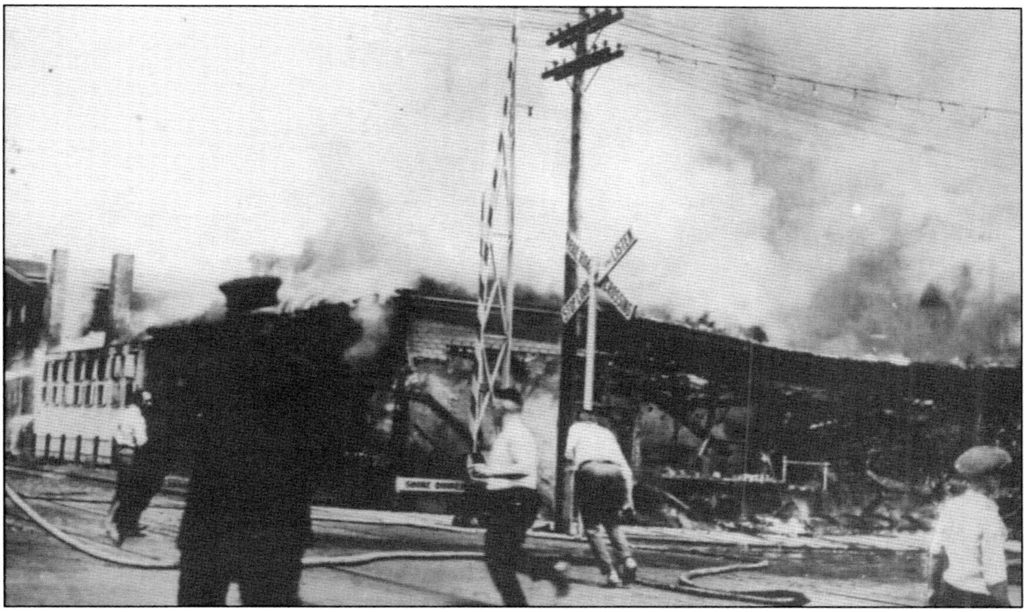

The fire started on the East Grand Avenue side of the building, in Katherine Fitz's hot dog stand. Saco, Biddeford, and Portland fire departments were called to assist. The fire was stopped on East Grand Avenue at William Whites Bowling Alley. This building still stands today and is known as Cocktails. A temporary building was erected in three days. The present-day Whitehall building was built on this location in 1924.

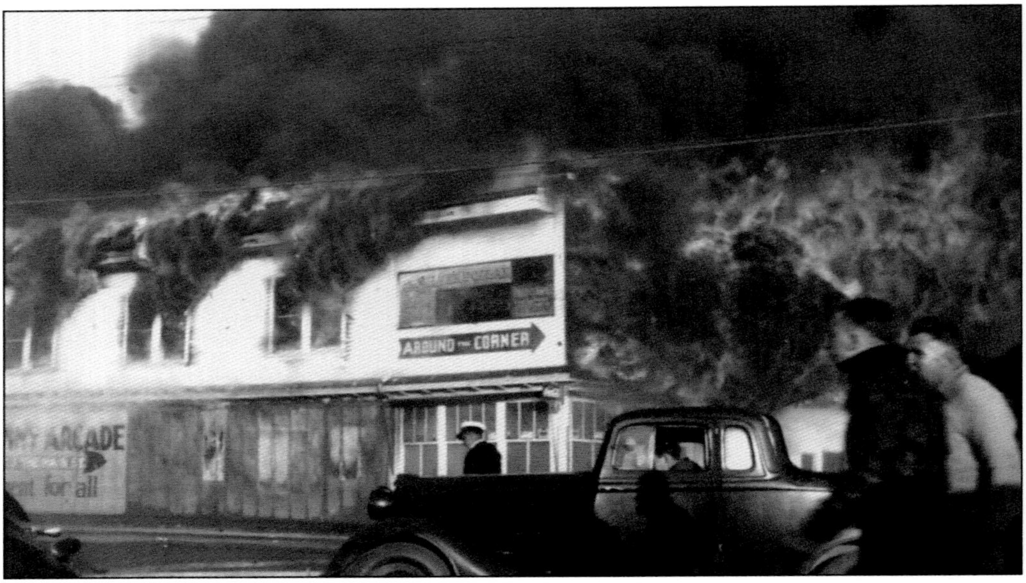


This was the scene on October 3, 1948. The entire block of the amusement area, known as Palace Playland, was destroyed. The fire started on Old Orchard Street in a ride called the Old Mill. The alarm was called in by a worker, Thomas Smith, who ironically became fire chief 22 years later in 1970. On December 23, 1972, this entire block was once again consumed by fire, with Smith as the fire chief.

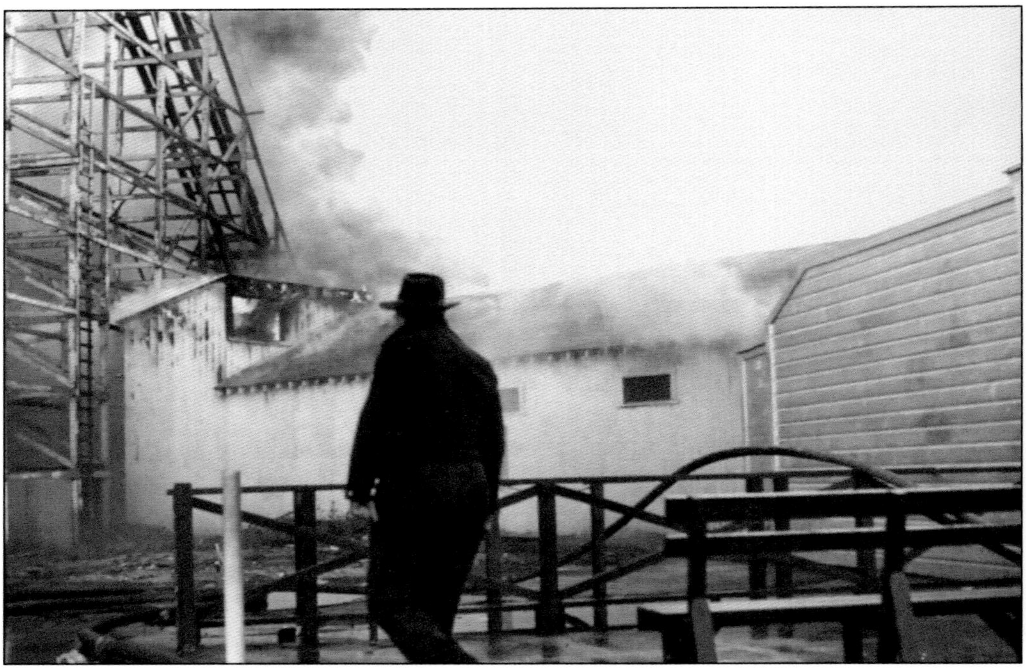

The area burnt was surrounded by Old Orchard Street, West Grand Avenue, Staples Street, and the oceanfront. The fire started at 3:45 p.m. When the smoke cleared, the famous wooden roller coaster, the Old Mill, two game concessions, two summer cottages, and two bathhouses were destroyed.

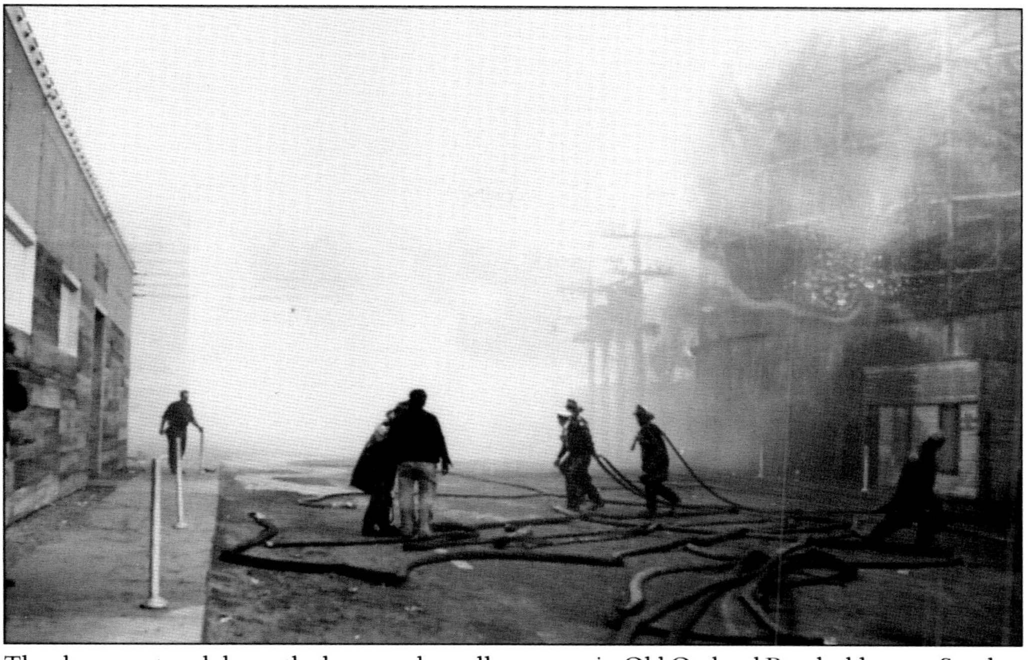

The above postcard shows the last wooden roller coaster in Old Orchard Beach ablaze on Sunday, October 3, 1948. A newspaper article mentioned the famous wooden roller coaster "looked like an oil well on fire." Damages from the fire totalled $250,000.

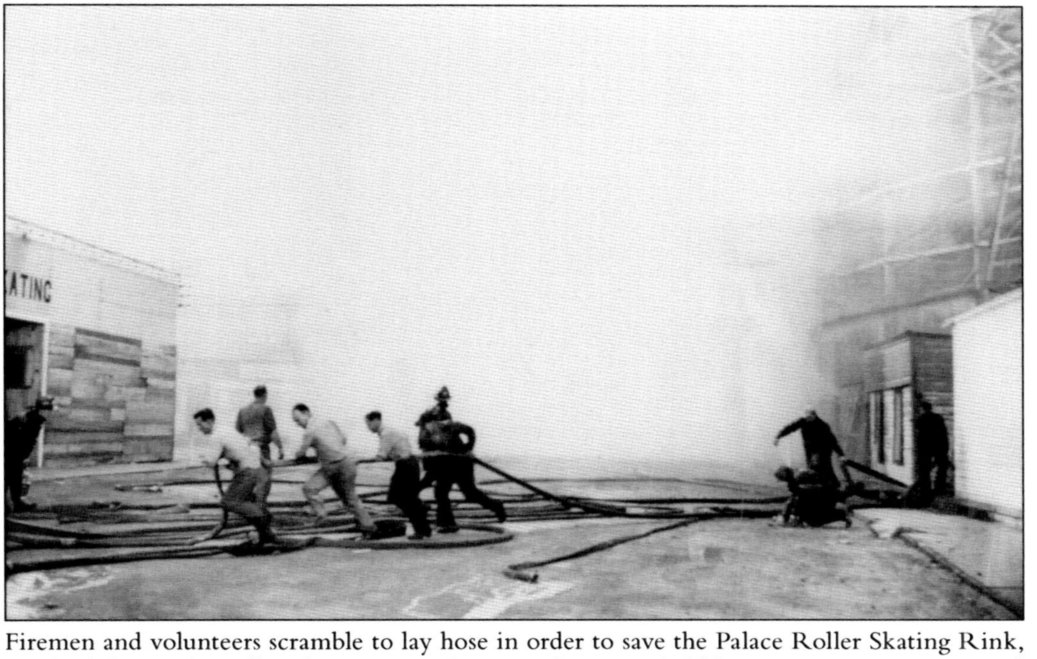

Firemen and volunteers scramble to lay hose in order to save the Palace Roller Skating Rink, on the left. Besides roller-skating, wrestling matches were held here. Later it was converted into a bar called Cocktails. The building was finally razed in March 2000. A log flume ride has replaced the skating rink, in what is now known as the Palace Playland Kiddie Park.

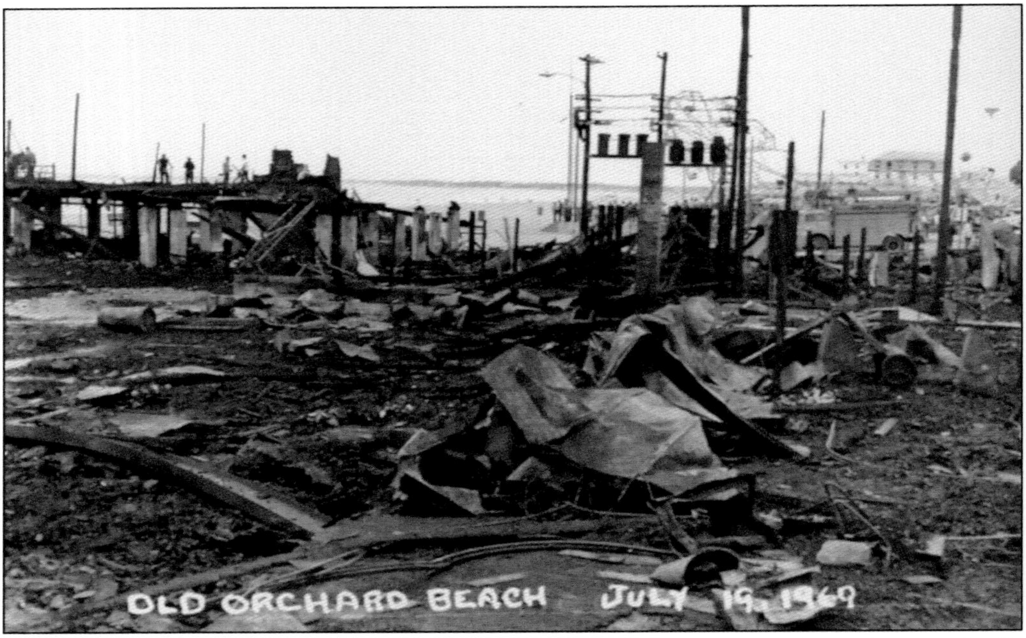


Fire again destroyed the Pier Block, seen in this image. On a warm Saturday night, on July 19, 1969, a penny in the fuse box started the disastrous fire. The Moon Spinner ride, in the White Way, was aflame when the firefighters arrived. Everything between Cortland Avenue, East Grand Avenue, Old Orchard Street, and the beach was a total loss. The fire started in the early evening and was brought under control by midnight. (Jim Hepburn collection.)

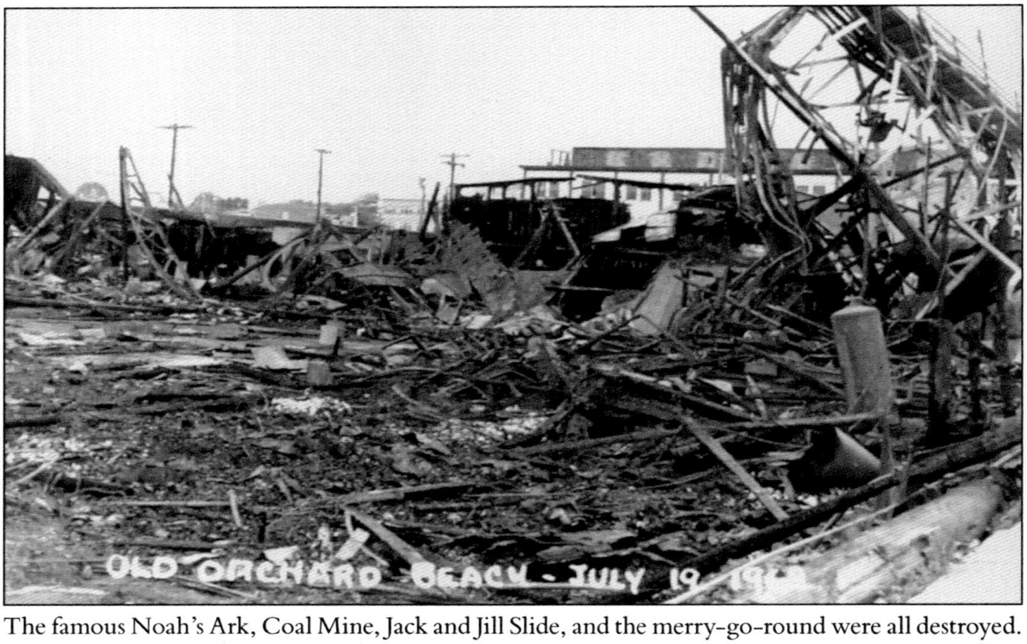

The famous Noah's Ark, Coal Mine, Jack and Jill Slide, and the merry-go-round were all destroyed. Flames were seen as far away as Sebago Lake. The total loss was estimated at $500,000. Two other famous events were happening that very night. One was the Ted Kennedy at Chappaquiddick incident, and the Apollo 11 crew being on the moon was the other. (Jim Hepburn collection.)

# *Five*

# The Pier

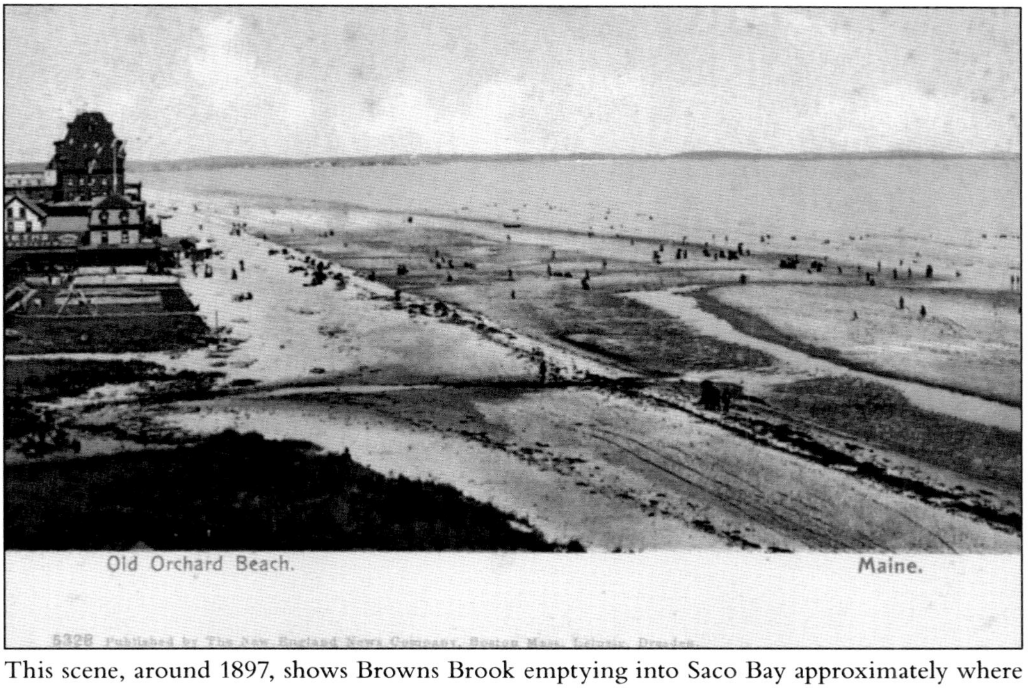


This scene, around 1897, shows Browns Brook emptying into Saco Bay approximately where the Palace Playland Kiddie Park is today. The pier was built in 1898. On March 17 of that year, actual construction commenced. The original twin pavilion was short-lived. The grand opening was on July 2. On December 4, the end of the pier was swept away during a northeast gale, only 156 days after opening. The ballroom, at the end, featured every well-known East Coast band. The big band era ended in the 1960s with the advent of rock and roll and record hops. Louis Armstrong was among the last big bands to play on the pier.

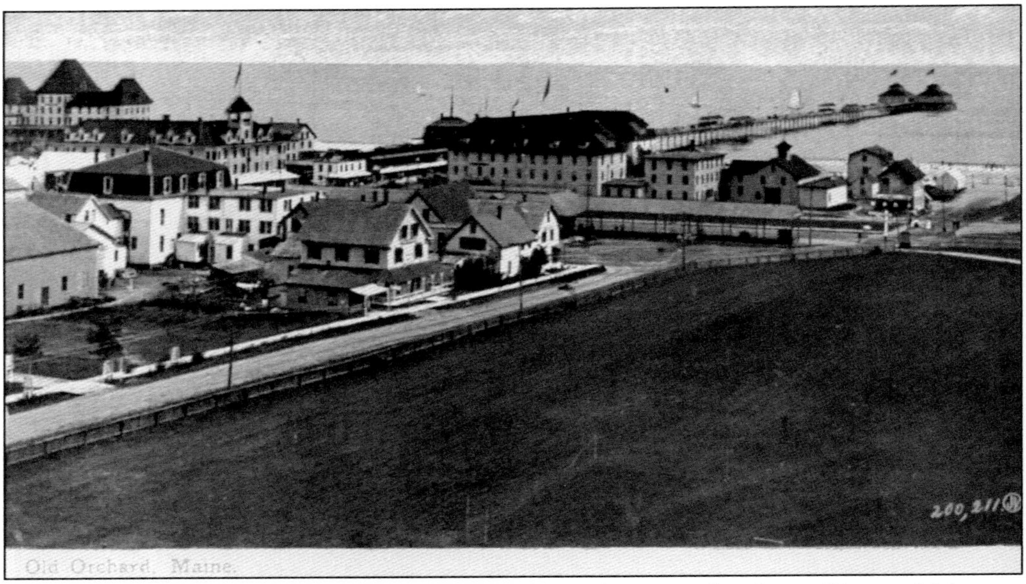


The postcard above is the only one known that shows the original twin pavilions, which were swept away on December 4, 1898. A second pavilion was built, in the spring of 1899, three stories high at the same location as the first one, as shown below.

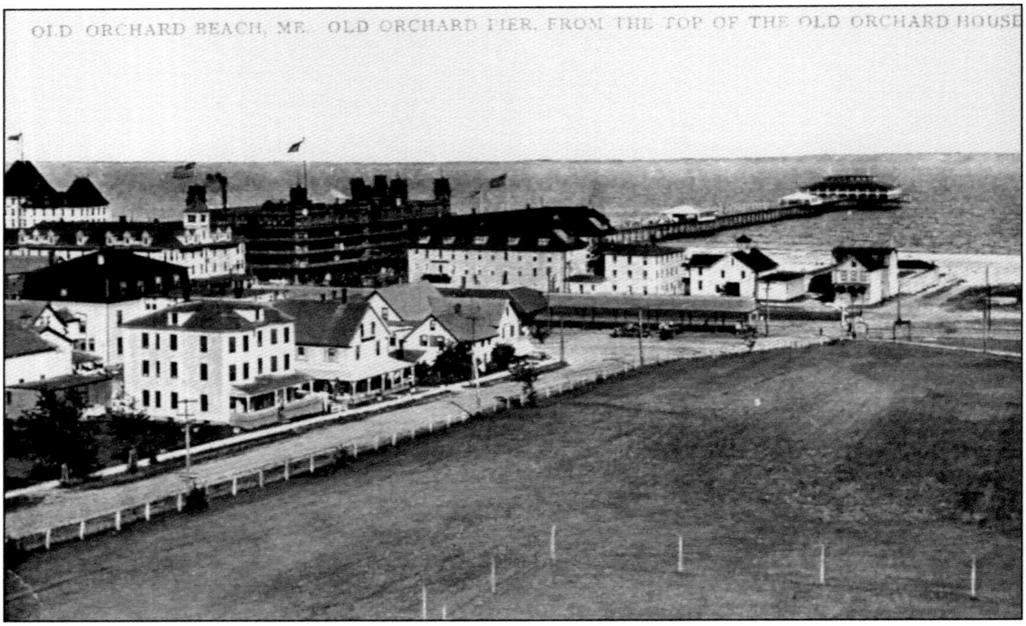


This postcard shows the new three-story pavilion and the Velvet Hotel in this 1907 view. The Velvet Hotel was moved to the foot of the pier in 1899. This view in 1907 was taken just before the great fire of August 15, which destroyed many of the hotels shown. The three-and-a-half-story Pullman House in the foreground, which was built in the spring of 1907, dates this photograph.

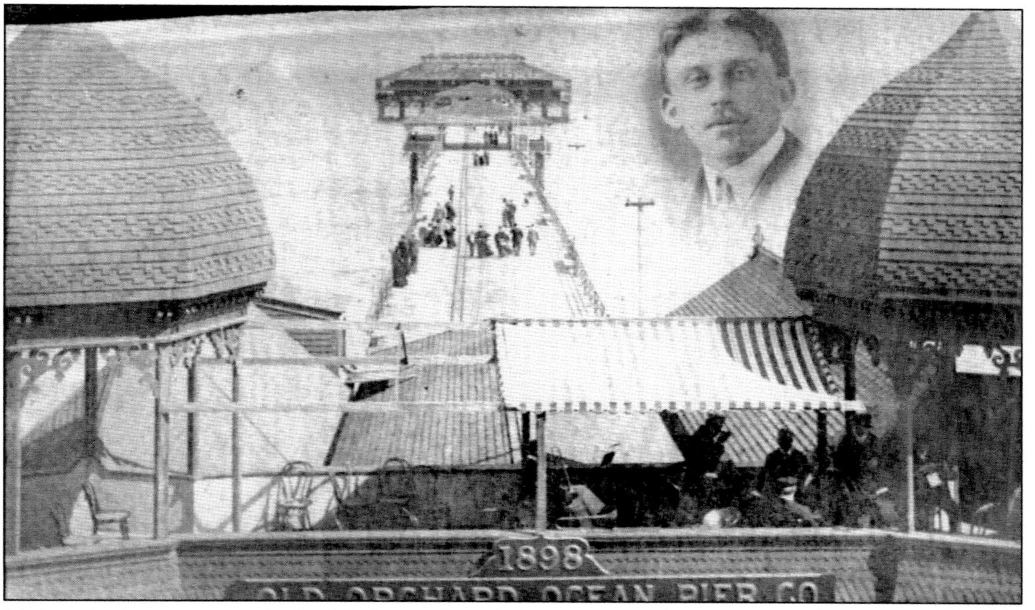


This real-photo postcard of 1899 shows the miniature railroad tracks extending out the middle of the pier. The rails were 12-inch gauge. The train made its inaugural run on July 8. The conductor was Howard A. Knowles, a 36-inch-tall person. The train cost $3,000, and the engine weighed 700 pounds. A one-way ride cost 5¢.

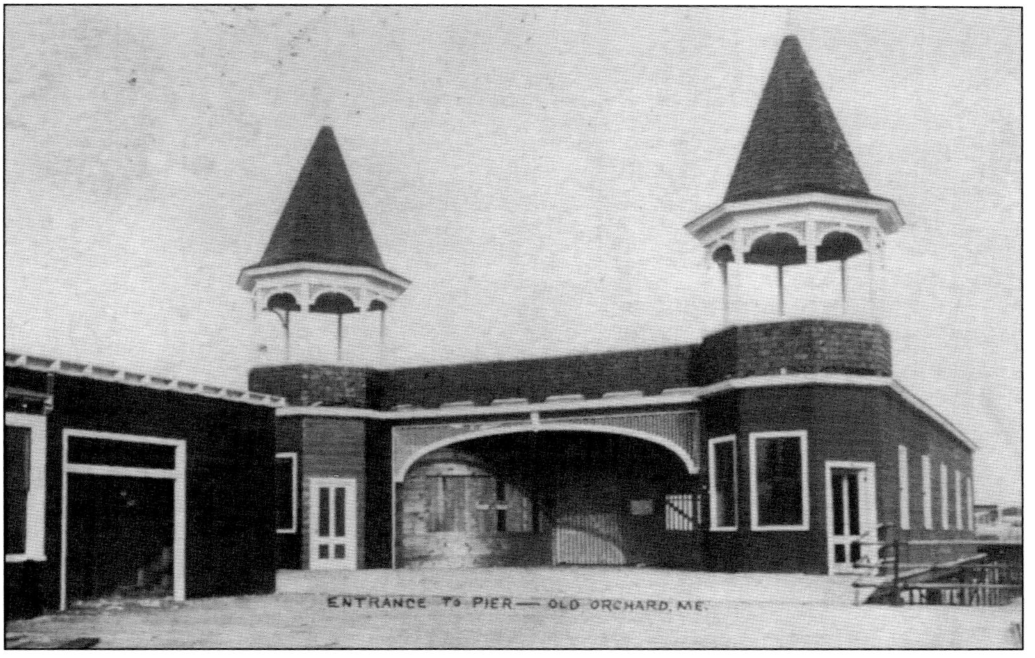


This is the new entrance to the pier. The 1907 fire destroyed the entrance to the old pier. This postcard view was taken in 1908. This entrance stood until it was destroyed by fire on July 19, 1969.

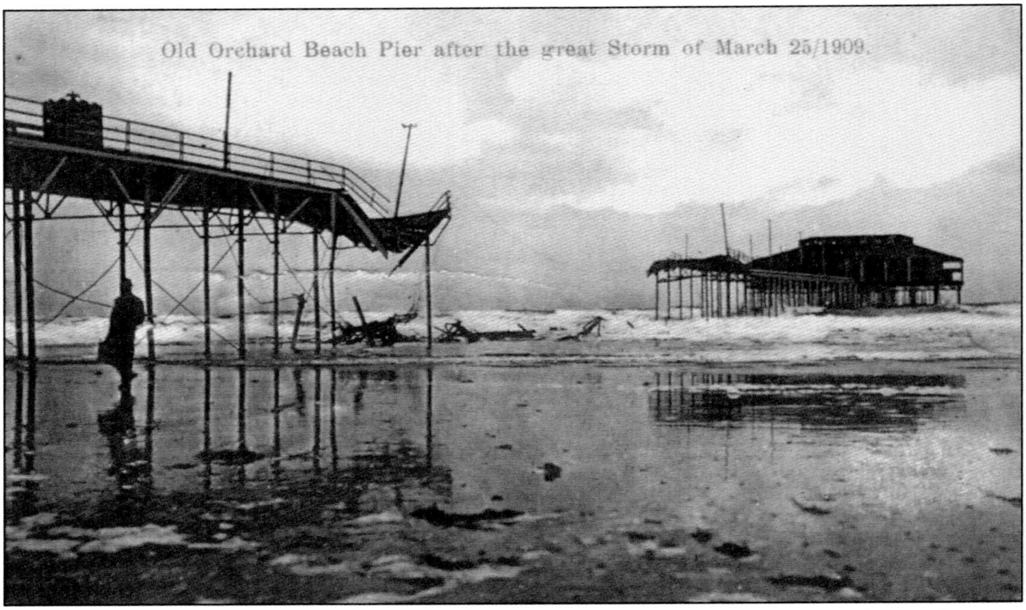


The storm of March 25, 1909, severely destroyed the center section, approximately 800 feet out, of the great steel pier. Large pieces of dislodged shore ice battered the pier during the night, causing the steel pilings to bend, twist, and disappear.

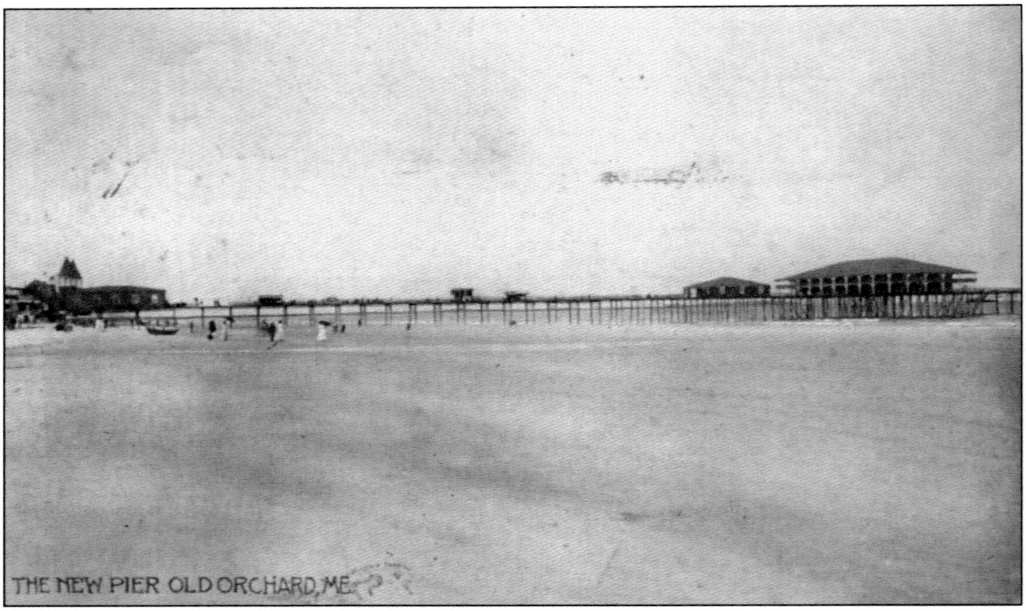


This view shows the new pier rebuilt in 1910. The outer three-story pavilion was cut into three sections and floated in to the 800 feet remains. The top story was removed. The reconstructed two-story pavilion remained in this location until March 1970, when it was razed due to deterioration and neglect.

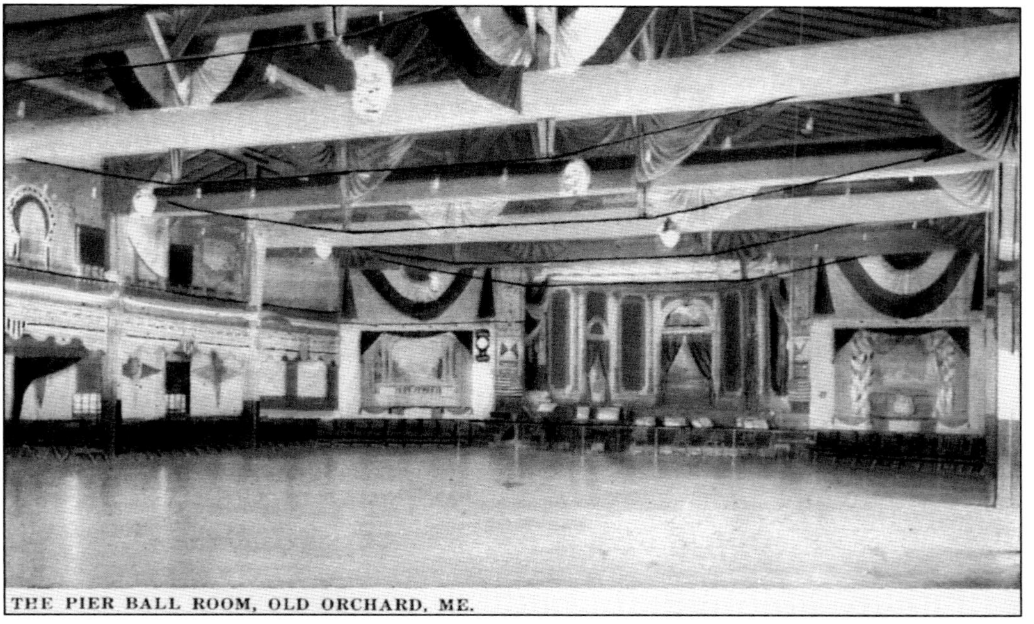


The Pier Ballroom is where all the big bands played. Some of the more popular ladies to play here were the Clooney Sisters, Helen Forest, Doris Day, Billie Holiday, Lena Horne, Abbe Lane, Peggy Lee, Helen O'Connell, Jane Russell, Dinah Shore, Keeley Smith, Jo Stafford, Kaye Starr, and Margaret Whiting, all featured with named big bands. Even Sally Rand, of Fan Dance fame, was featured here with Don Peebles and his orchestra, on Friday, August 20, 1937.

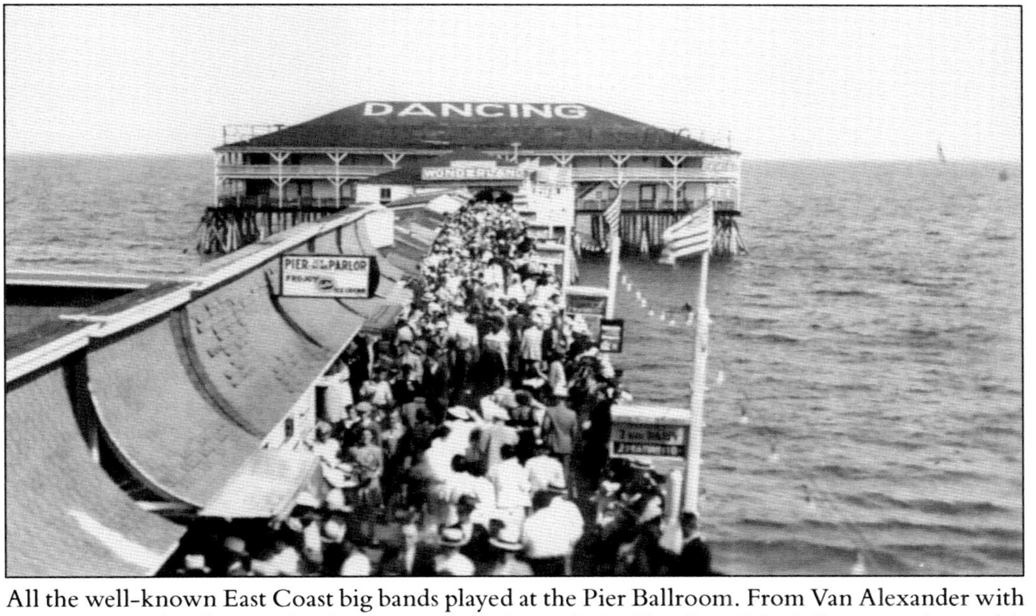


All the well-known East Coast big bands played at the Pier Ballroom. From Van Alexander with "A tisket, a tasket," to Paul Whitman with "Rhapsody in Blue," to Cab Calloway and even his sister, Blanche, all did gigs on the pier. On Saturday evening, September 17, 1938, one could see Tommy Dorsey, featuring Edythe Wright, Jackson Leonard, Allen Storr, and the singing trio, the Esquires, all for the $1.10 admission price.

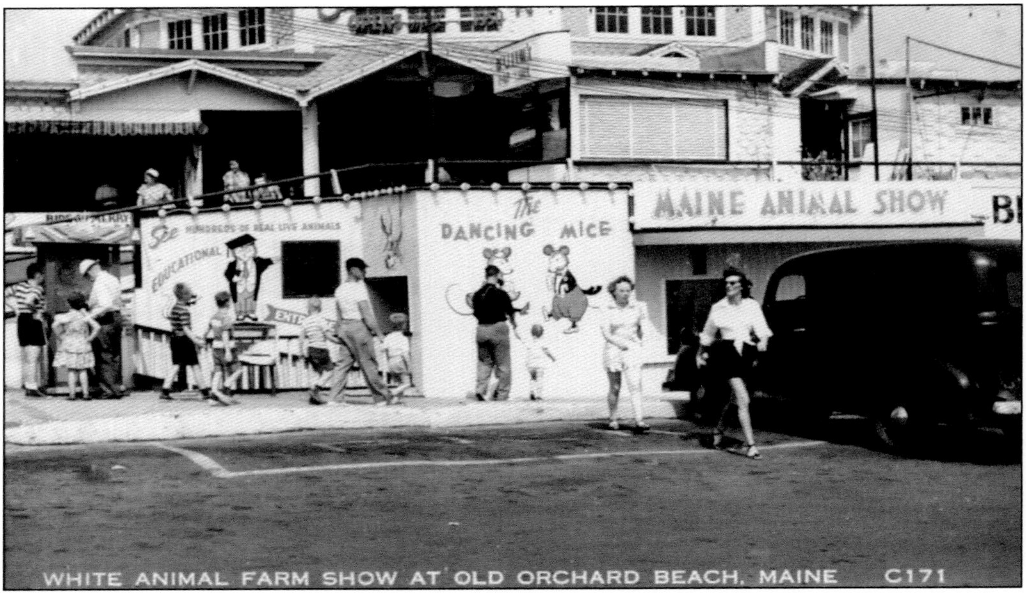


White Animal Farm was a popular attraction located under the pier ramp. Helen Perley, from Scarborough, had quite an array of animal attractions. Visitors could see the circus mice, snakes, rabbits, monkeys, exotic birds, frogs, lizards, and many others. This show was popular during the 1950s into the mid-1960s.

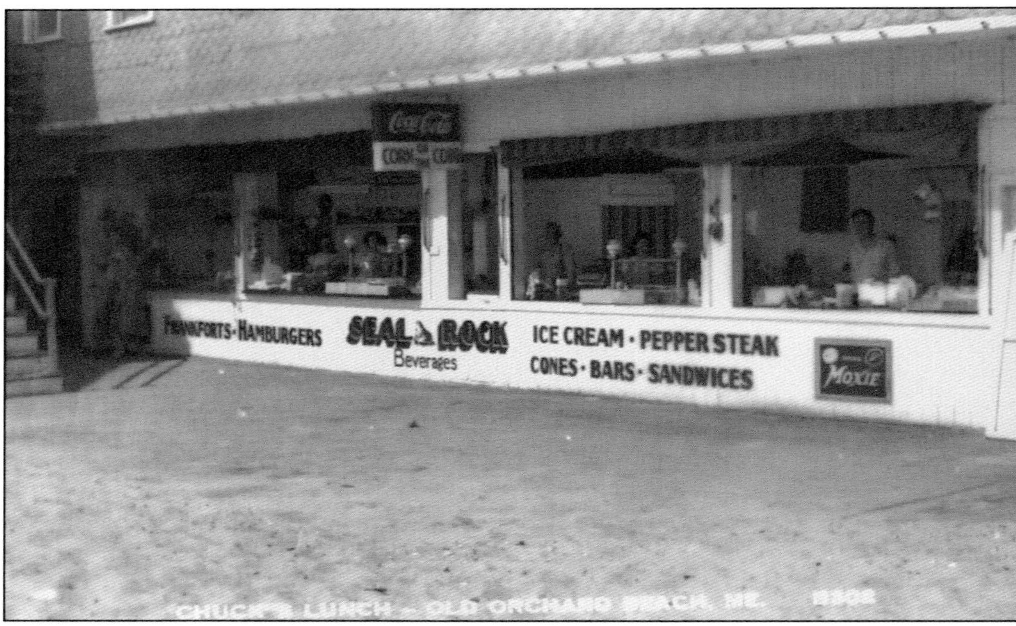


The real-photo postcard above shows Chuck's Lunch Stand on the oceanfront, next to the White Way. This is the only known postcard view showing this popular eat-in, take-out stand. It was popular from the 1940s until July 19, 1969, when it was destroyed by fire. It is said that it had the best hotdogs in town. The stairway, on the left, led up to the pier. If one walked between the stairs and the lunch stand, one would exit onto Old Orchard Street.

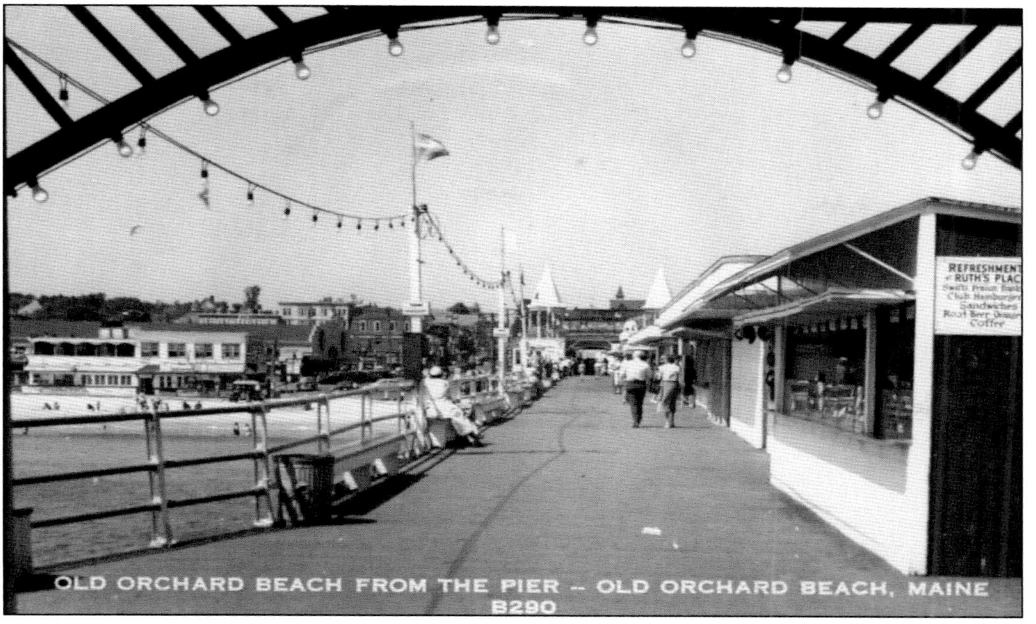


There are thousands of postcard views of the pier, but this is a rare view looking toward the shore end of the pier. The lighted arch above was the entrance to White City Arcade building, which housed many arcade machines. Ruth's place, the lunch stand on the right, was a favorite stop for Ruth's hotdogs, hamburgers, and Hires root beer. The great northeaster storm on February 7, 1978, destroyed White City pavilion and most of the pier.

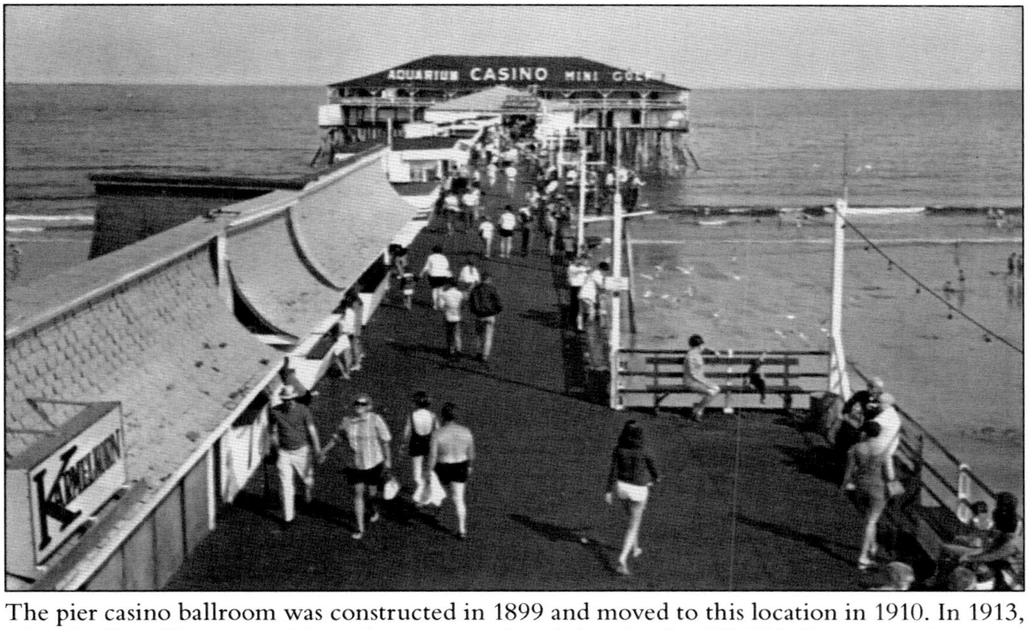


The pier casino ballroom was constructed in 1899 and moved to this location in 1910. In 1913, John Duffy, of Lawrence, Massachusetts, purchased the pier for $22,500. Large crowds were a common event on the pier. The largest crowd ever on the pier was to see Rudy Vallee and his Connecticut Yankees.

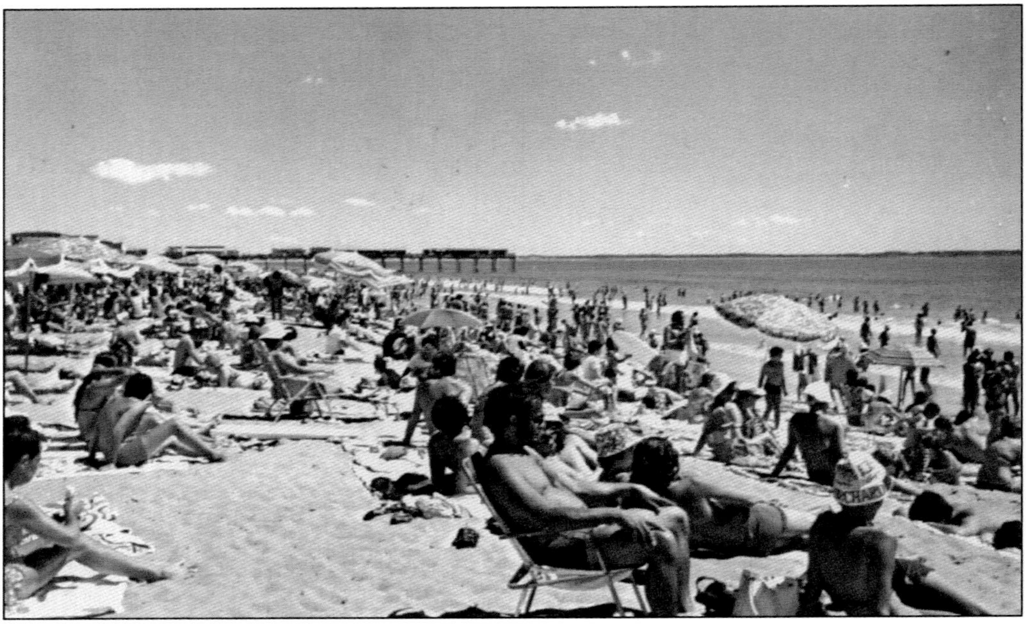

The postcards on this page are very unique. The above card shows the remains of the February 19, 1972, storm. White City pavilion was destroyed, and a second building was built for the 1973 season. This card shows the summer crowd of 1972, without the White City pavilion.

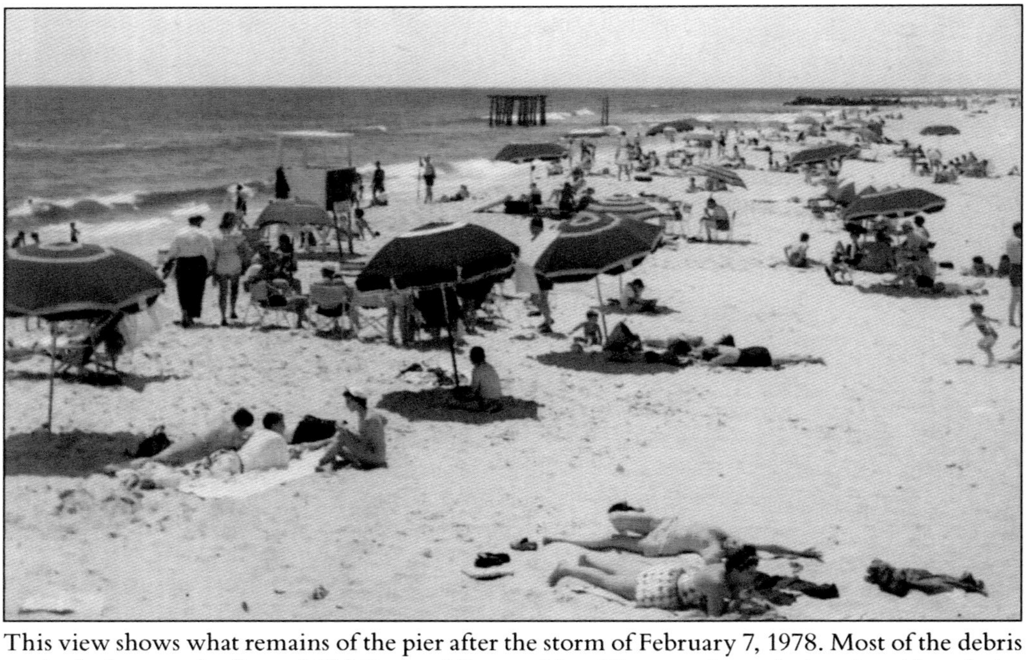

This view shows what remains of the pier after the storm of February 7, 1978. Most of the debris washed ashore at the foot of Old Orchard Street. After 80 years of popularity, the old steel pier was gone forever.

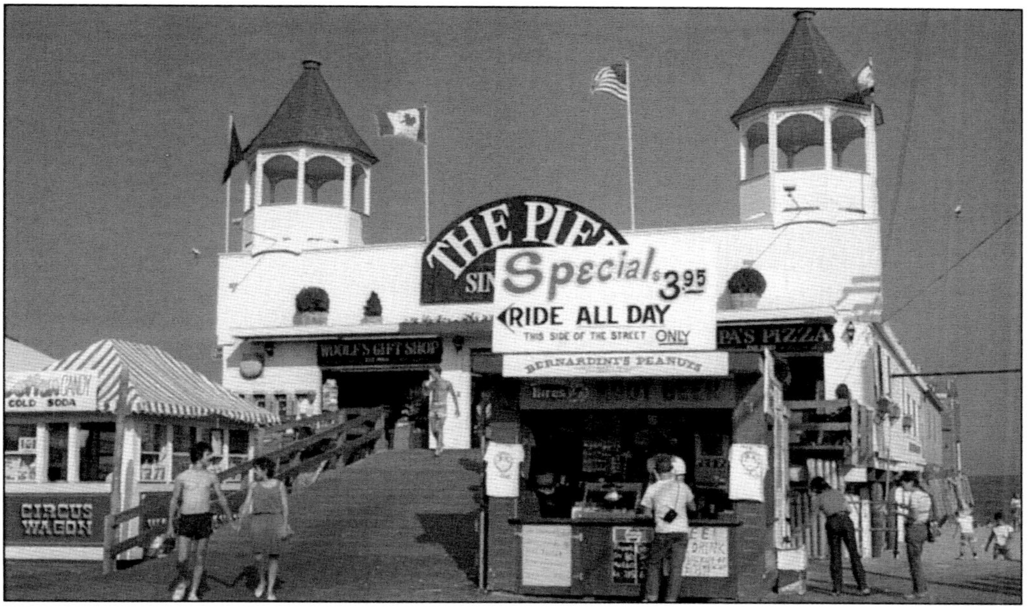

June 7, 1980, was the official opening of the new pier. Pier owner Catherine Duffy Petit, granddaughter of John Duffy, built the new 400-foot-long, 27-foot-wide pier, after the former pier was destroyed in the 1978 storm.

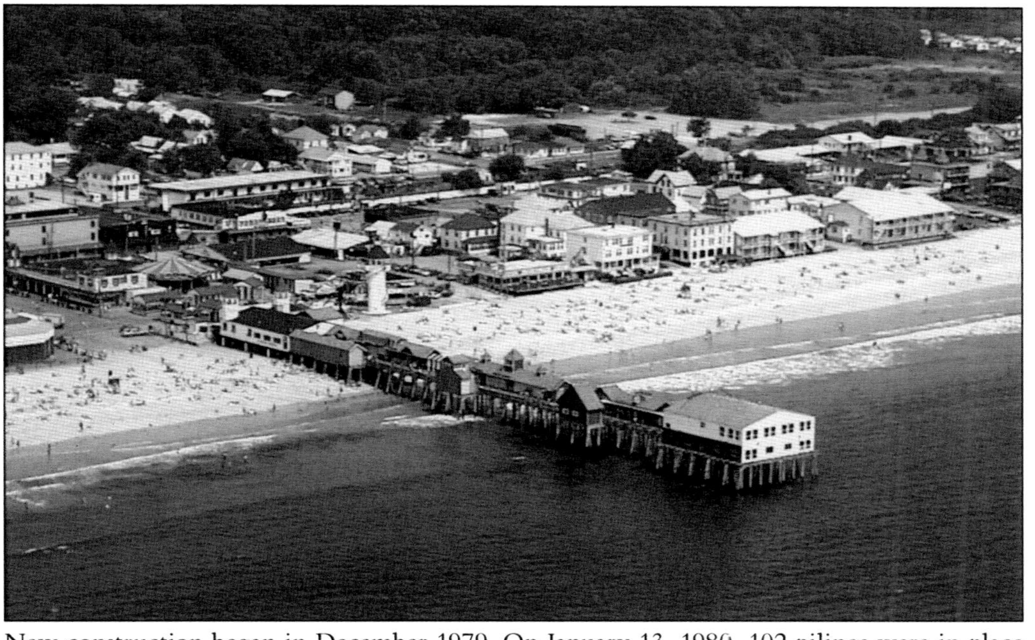
New construction began in December 1979. On January 13, 1980, 102 pilings were in place and the pier extended out 25 sections. In April, the twin towers were lifted into their proper places. They were built by local carpenter Evan Crosby. John Gibson, a pier and bridge builder from Yarmouth, was contracted to build the new pier.

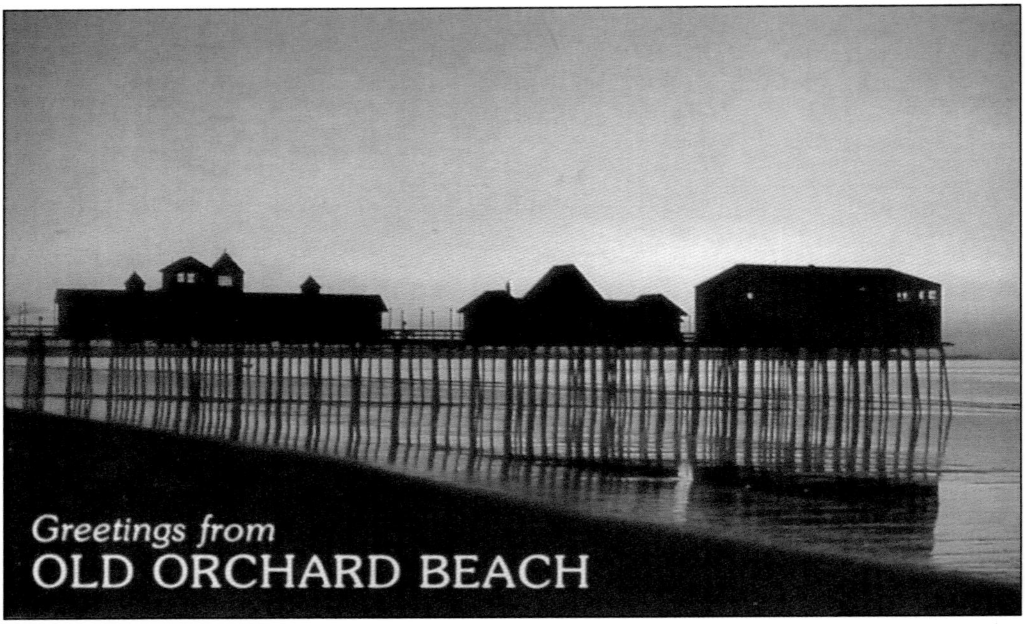

The new pier at sunrise is seen everyday. The new structure has survived 26 years of pounding storms, but ownership has changed hands several times. David Lewis gained control of the pier at the public bankruptcy auction. Today the Golzbein family retains ownership of the pier.

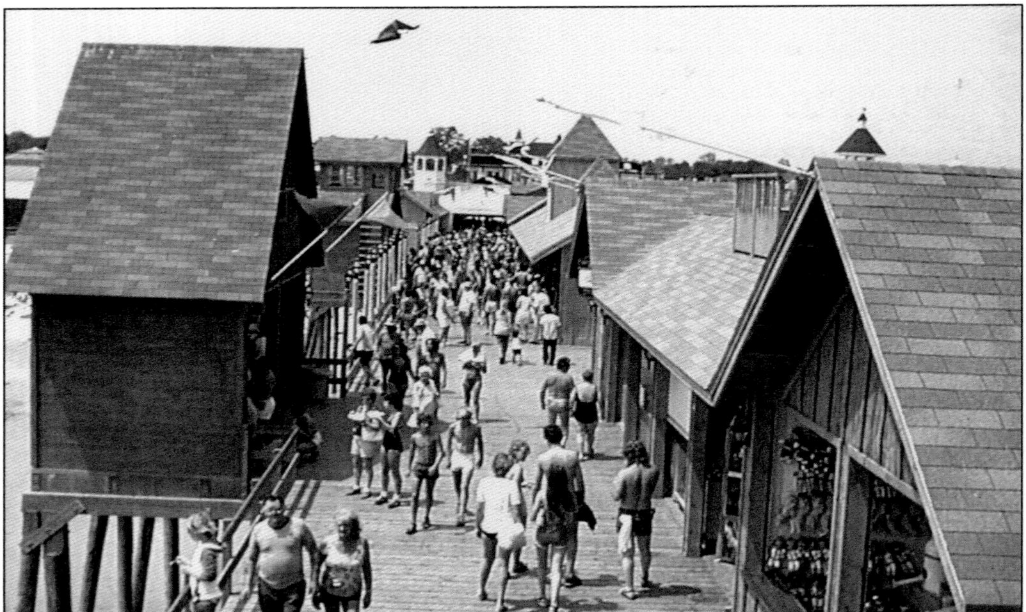
Today the pier, with its New England–style shops, never regained the elegance of the original 1898 steel pier. Local developer Tim Swenson has built the Grand Victorian Condominium at the entrance to the pier, where the original Velvet Hotel once stood. A new era has begun.

# *Six*

# For Your Entertainment

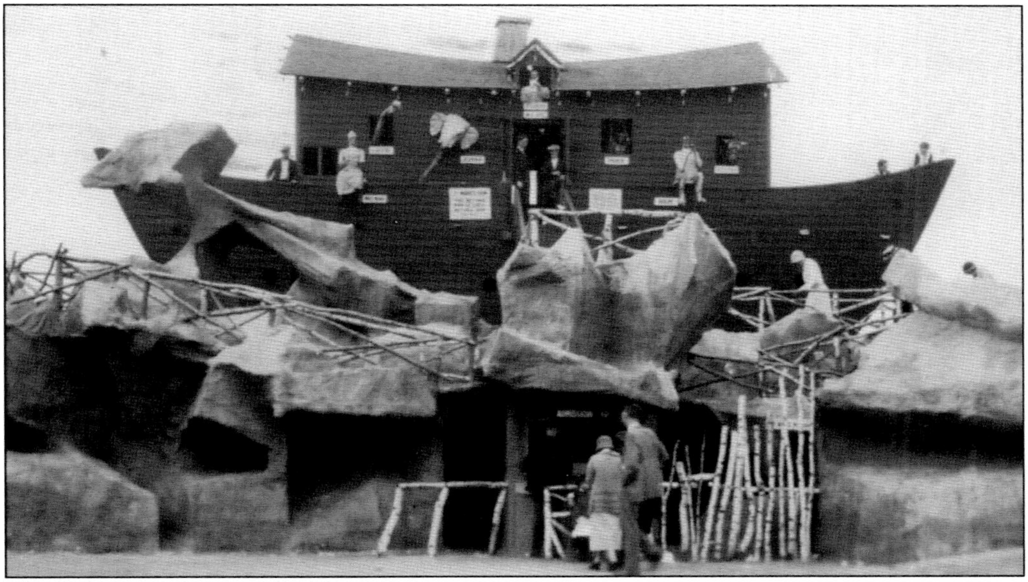

Noah's Ark, on the top of Mount Ararat, at the foot of Old Orchard Street, has opened its door and windows to the sun after all the cold and rain. This vermillian-colored ark, which can be seen for miles, is one of the latest amusements owned by John Duffy and Edward Rhoades. According to an unknown news article in May 1924, it has many windows, from which the elephant, giraffe, cobra, and monkeys look out, and in the doorway, looking his full 650 years, stands old Noah himself, while on the outside are seated Mrs. Noah and her son in well-worn garments, watching the sea dash up over the white sands. Duffy and Rhoades are also erecting the big merry-go-round and organ at the entrance to the pier and under the pier the scooter is in operation, furnishing amusement for many.

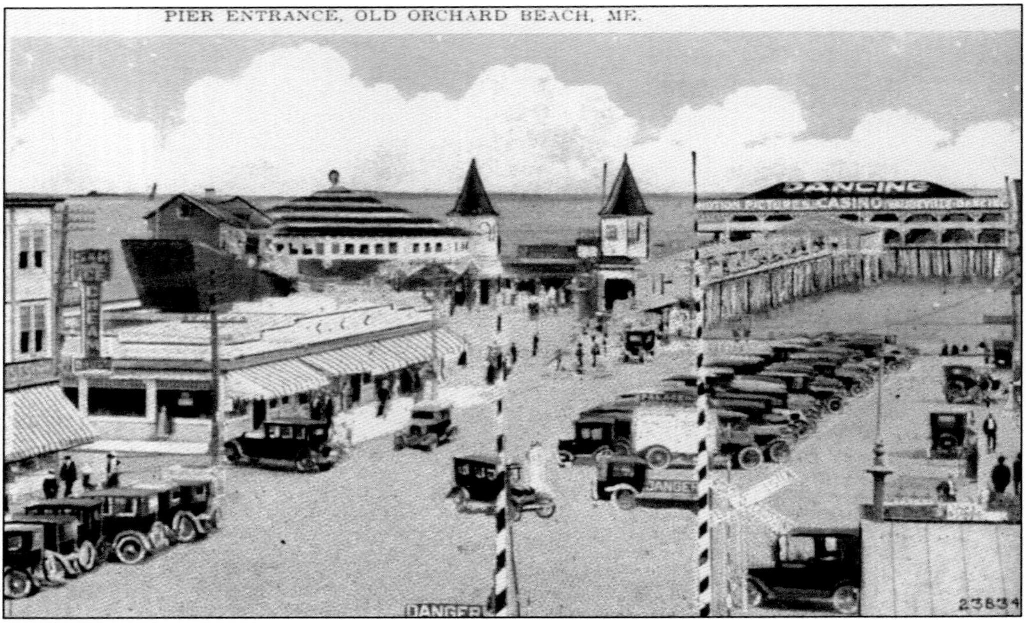


This postcard view was shot from atop the Seagate building, present-day Lisa's Pizza, showing the new John Duffy and Edward Rhoades Pier block. Today the Grand Victorian Condominium is being constructed on the same location. The Grand Victorian Condominium ribbon-cutting ceremony was held on Thursday, October 19, 2006, at 2:00 p.m.

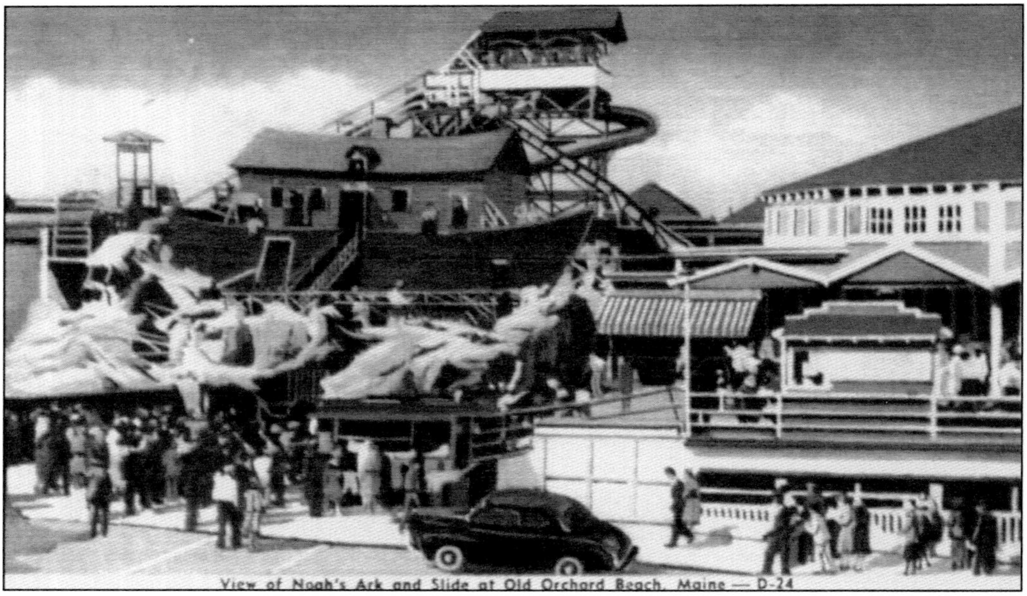


The Jack and Jill Slide added the final touch to the amusement center. The slide was built in 1930. Underneath Noah's Ark was the Coal Mine with its live donkey-drawn carts filled with youngsters and their elders. The Coal Mine was an actual reproduction, in miniature, of a famous Kentucky mine. All of the above went up in flames on July 19, 1969.

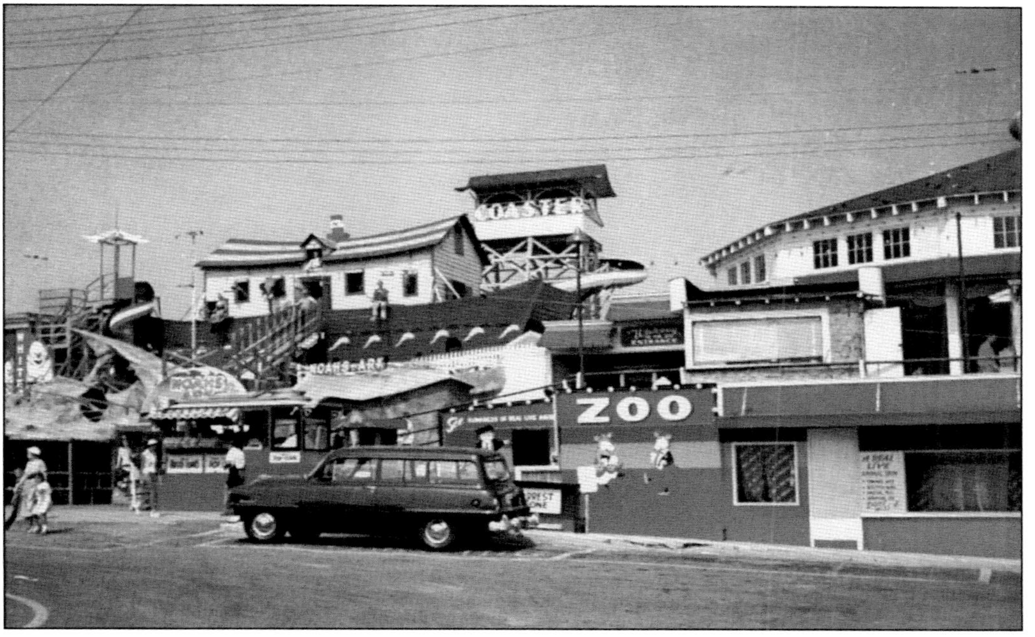


Located underneath the pier ramp, replacing the scooter cars, was Helen Perley's animal farm. Perley was the sister of local judge Wesley Mewer. Some of the animals were raccoons, guinea pigs, ducklings, snakes, turtles, skunks, and chimpanzees dressed in children's clothes.

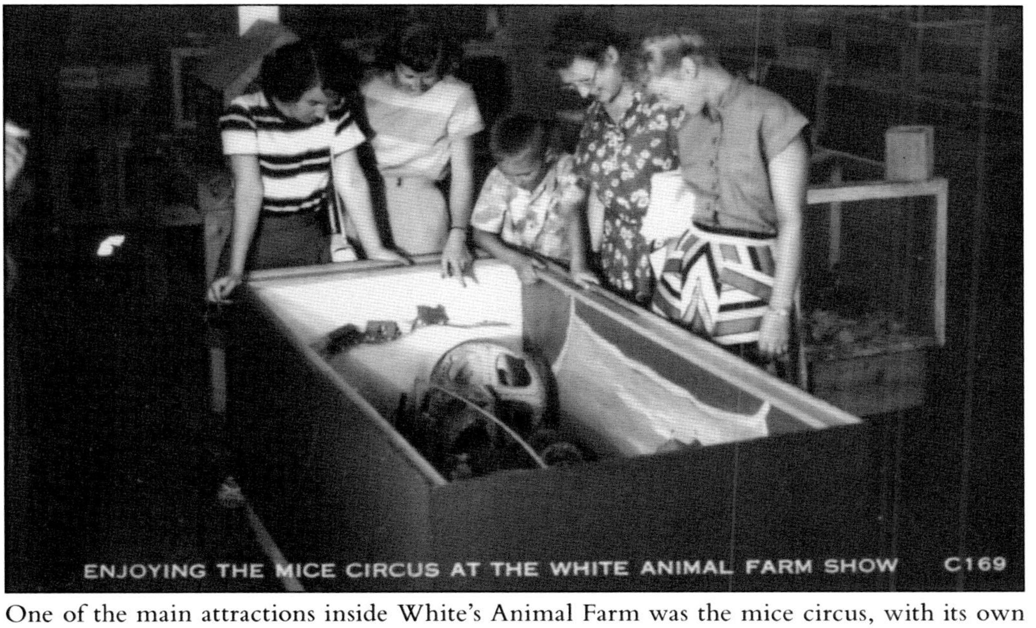


One of the main attractions inside White's Animal Farm was the mice circus, with its own Ferris wheel. One could experience all this and more for 25¢ in 1959. The above view is the only known postcard that shows the interior of White's Animal Farm. This card was made by Eastern Illustrating and Publishing Company of Belfast, Maine.

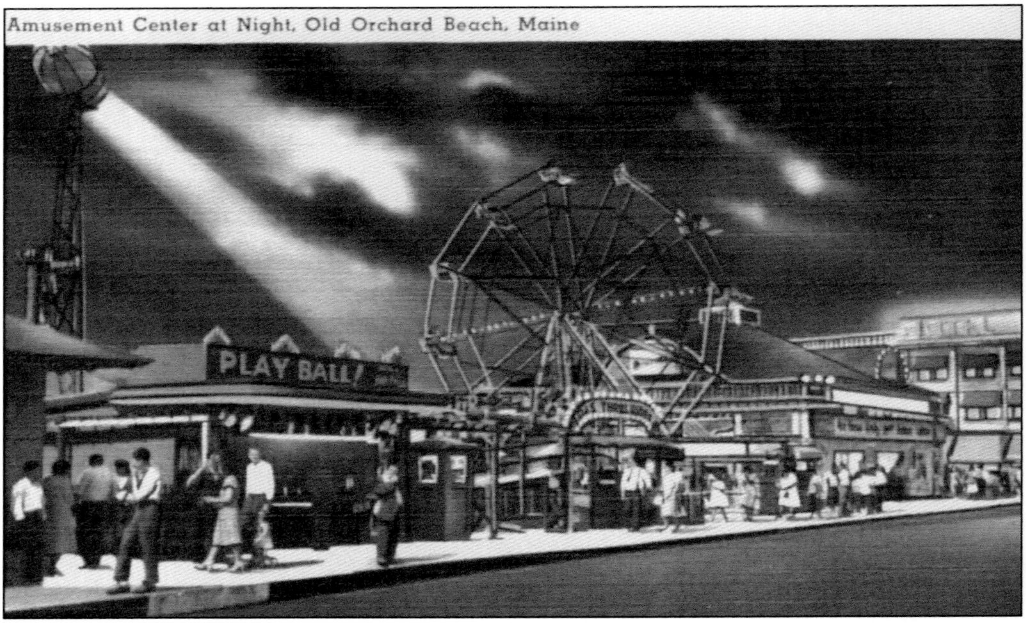


It is hard to imagine all these rides in such a small area. All of these rides, including the rocket ride, a Ferris wheel, and several others, were situated along West Grand Avenue, between the public comfort station and Reed's Restaurant, today called J. J.'s Eatery and Rocco's Pizza. Today a clothing store, formerly Smith's Arcade, is located where the rides once were.

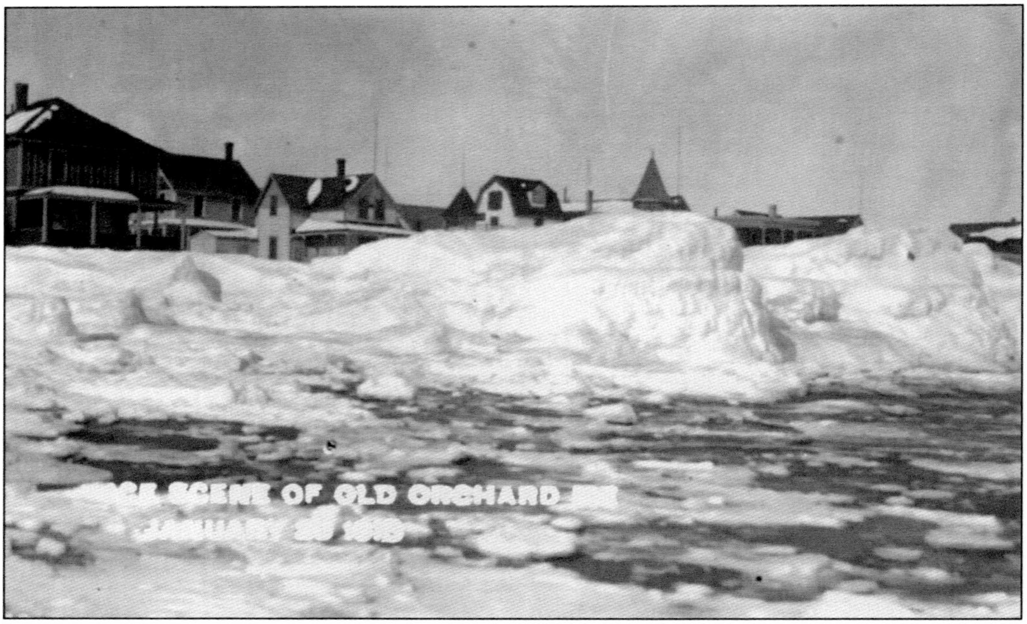


January 23, 1918, was when this real-photo postcard was taken, it was said that was the year that Saco Bay almost froze over. The ice formations were such that a person could walk along the beach and walk right over the pier without missing a step. The photograph was taken at the foot of Brisson Street.

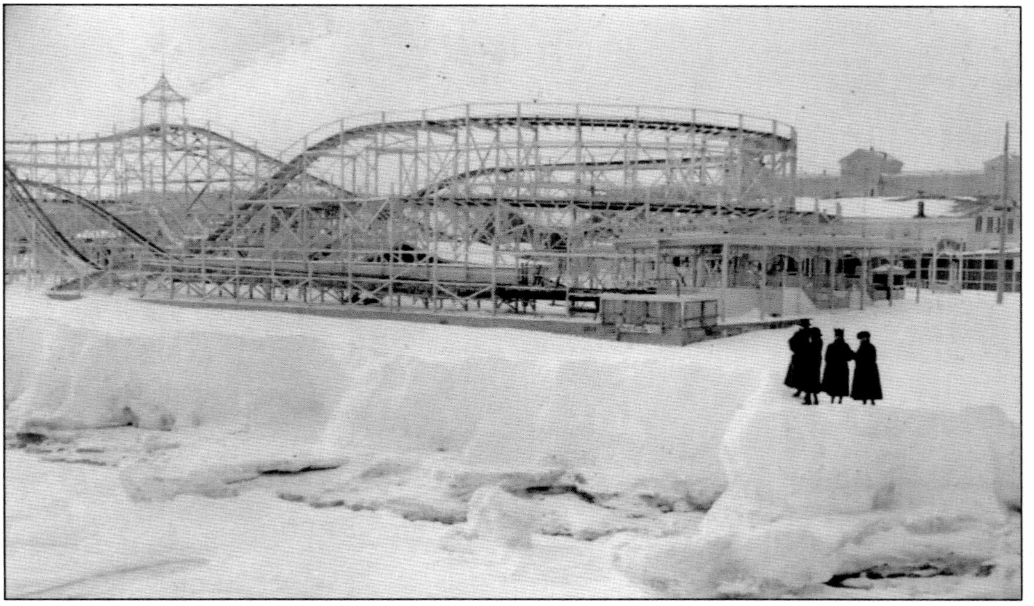

This real-photo postcard, taken in February 1918, shows the first roller coaster in Old Orchard Beach. It was built in 1917 and continued until 1929. It was the largest roller coaster built in Old Orchard Beach. It was called the Jack Rabbit. Note the ice formations.

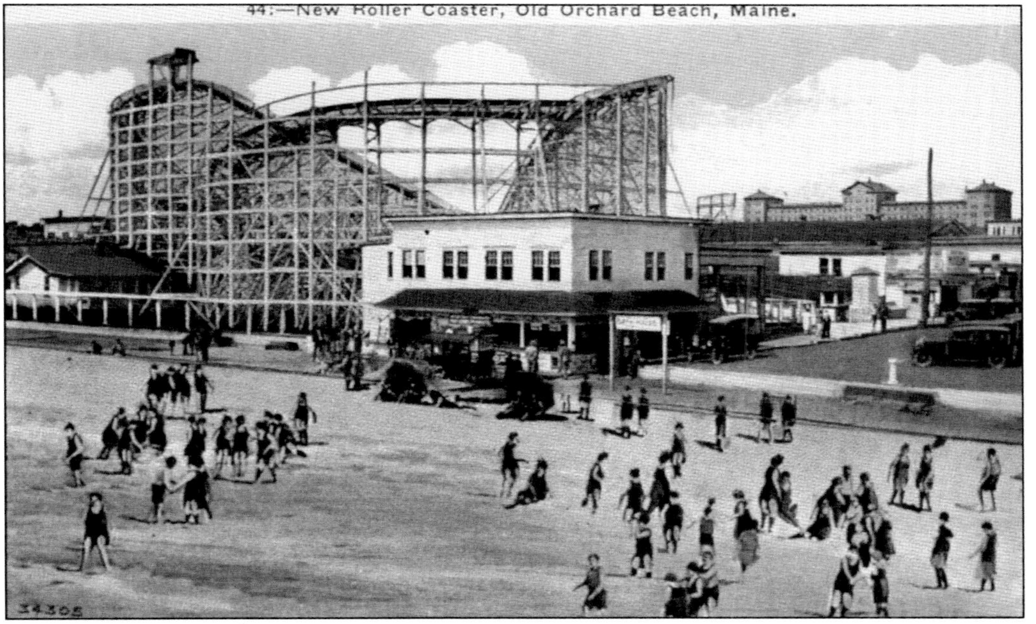


The new roller coaster, shown in this August 26, 1934, postcard, was Old Orchard Beach's second roller coaster and was called the Cyclone. It was built in 1930 and came crashing down in flames on Sunday, October 3, 1948. This was the last wooden roller coaster built in Old Orchard Beach. The two-story Bricky's Spa Dine and Dance Hall, on the corner, survived the fire that took down the remaining block.

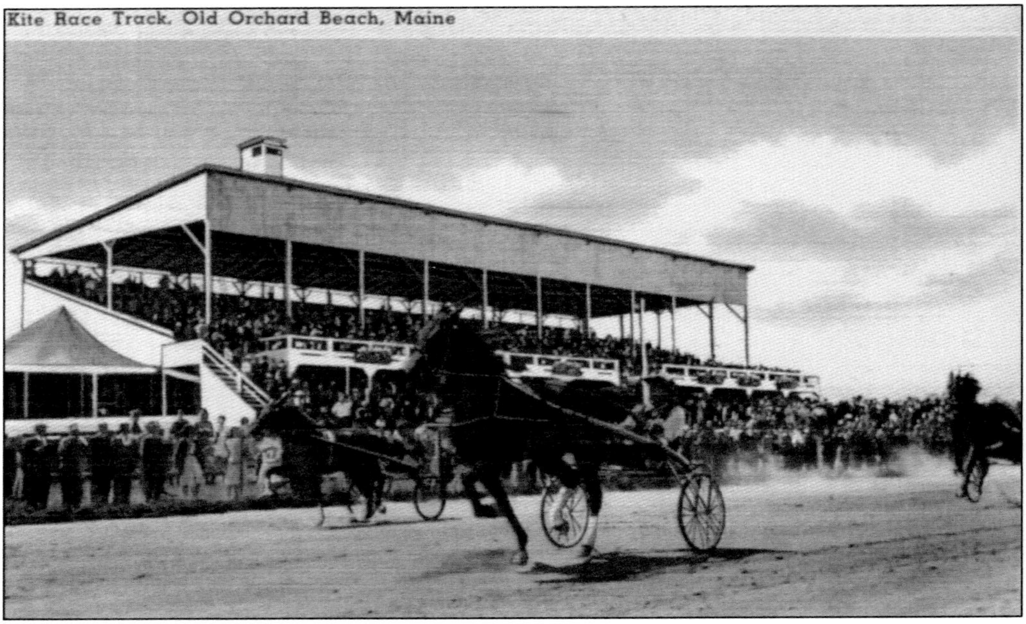


The Kite Track was the brainstorm of local businessman/merchant Millard F. Porter. The track was built in 1892. The Breeders Mile Track Association was formed, stock was issued, and a new racetrack was up and running. The postcard view above shows the trotters coming down the finish line.

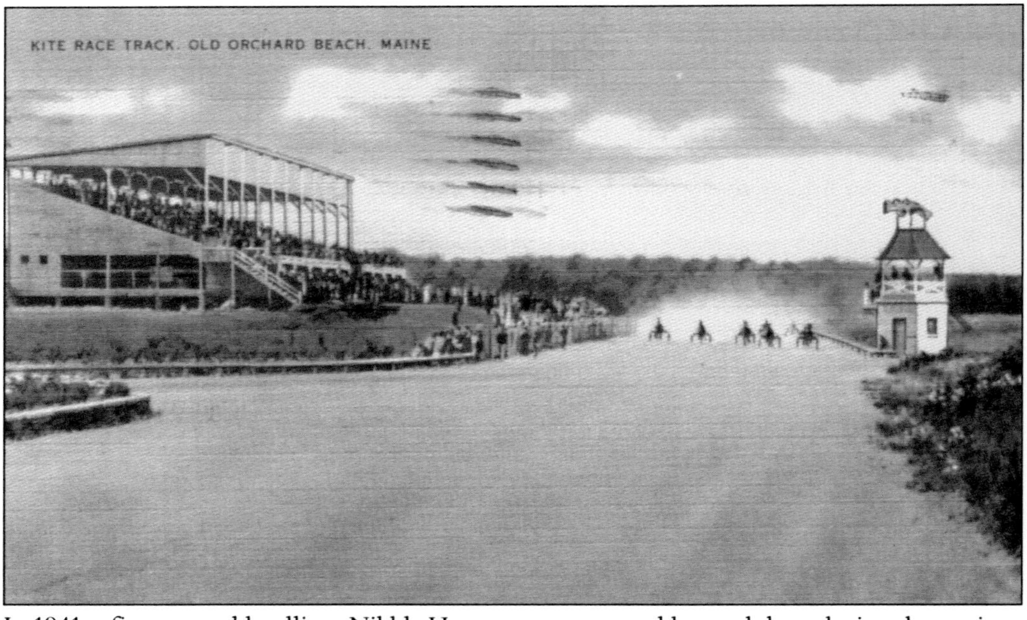


In 1941, a five-year-old stallion, Nibble Hanover, set two world records here during the matinee racing card. Nibble Hanover raced around the kite-shaped mile, oval track in 1:58.75, in his first heat. This was the world record of that time. He ran his second heat in 1:59, establishing a new world record.

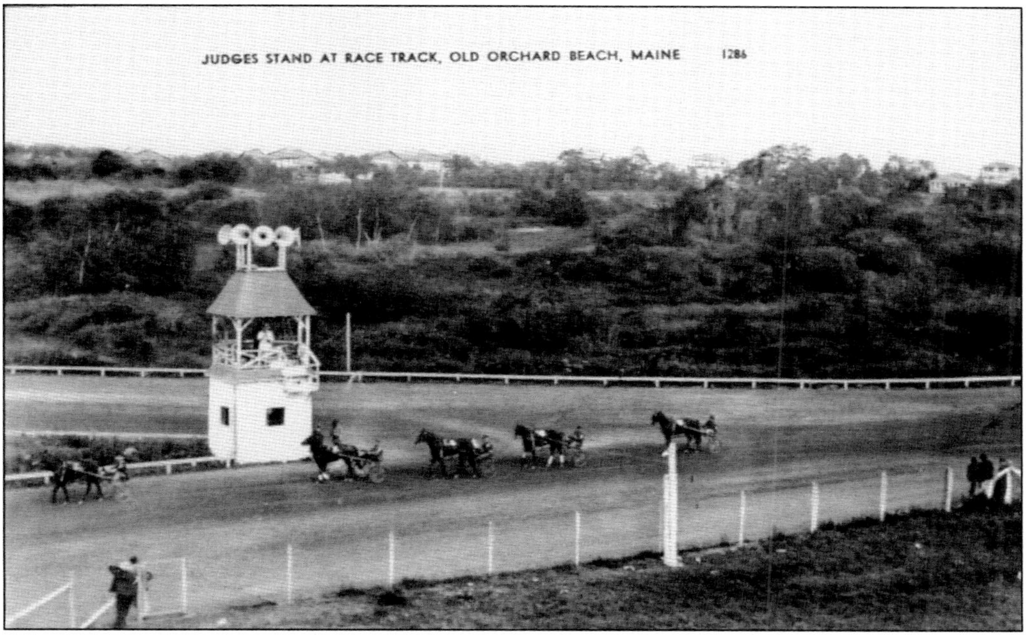


The official judge's stand is shown in the above view. The Kite Track had two lives. The first was 1892 to 1902. The second life was 1936 until 1950. The final race of that year was Thursday, July 3. Much of the field equipment was sold off to the new Scarborough Downs track.

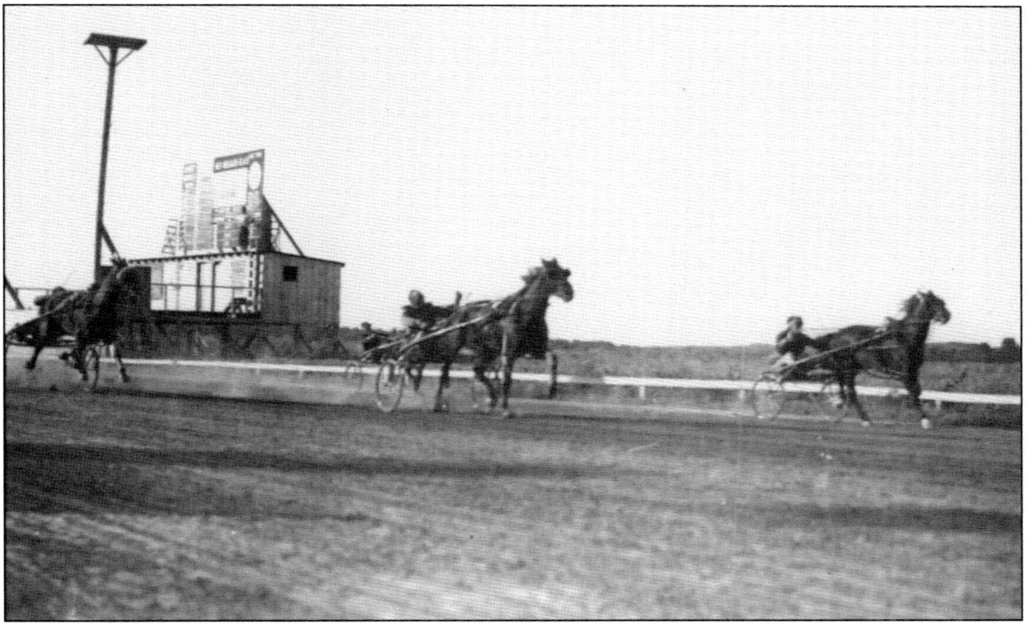

As early as June 1937, motorcycle races were held at the Kite Track. Crowds of 5,000 spectators and over were common. On August 2 and 3, 1941, the second annual Gypsy Tour was held here. It was estimated that 3,000 motorcyclists from various parts of New England participated in the Annual Maine Gypsy Tour conducted by the Triangle Motorcycle Club Inc. of Portland. The featured race was the 50-mile event.

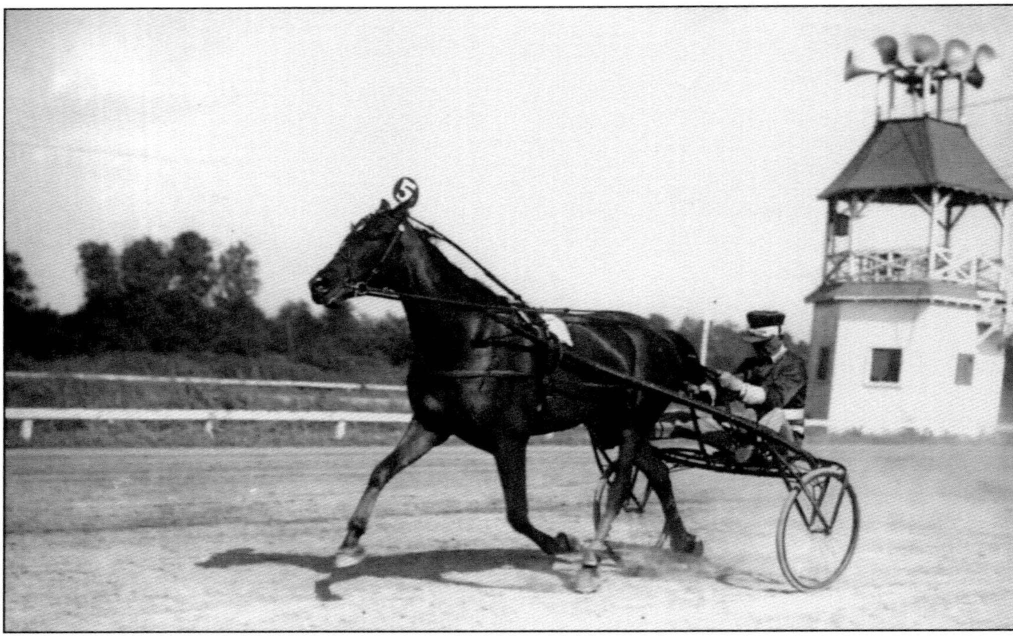

Sep Palin, seen here, paid the unheard price of $73,500 for a pair of untried colts, Victory Song and Bombs Away. In 1975, the State of Maine purchased the old Kite Track land. Today it is a game management area full of deer, duck, fox, coyote, geese, otter, and muskrats. The outline of the old kite-shaped track is still barely visible. The footings of the grandstands can still be seen, if one looks hard enough.

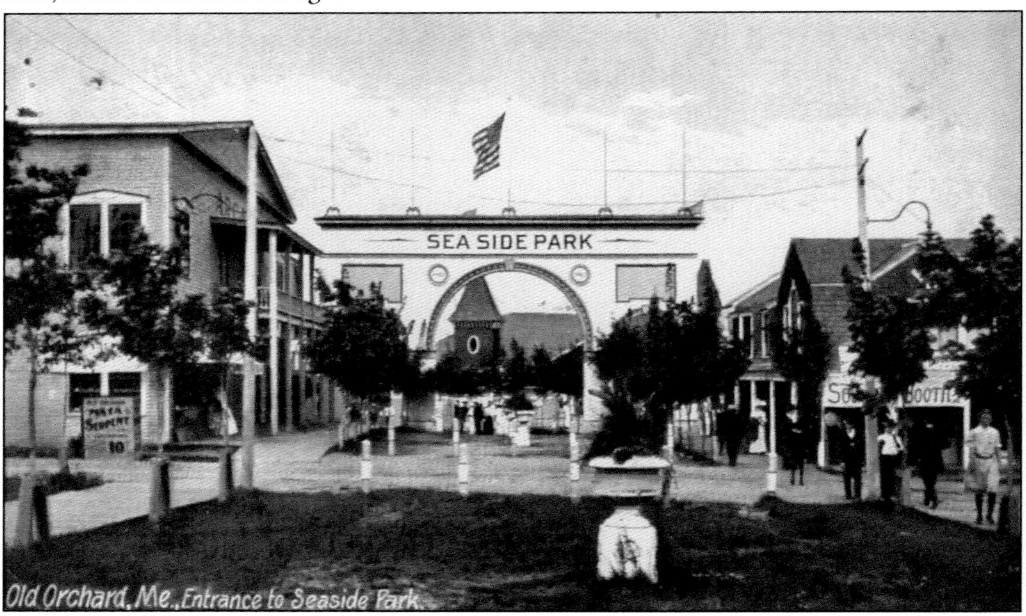


The arch entrance to Sea Side Park was designed by John Calvin Stevens (1855–1940), the notable Portland architect. The arch entrance was on Imperial Street but could be approached from Old Orchard Street through a village green–style entrance. The building on the right was the ticket office and is still standing today. It is called the Imperial Waters Motel at 18 Imperial Street.

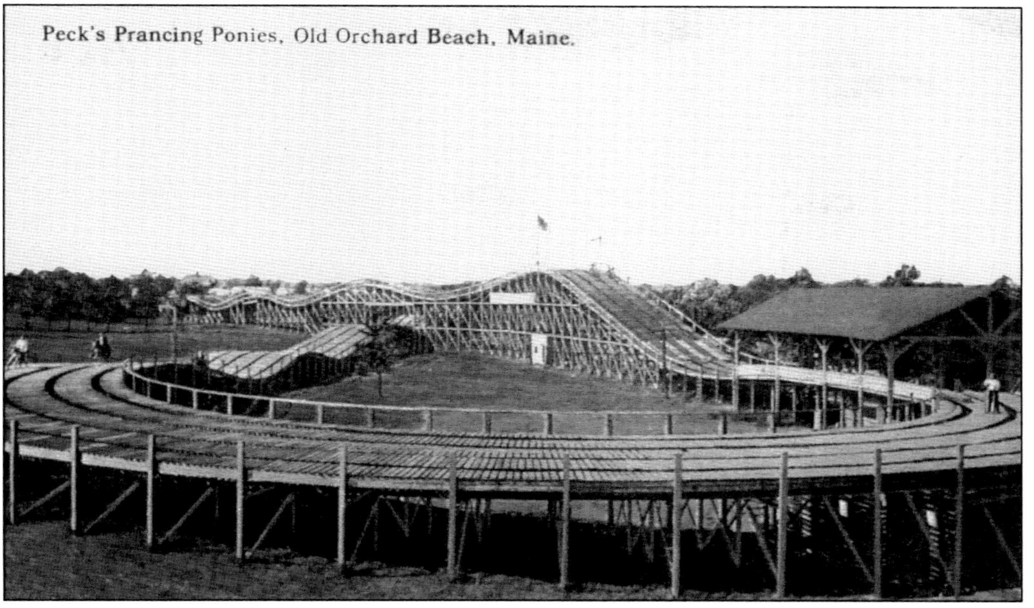


In 1902, the Maine Investment Company Ltd. managed by Wesley G. Smith converted a field of 25 acres of land, comprising what was once intended for house lots by Ebenezer Staples, into an amusement park named Sea Side Park.

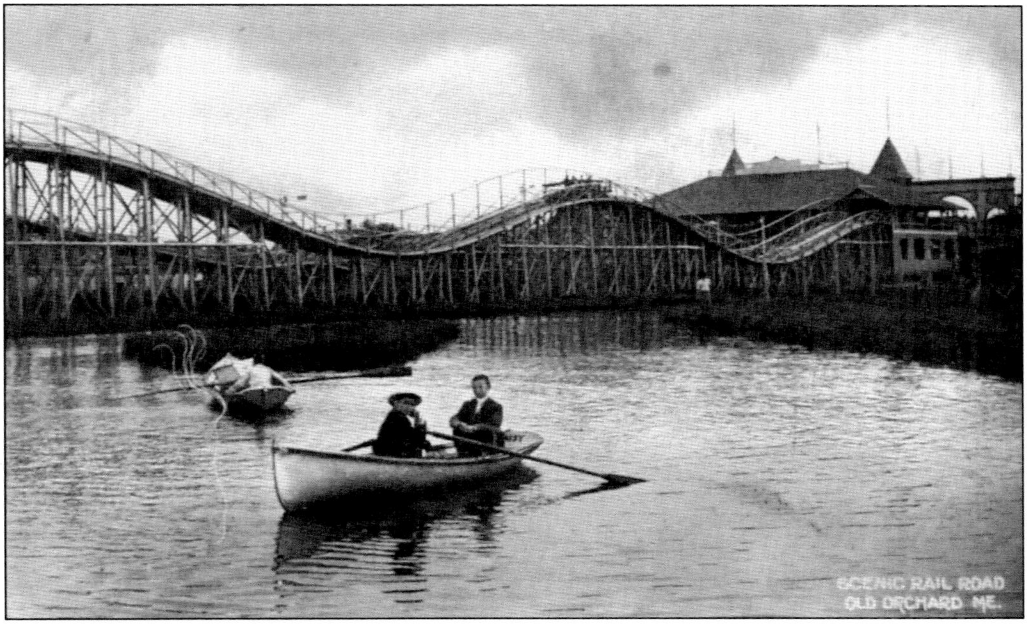


The largest and most expensive structure in the park was the scenic railway ride, built at a cost of $20,000. The price of 10¢ per ride entitled the passenger to two trips around the 2,300 feet of bewilderment. Three rides could be had for 25¢. A cable run by electrical power pulled the cars up 40 feet, then gravity sped one around and into a tunnel where strategically placed mirrors made the passengers appear that they were about to crash into other cars.

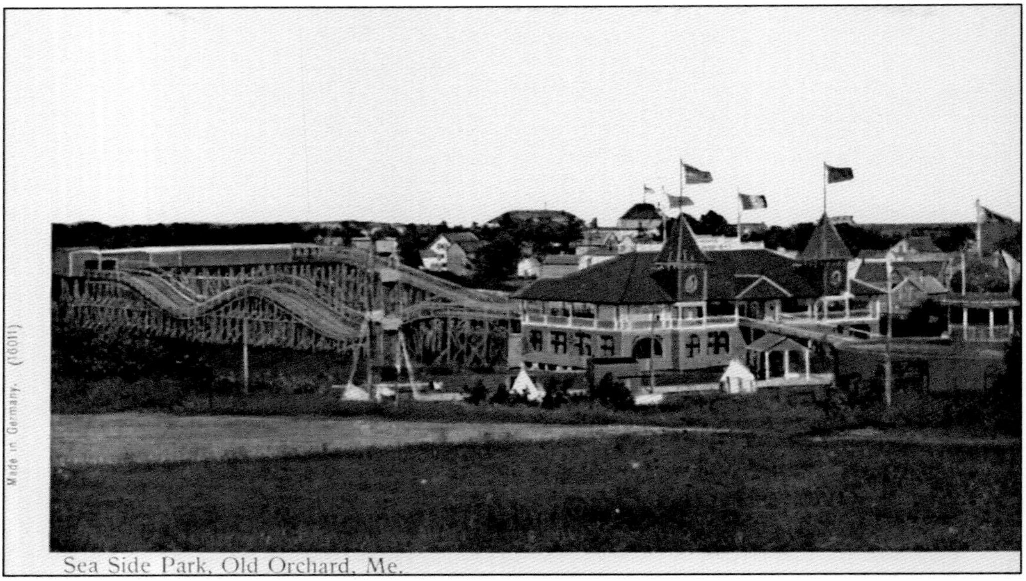


The postcard above shows the scenic railway pavilion, which was one of the main attractions at Sea Side Park. Competition from downtown rides took its toll. The park was built on peat and could not hold the heavy machinery that the downtown rides could. In 1924, Seaside Park was officially closed.

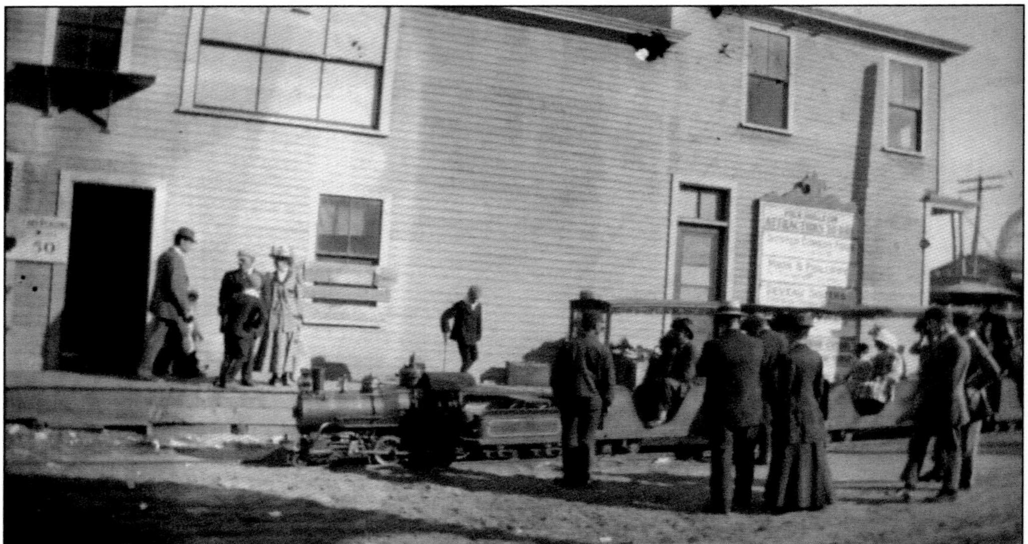

This rare real-photo postcard shows the miniature railroad on Milliken Street loading passengers for a ride up Imperial Street to the entrance of Sea Side Park. Originally the train was located on the pier but was not very successful there.

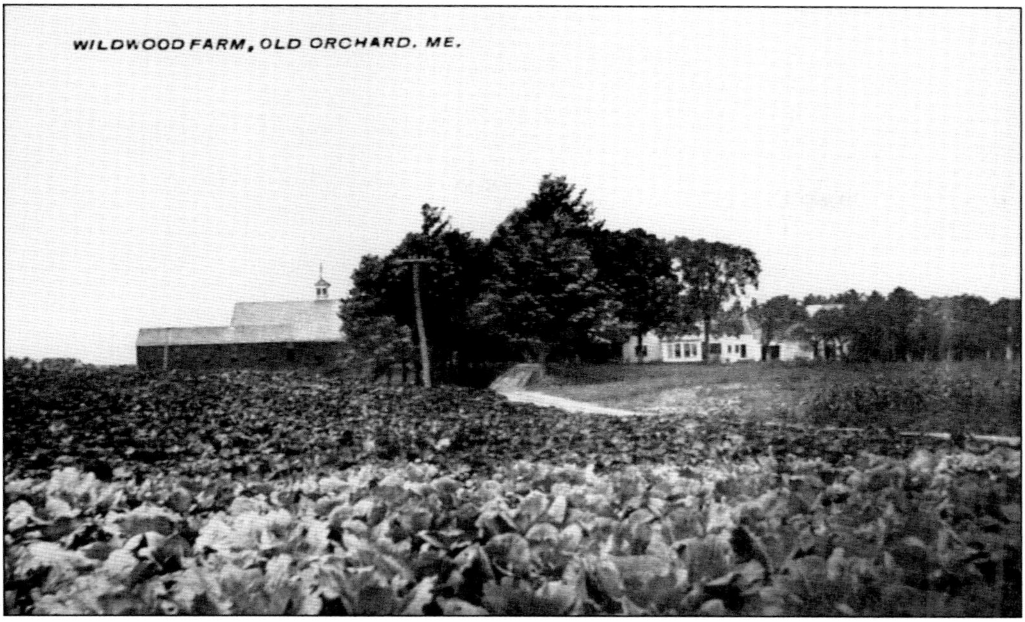


This view looking out Cascade Road toward U.S. Route 1 shows Wildwood Farm. The large barn on the left is where Dunegrass Golf Course is today. The old farmhouse on the right became the country club for the Old Orchard Beach Golf Course, until it was destroyed by fire in 1935. The crops in the foreground are potatoes, and there are 18 acres of them. Wildwood, also known as Murch Farm, boasted of the 5,000 bushels it grew each season. They were the major supplier of vegetables to all the large hotels of Old Orchard Beach.

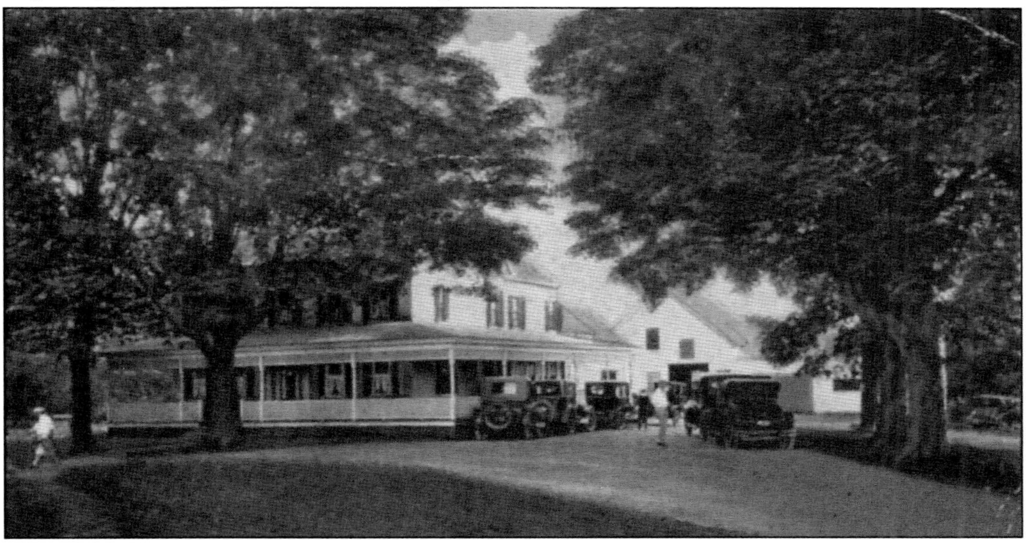

The exact date of the *c.* 1730 farmhouse is not known, but in 1825, General Marquis de Lafayette is said to have stopped at this farm to visit his old Revolutionary War friend John Means, during his tour to Maine. There have been numerous owners of Wildwood Farm over the years: Mark Leavitt, the Davis/Googins family, George Means, Millard Porter, George Murch, the Old Orchard Beach Country Club Business Group, Bernard Osher Group, and today the David and Glenna Ahearn family.

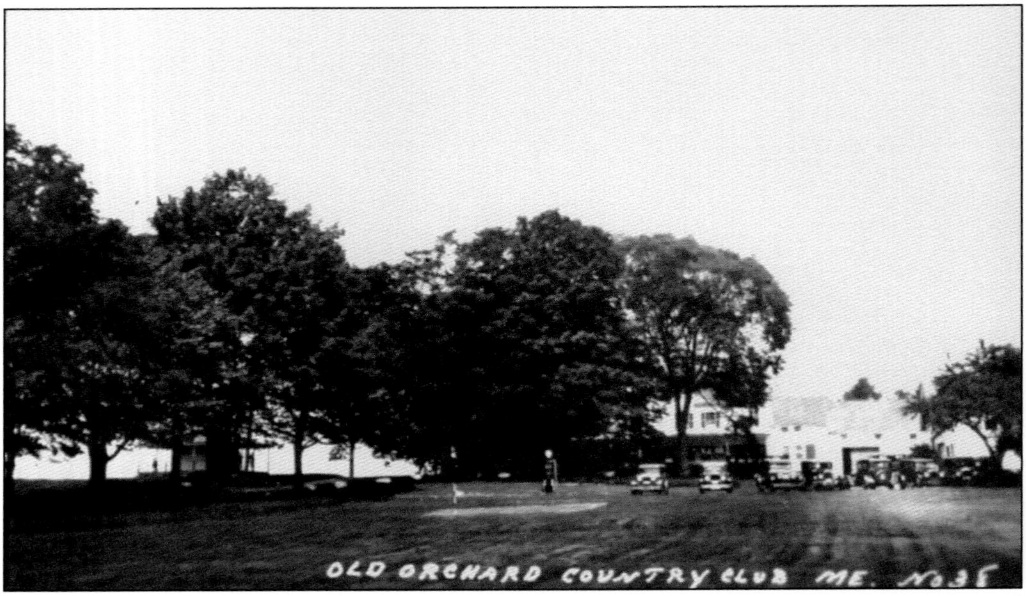


One famous story about the country club happened on September 28, 1937. Paramount Newsreel photographer Al Mingalone did a "balloon jump" to film the golf match from the air. A harness holding Mingalone was hooked to 28 helium-filled balloons and was tethered to a car bumper. A strong wind pulled the suspended cameraman up too fast and the line snapped, sending Mingalone in the direction of Biddeford. Local Catholic priest Fr. Jim Mullen followed the drifting cameraman with his car and shot out several balloons over Beach Street in Saco with his 30-30 rifle. Mingalone safely landed in North Kennebunkport, 10 miles and 25 minutes later and was much relieved.

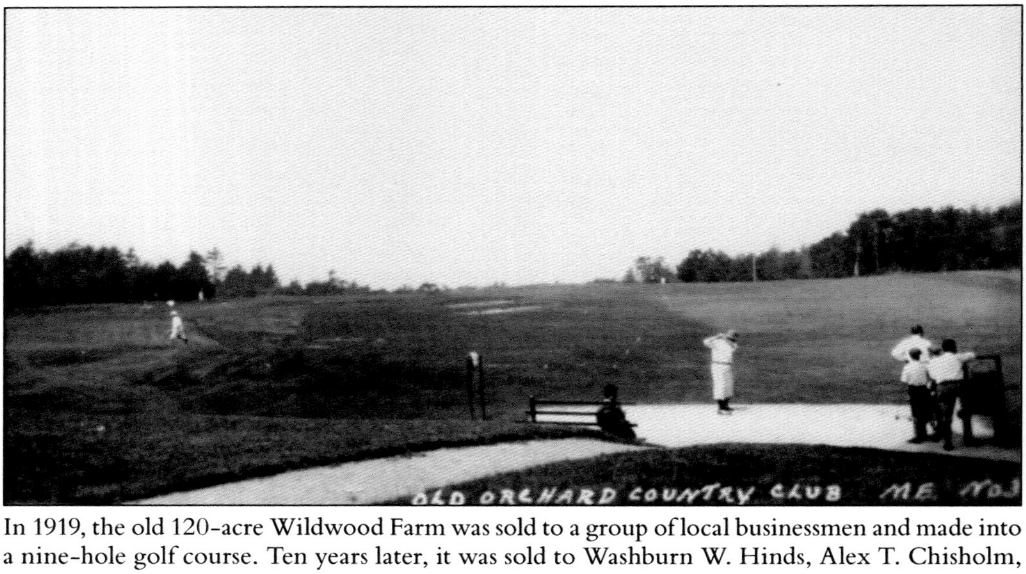


In 1919, the old 120-acre Wildwood Farm was sold to a group of local businessmen and made into a nine-hole golf course. Ten years later, it was sold to Washburn W. Hinds, Alex T. Chisholm, and Edward J. Chisholm. They added another nine holes to make it one of the finest courses in northern New England at the time. In 1933, Howard A. and Wilfred L. Duffy acquired ownership and management. Ben Houser, former major-league baseball player, became the club professional.

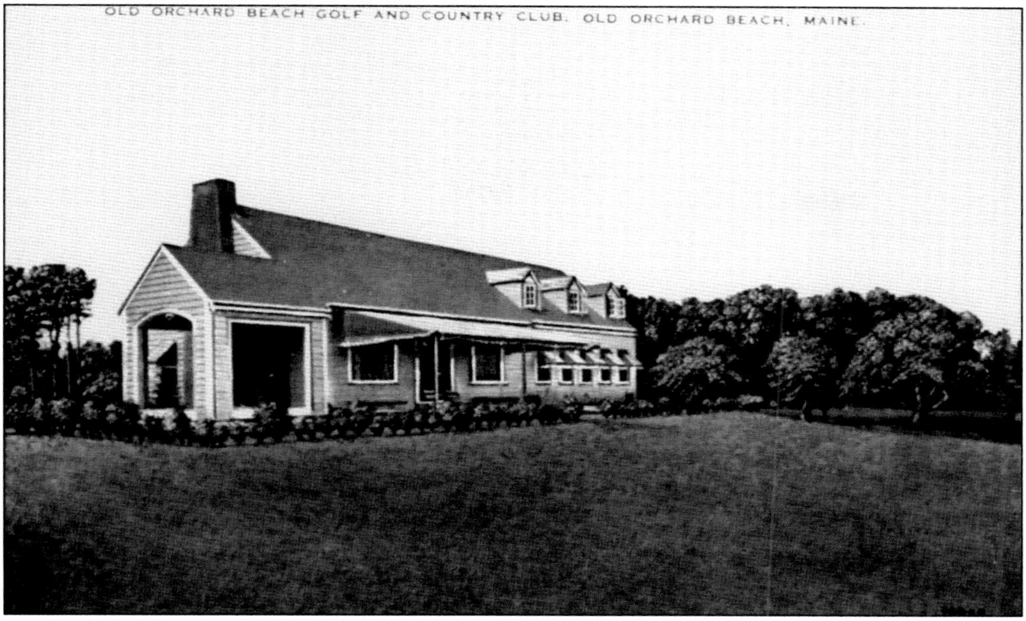

The original Wildwood Farm house was made into the clubhouse in 1919 by Charles Harrison Campbell, one of the original members of the 1919 group of owners. This clubhouse burned in 1935, and the new, still-standing clubhouse was built. In 2006, it is a private house, owned by the Ahearn Family. Probably the two most famous golfers to play here were Babe Didrikson Zaharias (1911–1947) and "Slamming" Sam Snead (1912–2002) in an exhibition match.

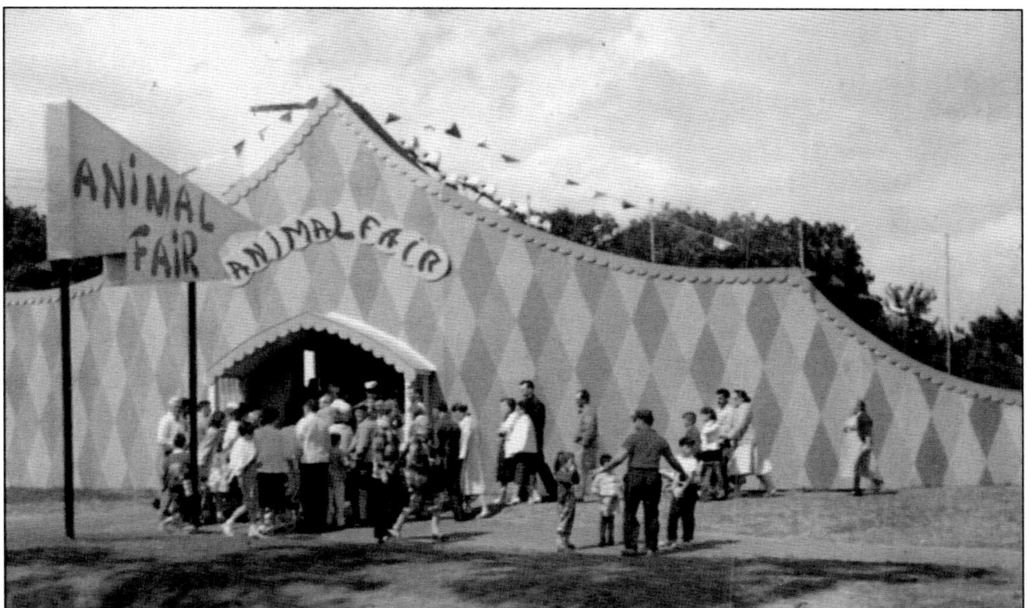

In 1958, the 20-acre Animal Fair was opened on the Cascade Road. The view above shows customers entering the Animal Fair facade into the old golf course clubhouse, which can be seen behind. The Animal Fair sprawled across 20 acres of rolling land and was home to several hundred animals from all over the world.

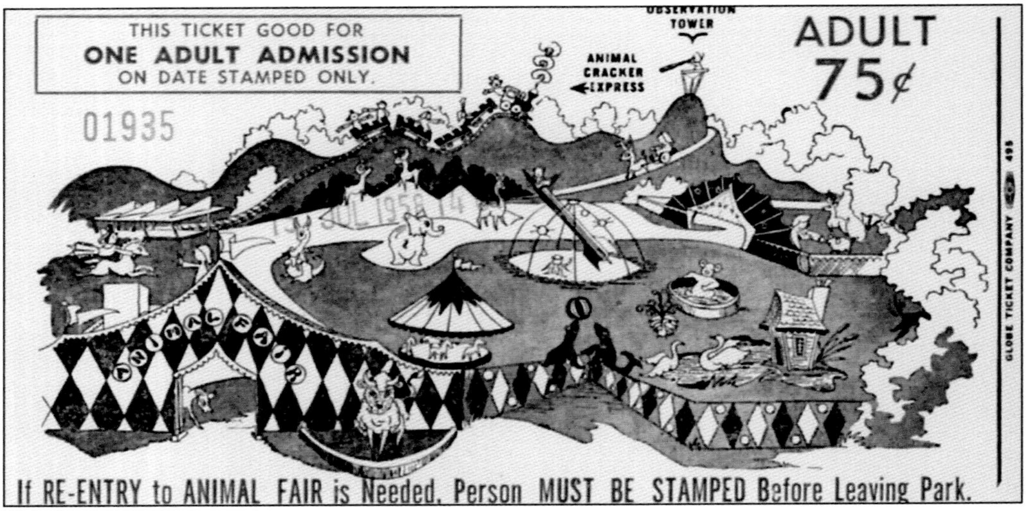


In April 1958, workmen began working seven days a week, constructing the buildings and pens. William Tracy of Tracy Parade and Design Company of North Bergen, New Jersey, was in charge of developing the Animal Fair owned by Bernard Osher. The above ticket is dated July 15, 1958. Weekday admission was 50¢, and children paid 35¢ to enter.

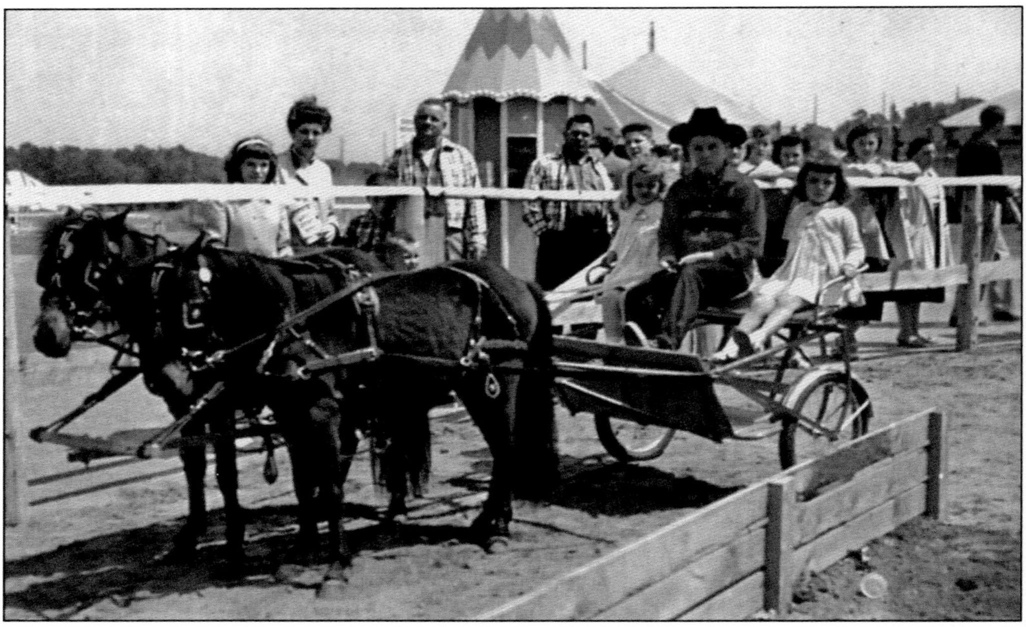

The *Portland Press Herald* of May 21, 1958, reported that "Visions of Africa, Australia, the old West and the Maine woods appeared at the famous beach front resort town this morning, as the first load of animal arrived for an 'Animal Fair' to be opened, May 30." In the above image, children are taking a ride on twin Shetland ponies.

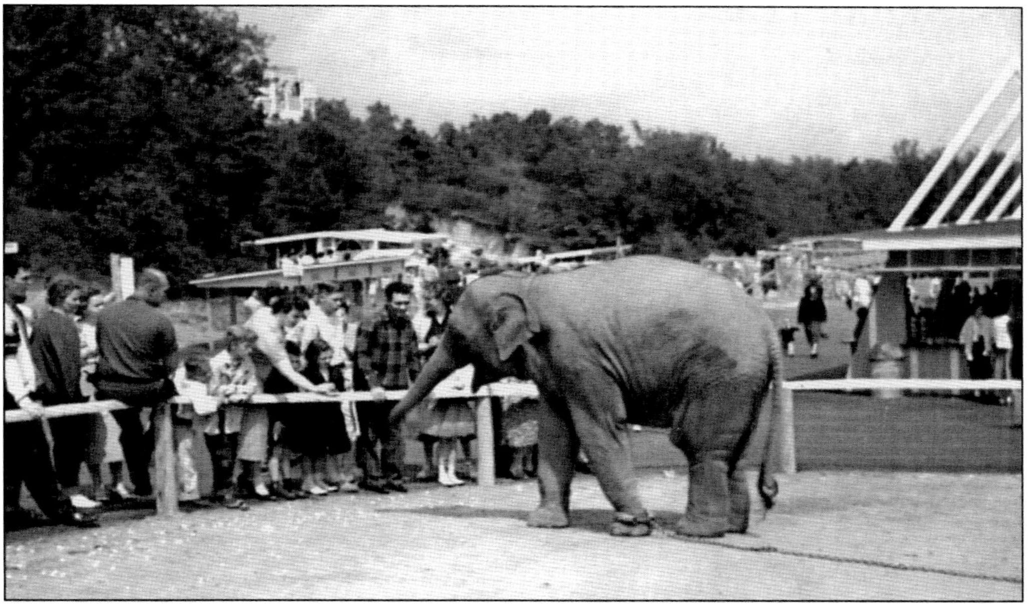

"Animals from five nations find homes at the Animal Fair," said Clayton Feeney, of Standish, manager of the Animal Fair. A 100-yard-long mining tunnel, complete with simulated wood-burning trains, or a visit to two ponds, which held sea lions, swans, ducks, seals, and other waterfowl, were among the many attractions at the new amusement center.

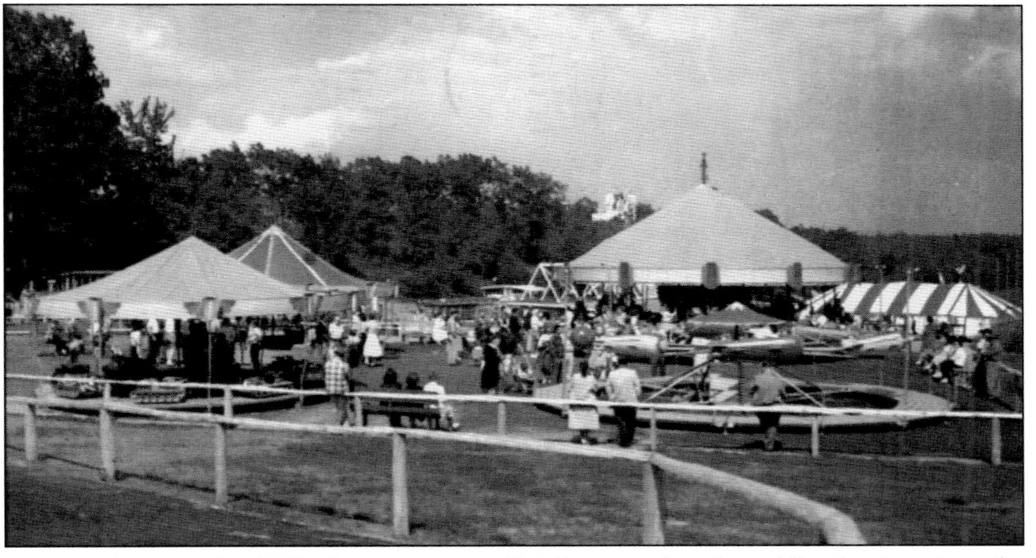

On Saturday, June 21, 1958, the gates were officially opened to the public, despite rain and a cool breeze. The Animal Fair was spread over 20 acres of scenic Maine beauty and inhabited by several hundred animals in their natural surroundings. There were special areas for feeding the animals, many kiddie rides, and areas for group outings for the young and old to enjoy. Prior to the official opening, the seventh-and eighth-grade school kids were allowed a sneak preview. The author and good friend David Ahearn were among that group. Today Ahearn and his wife, Glenna, own the old Animal Fair property and operate Powderhorn Campground. The Animal Fair closed its doors in 1962.

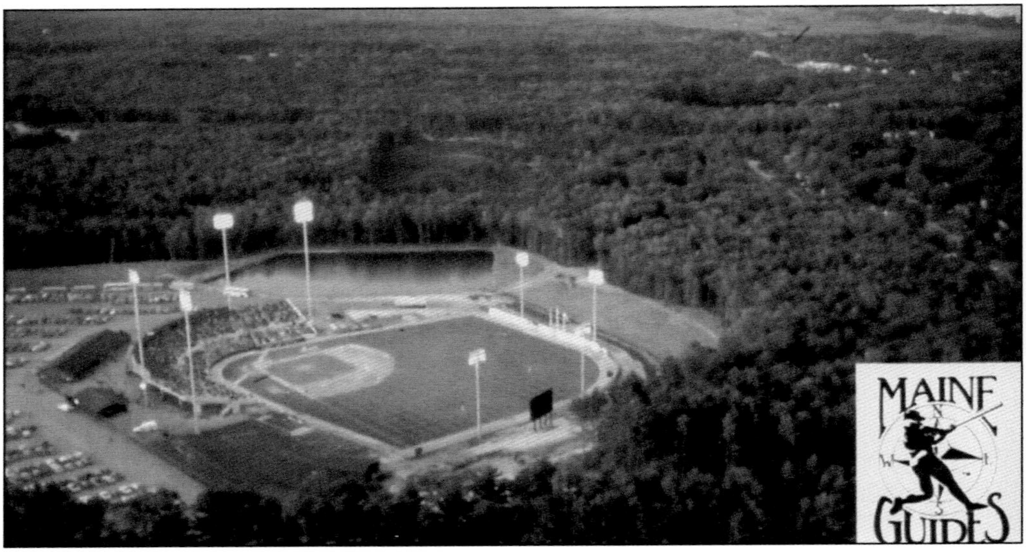


The ballpark was the home of the Maine Guides, a Triple A baseball team. Construction commenced in 1983 on the old Titcomb farm property that was owned by the town and sold to team owner Jordan Kobritz. After a rainout the previous day, the opening game was held on April 18, 1984. *Sports Illustrated* magazine called the ballpark "the prettiest little park in the country." Unfortunately, Triple A baseball and later concerts failed and the town was left with the $2.2 million note it had cosigned with the Finance Authority of Maine (FAME). Today the ballpark is closed, desolate, overgrown with weeds, and slowly crumbling.

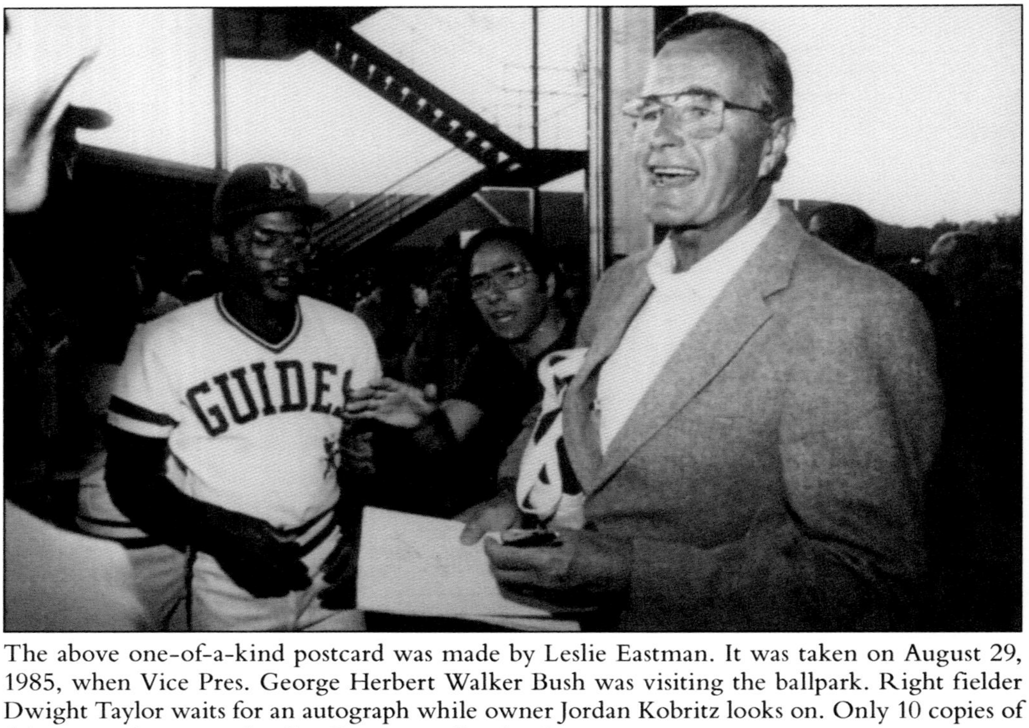

The above one-of-a-kind postcard was made by Leslie Eastman. It was taken on August 29, 1985, when Vice Pres. George Herbert Walker Bush was visiting the ballpark. Right fielder Dwight Taylor waits for an autograph while owner Jordan Kobritz looks on. Only 10 copies of this postcard were made. (Les Eastman collection.)

# *Seven*

# Things Remembered

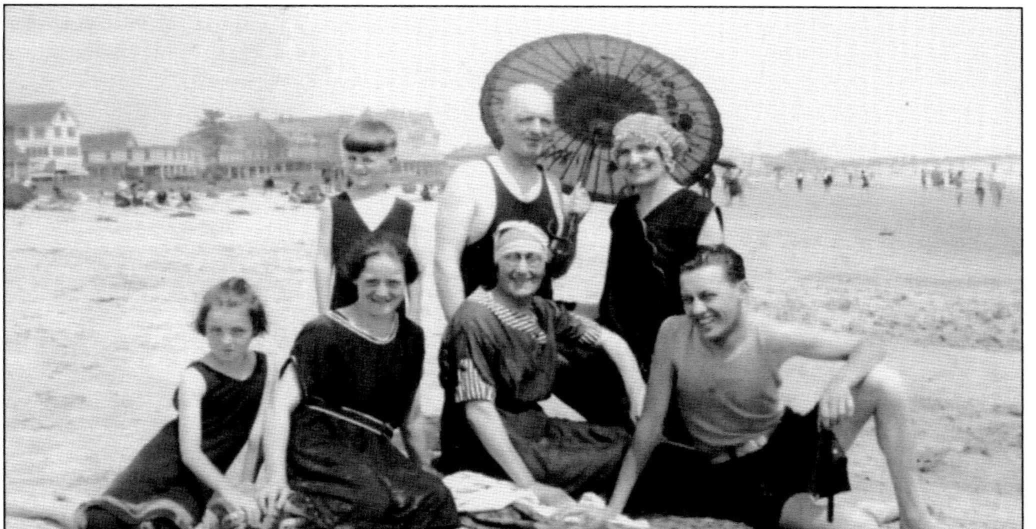

Everyone enjoys going to the beach for a day of fun, including this happy group above in this *c.* 1920 real-photo postcard. A local beach photographer took this picture at the foot of Atlantic Avenue. In 1929, town elders petitioned the state legislature and changed the name from Old Orchard to Old Orchard Beach, realizing the importance of its best tourist attraction, the beach. Most everything has changed in town since this photograph was taken, except the sands of Old Orchard Beach. Actually today there is more sand here than there used to be, because of the man-made breakwater, also known as "the jetty," that was built in the mid-1800s on the north side of the Saco River at Camp Ellis in Saco. The sands of Saco Bay are deflected toward Old Orchard Beach.

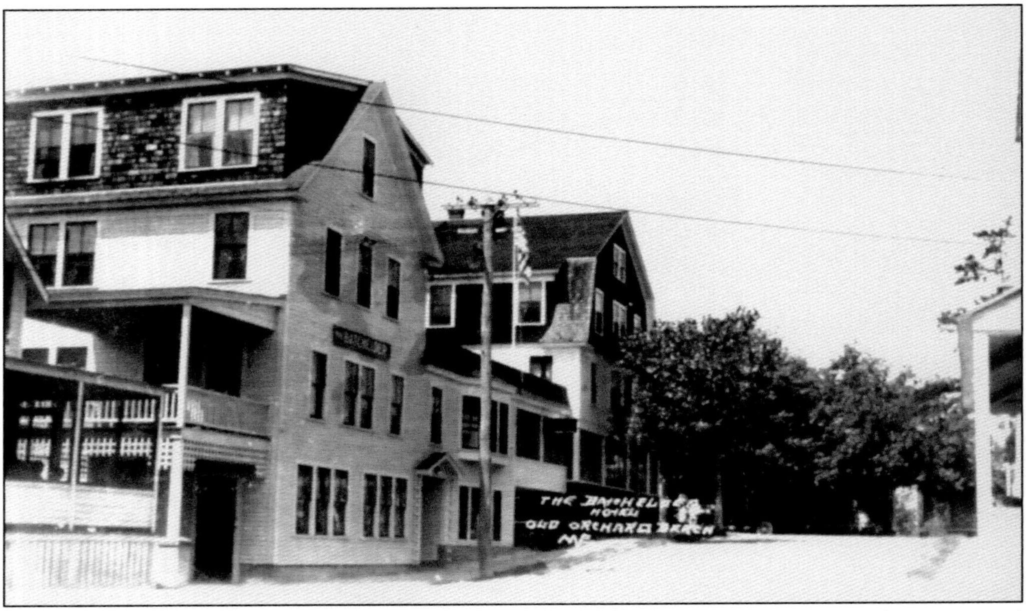

The postcard above shows the Batchelder Hotel that was located at 95 West Grand Avenue and ran down Camp Comfort Avenue. The exact date of the hotel is not known but is believed to have been built in the 1880s. Ownership, as well as the name, has changed many times over the years. Around 1900, Ivan Batchelder owned most of the buildings on the right-hand side of Camp Comfort Avenue. The restaurant/lounge had many different names such as the Saxony, the Hillbilly Ranch, and the Red Carpet Lounge, when the two buildings shown above were destroyed by fire on May 25, 1976.

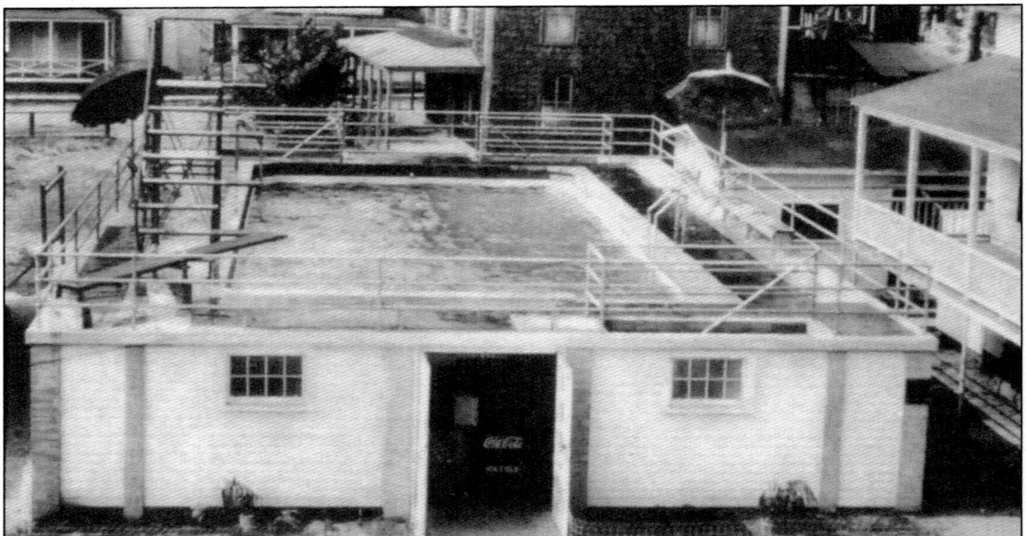

The first aboveground, outdoor swimming pool in Old Orchard Beach was the Batchelder swimming pool. Besides its guests, the public was welcome to swim or dive off the diving board or platform. Local cement contractor Clinton Mewer built the 20-by-45-foot pool in 1937. The demise of the pool came in the late 1950s, when it was believed that someone contracted polio from swimming in the pool.

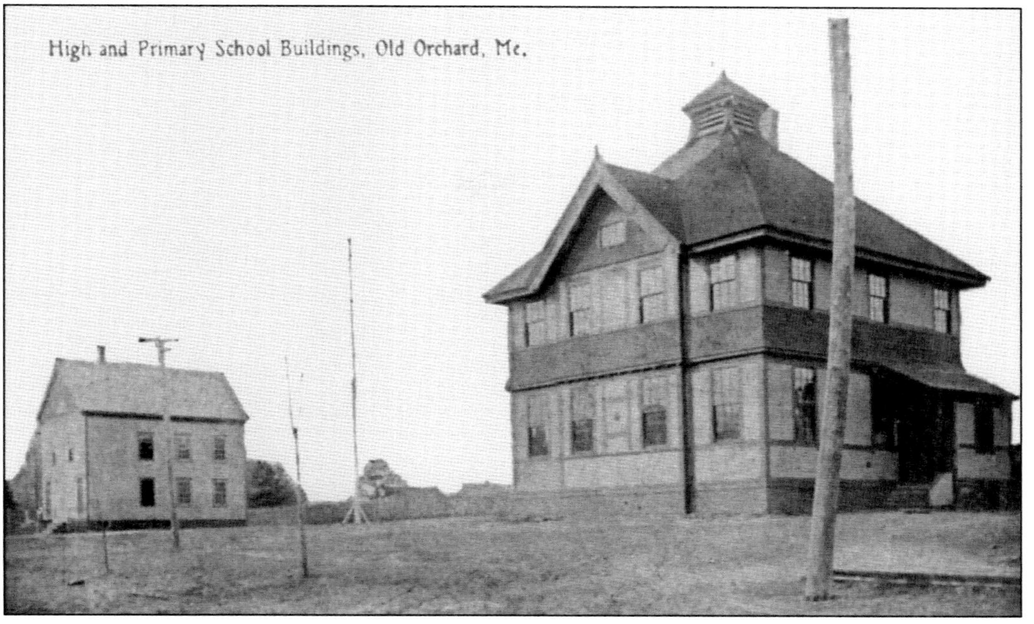


The primary school district No. 3 on the left was built in 1891 and remained a schoolhouse until it was given to the American Legion in 1924. It was moved directly across School Street and is still standing today. The old high school, on the right, was built for Old Orchard students by the City of Saco in 1881. It was razed in three and a half hours in 1982, and Centennial Place was built in 1983, for senior citizens housing.

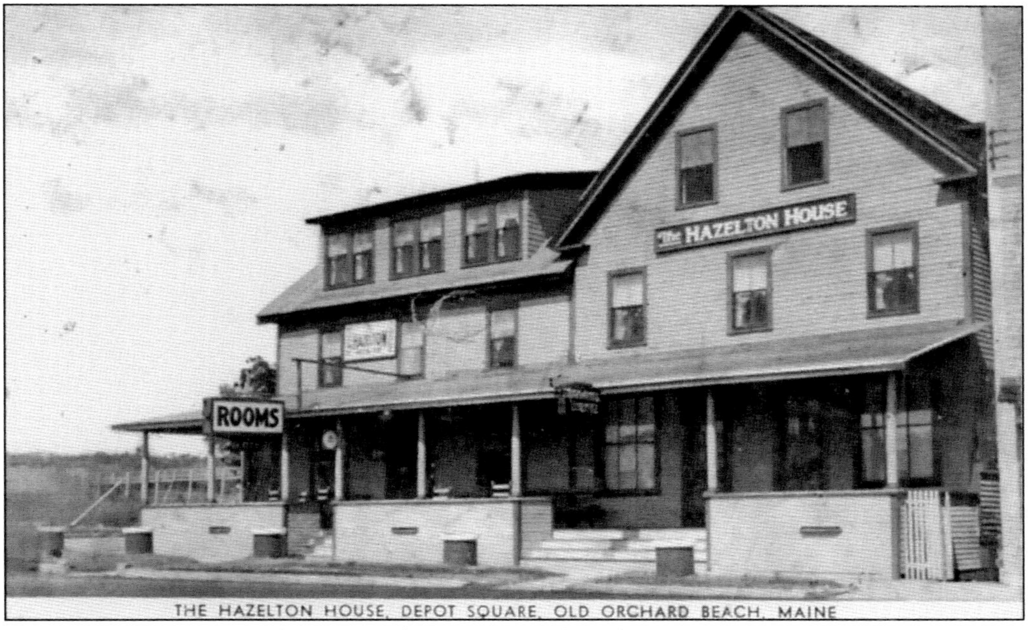


The Hazelton House, on the corner of First Street and Staples Street, was torn down in June 1965. It was also called the Jones House and the Marshall House. Famous inventor Alexander Graham Bell (1847–1922) is said to have stayed overnight here. Today a paved parking lot occupies the site, which is owned by the Kerr family.

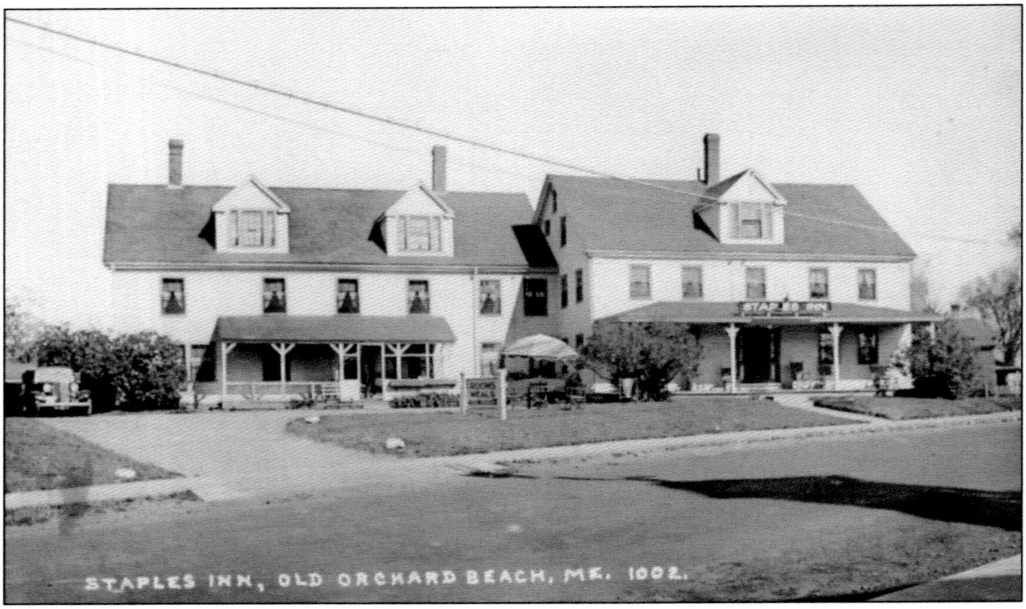


The old Captain Bonython home at 8 Portland Avenue is considered one of the earliest homes still standing. Built around 1730, the one-story farmhouse came into the possession of Elisha Staples in approximately 1790. Later the one-story cape's roof was raised and became the 2.5-story farmhouse that today is still used as a hotel. It was expanded in 1860 into one of the largest hotels in Old Orchard Beach. In 1875, the hotel burned, but the current old cape-style homestead survived. Saved from demolition in 1997, the elegant Staples Inn is now listed on the National Register of Historic Places.

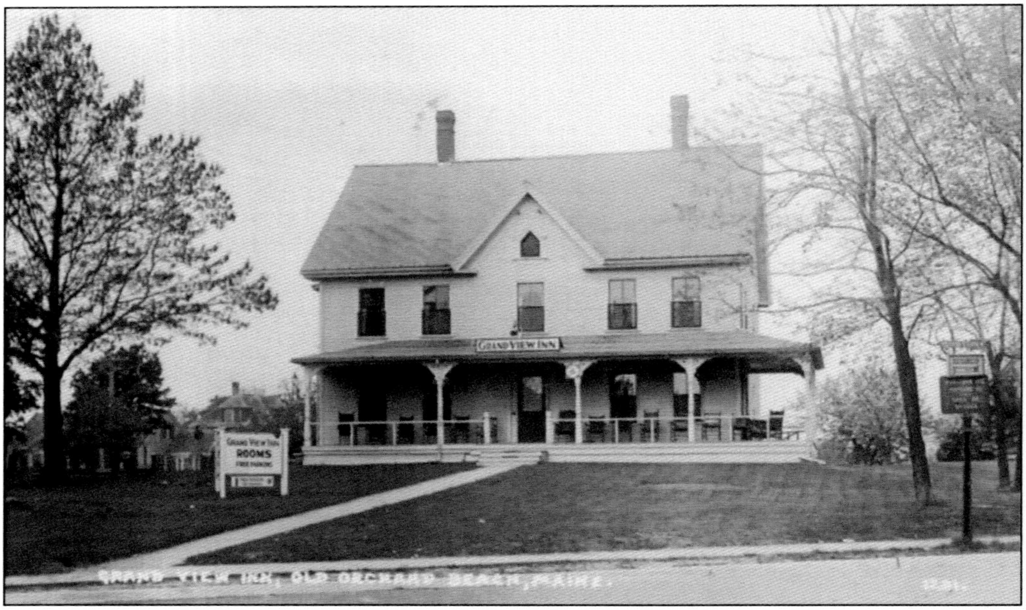


The Grandview Inn was built on the same lot as the 1875 fire of the Old Orchard House. In 1878, Ebenezer Staples built the 30-by-40-foot, 2.5-story inn. It was razed in 1944, and seven years later the Saco and Biddeford Savings Bank was built on the same site.

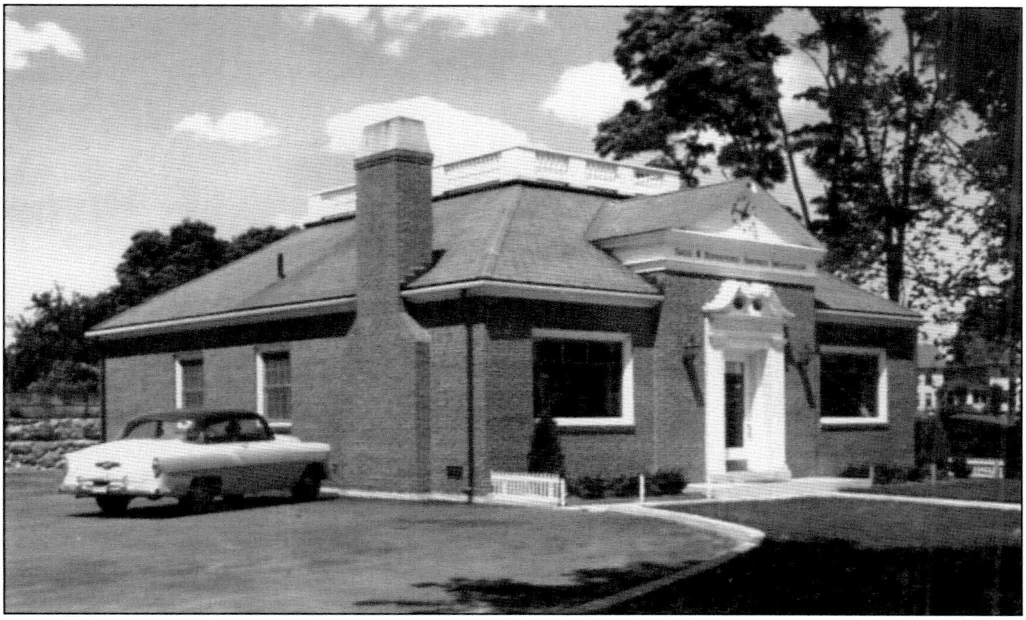

On November 24, 1951, Saco and Biddeford Savings Bank opened on the site of the old 1878 Grand View Inn. One odd novelty about the bank is that there have been only three managers in the bank's 55-year existence. William Deans was first, followed by Mel Wilbur, and it is currently managed by Carolyn Lamontagne. The brick-style bank was designed by architect Phil Snow.

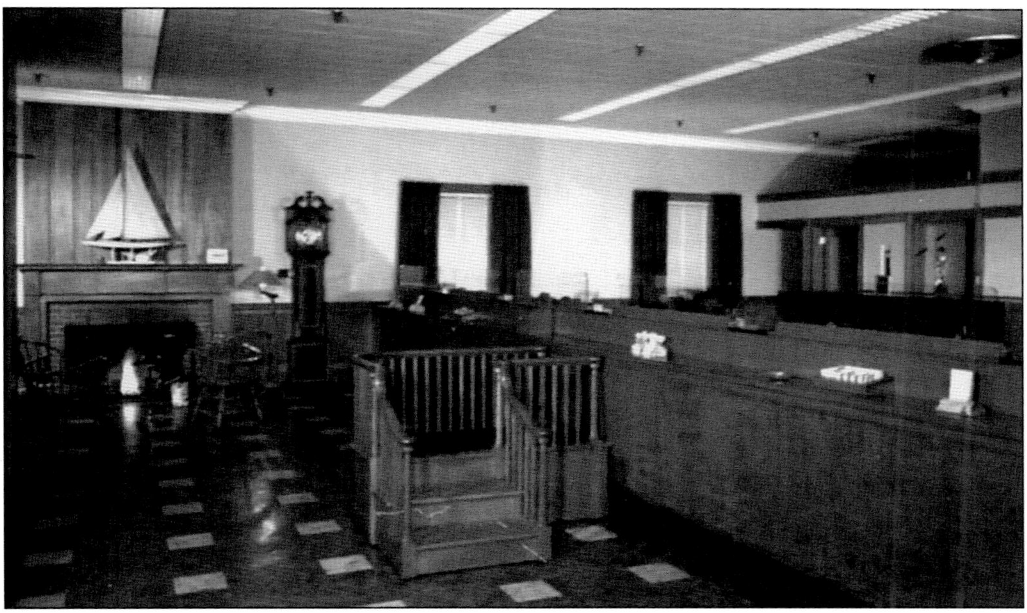

The above interior view shows the grandfather clock made by Harold Yeaton, in 1951. The Old Orchard Beach branch bank has undergone several renovations since being built. The first remodeling came in 1979. The second expansion happened in the 2002–2003 season, with a large addition in place. In 1996, the first ATM machine in Old Orchard Beach was added. Saco and Biddeford Savings Bank is the oldest mutual savings bank in Maine, since 1827.

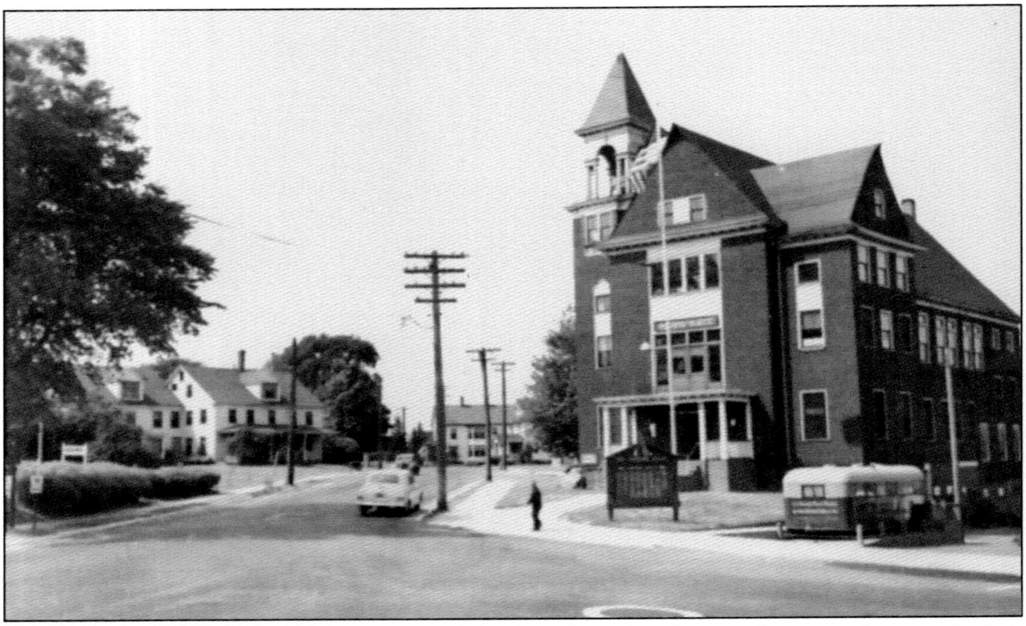

This rare photograph postcard shows the original York National Bank alongside the town hall. It was moved there in 1947. A wooden platform was constructed for walk-up customers to conduct their banking needs. The trailer was moved on-site from May 15 to September 15 each year and removed for the winter. In 1951, the trailer was left on location continuously until the new glass bank was built across the street.

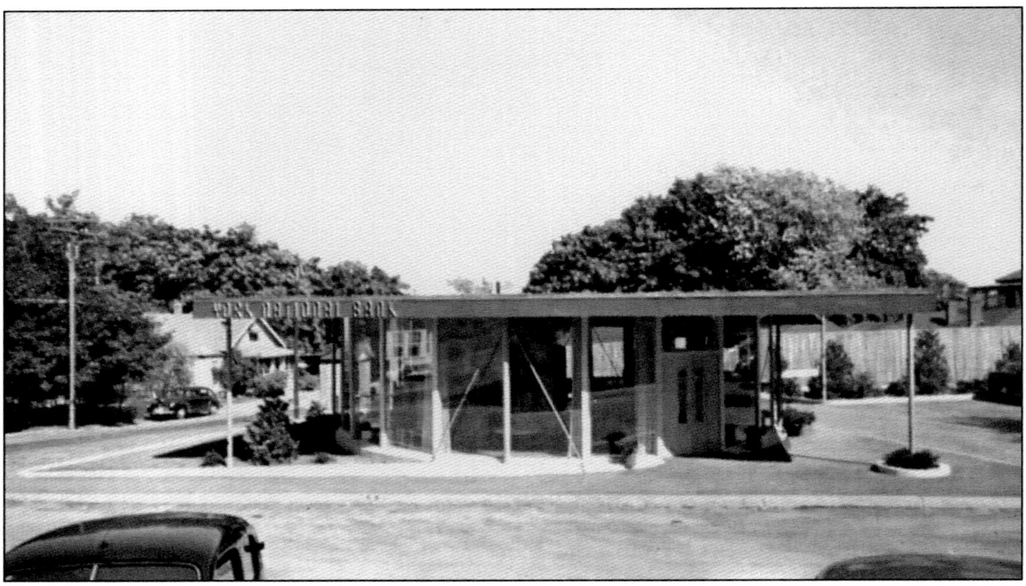

In June 1952, the new glass York National Bank was opened to the public. The exterior walls were glass, the vault was decorated with enameled porcelain, and the furniture was blond Scandinavian wood. The first manager was a local resident, Rupert Davis. Another well-known local, Jeffrey Thompson Jr., later became manager.

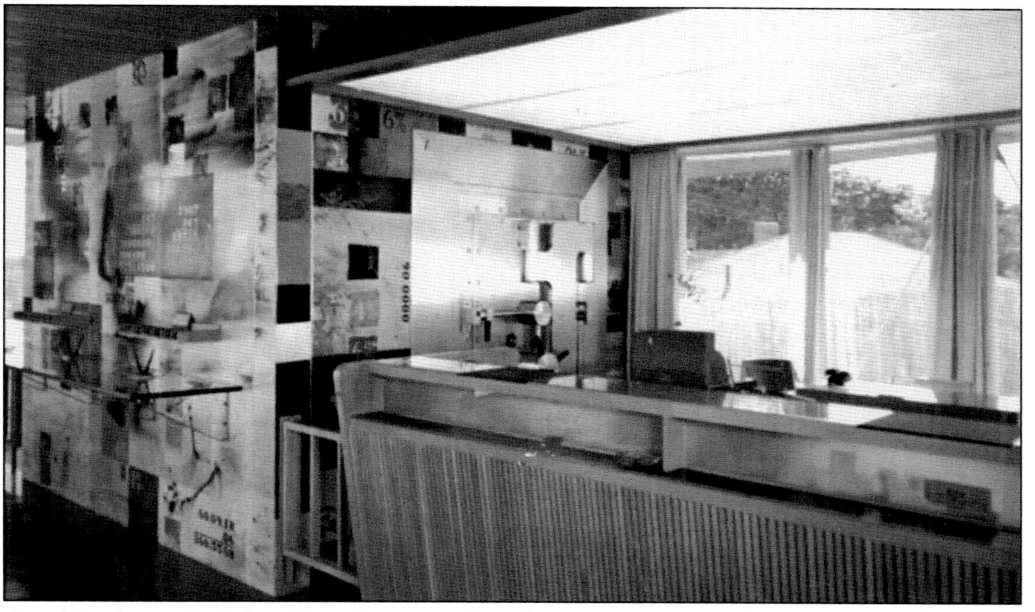

Canal Bank acquired the old York National Bank in 1959. In 1982, the bank was moved to the Cascade Plaza out on the Cascade Road. The old York National Bank was purchased by the Town of Old Orchard Beach and was razed on Saturday, March 27, 2004, and is now a paved parking lot for town hall parking.

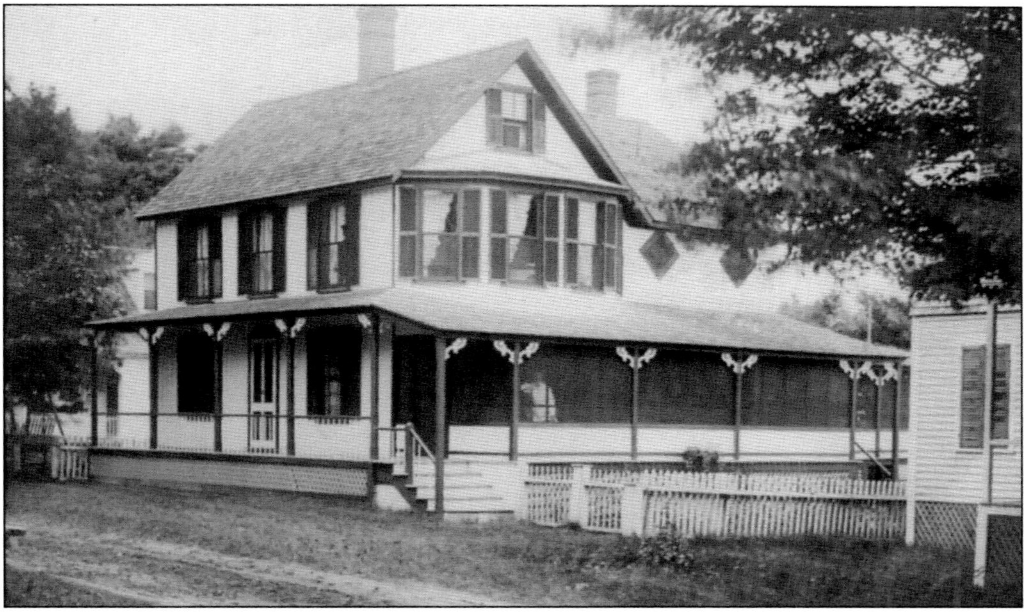

The above real-photo postcard, around 1912, shows the summer home of Maine First District United States House Representative Amos L. Allen (1837–1911). The house was built by local carpenter James Porter in 1880. The present-day owners, Robert and Sandra Scarpelli, own the home on Cedar Avenue.

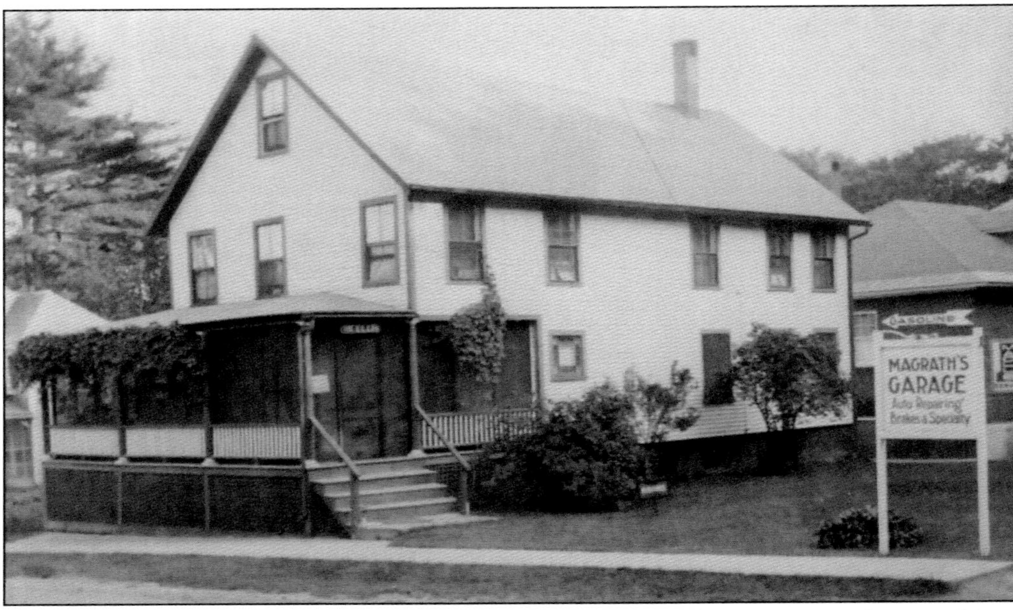


The Ellis, the home of Mary and Harry Magrath, was located on Fountain Avenue. Many well-known families have lived here over the years, including the Morton family, the Charles Sherman family, Lynedale Realty Company, and the Joseph and Edwina Jordan family. Today Joseph C. Jordan Jr. is the owner. The brick house behind the Magrath House is the parsonage for the Methodist church today.

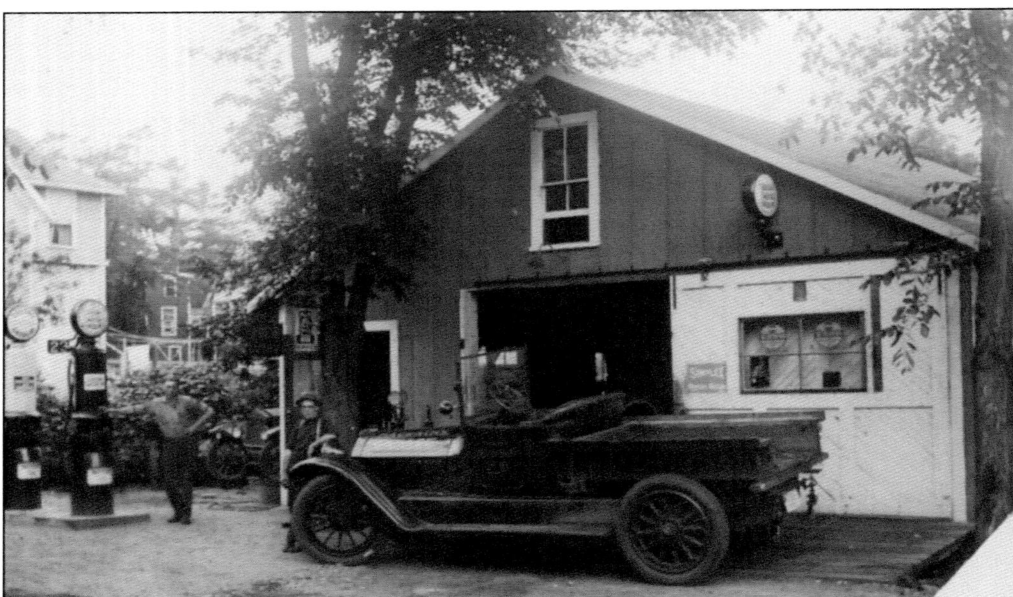

This rare real-photo postcard is Harry Magrath's garage, located at 10 Fountain Avenue. This popular neighborhood garage shows the garage in the 1930s. The gentleman leaning on the truck is Harry Magrath. Today the garage is long gone, and the lot is used for parking for the Methodist church.

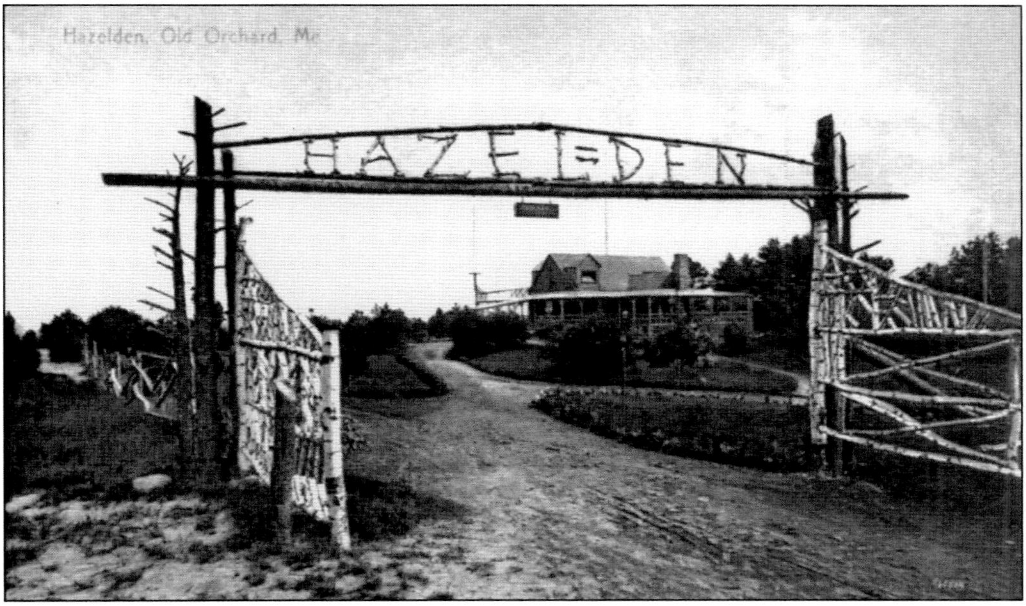


The stick entrance to Hazel Den, located on the corner of Hillside and Park Avenues, was built by Franklin Herbert Hazelton in 1898 as a summer retreat. Hazelton was the manager of Equitable Life Assurance Company of Portland. Hazelton married Magdalene, the daughter of Rev. Israel Luce, founder of the campgrounds. The one-room cabin was open for tours. In 1901, over 500 visitors toured the den. Even Pres. Theodore Roosevelt visited the Hazel Den around 1900.

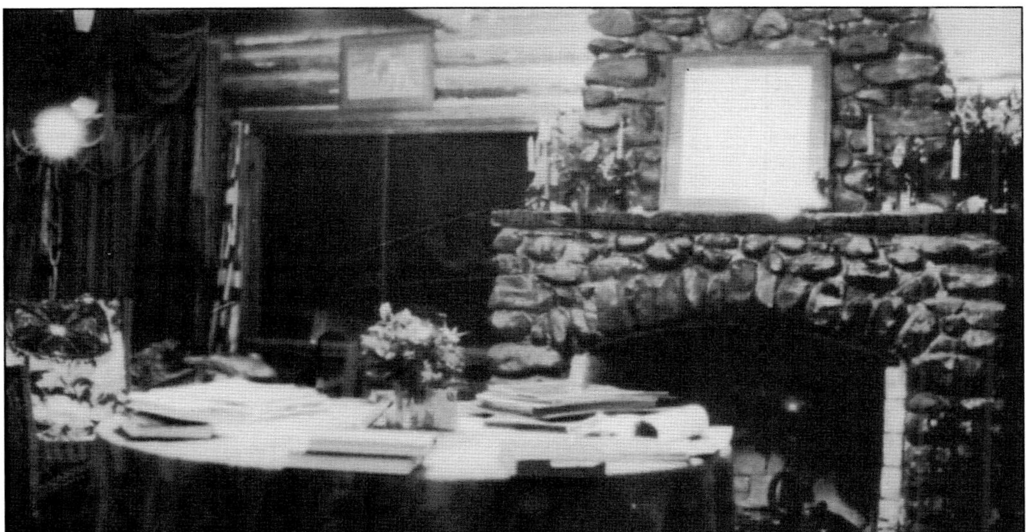

This rare view shows the interior of Hazel Den. The fireplace was constructed with locally gathered fieldstones. The famous log cabin was the principal feature of the grounds. Numerous musicals and other high-class social events were held there. Magdalene (Luce) Hazelton died in 1910, and Frank Hazelton passed away in 1924. Today this property is part of the Wild Acres Campground. The Hazel Den is scheduled for demolition in the very near future.

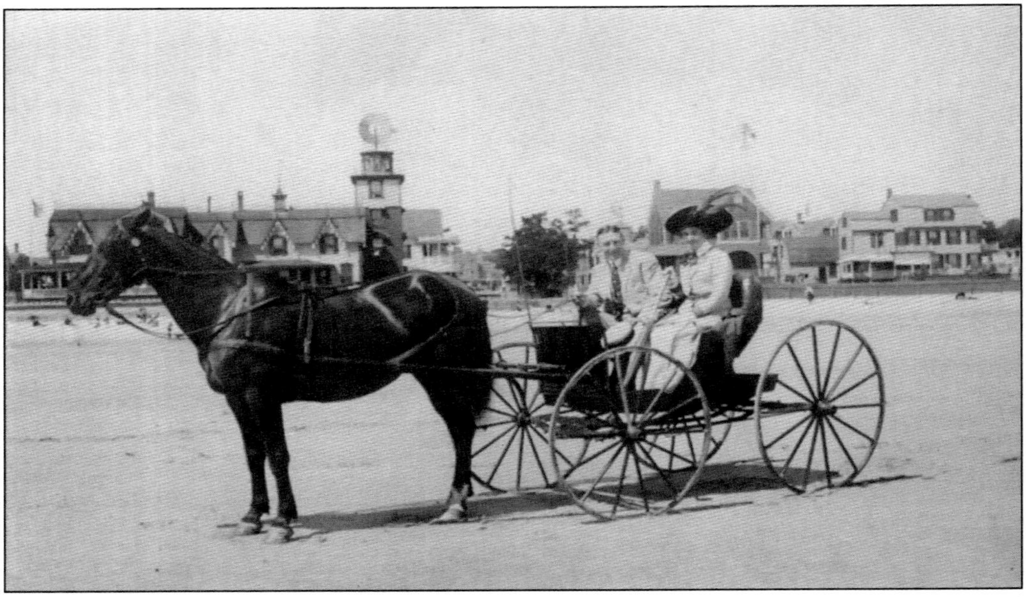

This *c.* 1912 real-photo postcard depicts people out for a Sunday stroll. Pictured in the background is the Thomas Goodall house located on the oceanfront between Pearl Street and Bay Avenue. Built in the 1870s, it was the summer estate of Thomas Goodall Esq. of the Goodall-Sanford Mills. It was razed in 1982, and in the history of Old Orchard Beach, the first condominium (Golden Shores) was built in 1983.

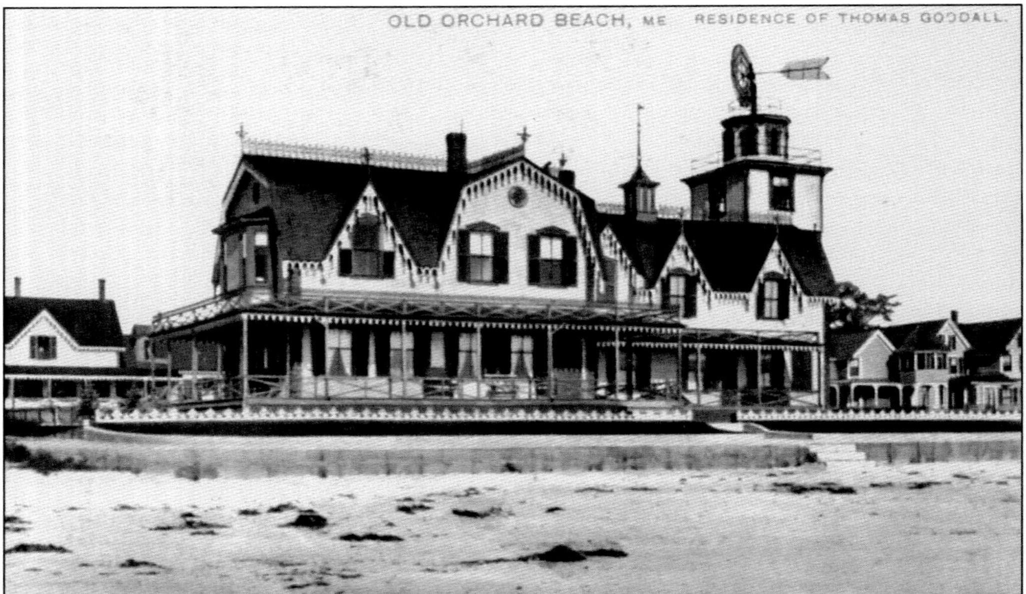


The tower room, with the windmill on top, was where Thomas Goodall displayed his replica of New York Harbor, complete with mechanical ships and flashing lighthouses. Once a week, the room was opened to local youngsters to admire his water display.

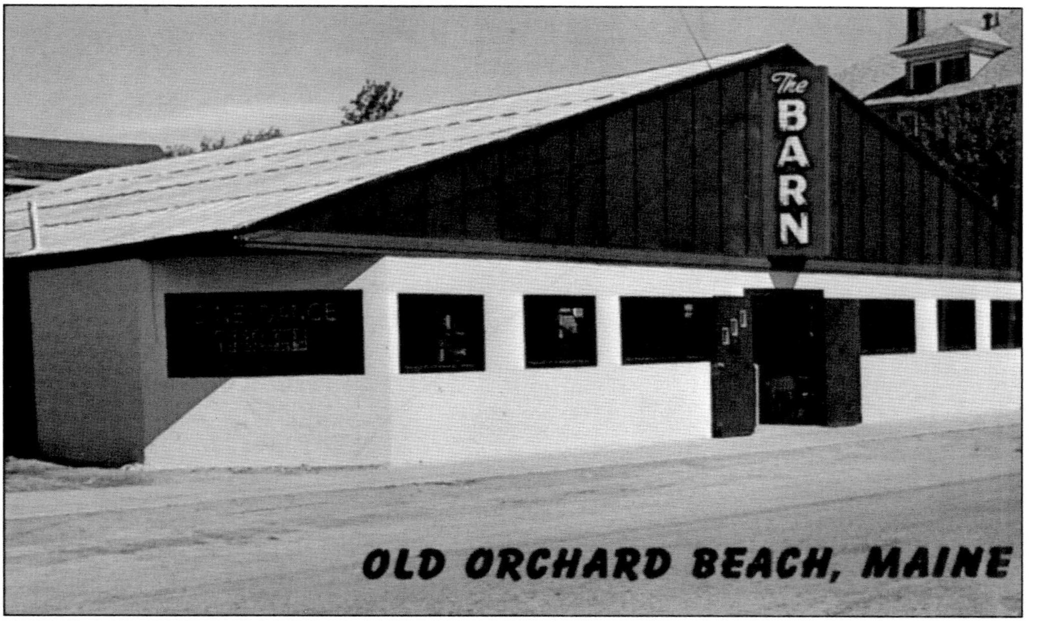


The Barn was located on the corner of Milliken and Imperial Streets. Originally it was a fuel and range oil business run by Oscar Larochelle. In the early 1960s, it was the hottest rock-and-roll establishment in town. The summer of 1962 featured Little Lou and his band from Boston. Waiting lines wrapped around the corner to hear Little Lou and his band doing their rendition of Joey Dee and the Starliters hits "Peppermint Twist" and "Shout." The Barn was later razed and Dy-No-Mite boutique was established.

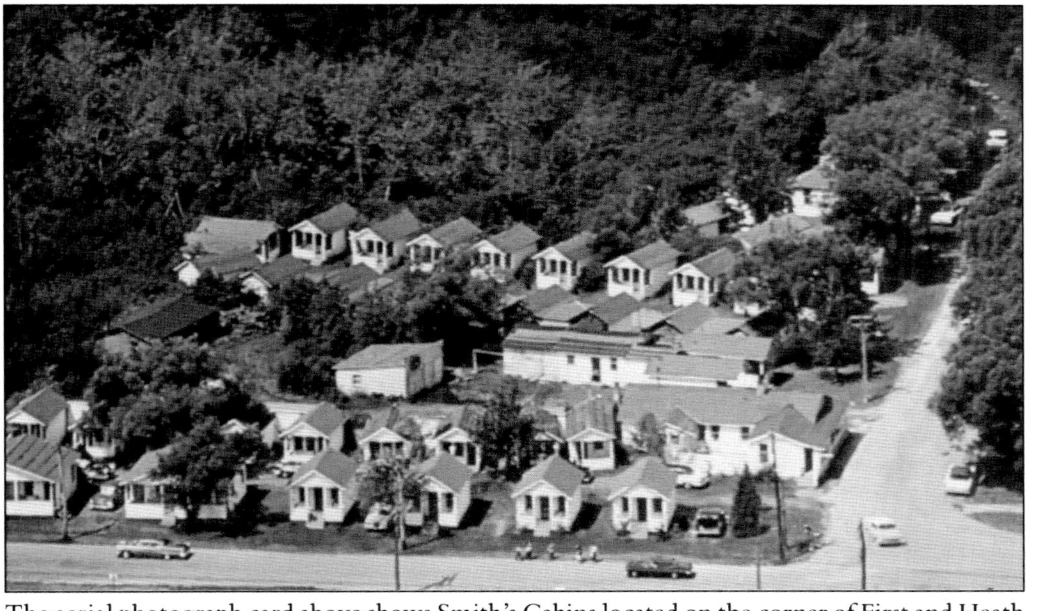

The aerial photograph card above shows Smith's Cabins located on the corner of First and Heath Streets. Originally built around 1937 by Edwin and Nan Smith, the 50 cabins were very popular and close to the beach. They were razed by Sidney Sclare in 1968, and the two-story Americana Motel was built on the site in 1969.

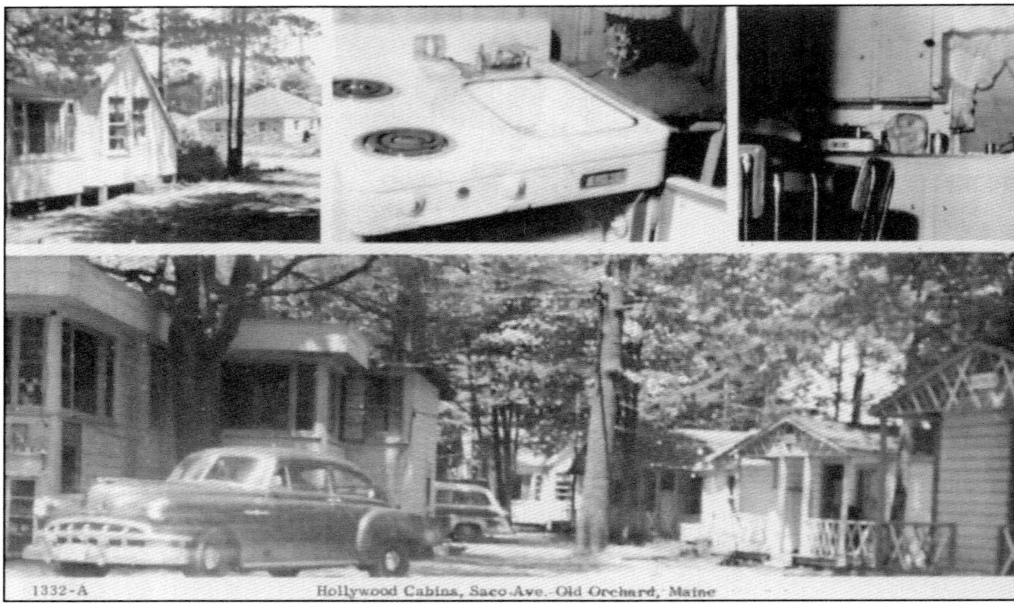

Located where present-day King Real Estate is at 198 Saco Avenue were the Hollywood Cabins, owned by the Lacasse family, situated in a pine forest in the halfway section of Old Orchard Beach. They advertised that each cabin had its own private bath, hot water, shower, kitchenette, and radio. Every fall, one could plan on stopping by and purchasing fresh apples, sold by Leo Lacasse, out front of the cabins.

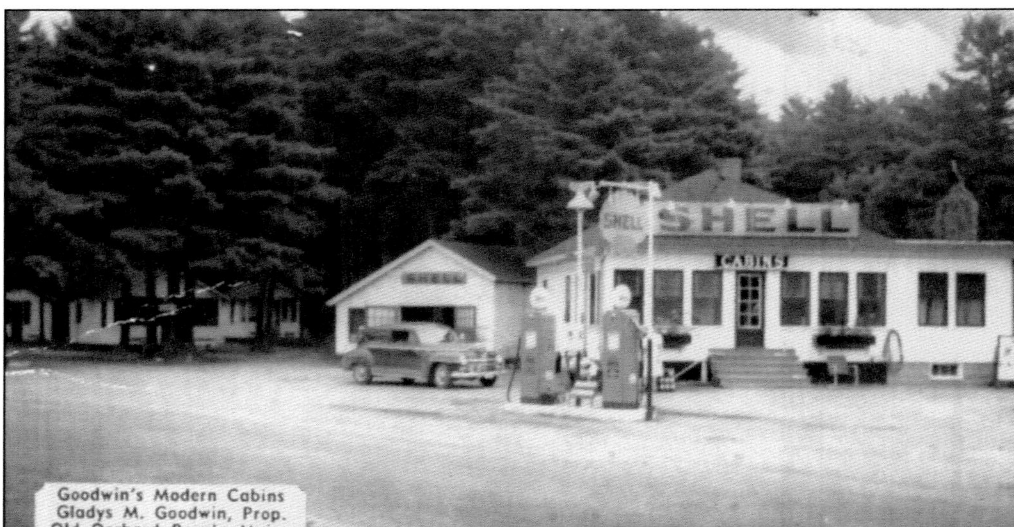

Goodwin's Garage was located where the present-day 7-Eleven store is located, in the halfway section. The house, cabins, and garage were built by Charles Goodwin. It was later sold to the Fred Larochelle family. Eventually the cabins were sold; the house was moved to 222 Temple Avenue. The pine trees were cut, and the lot remained vacant for many years. In 1986, the 7-Eleven store was built. Later the name was changed to Christy's and then was changed back to its present name, 7-Eleven.

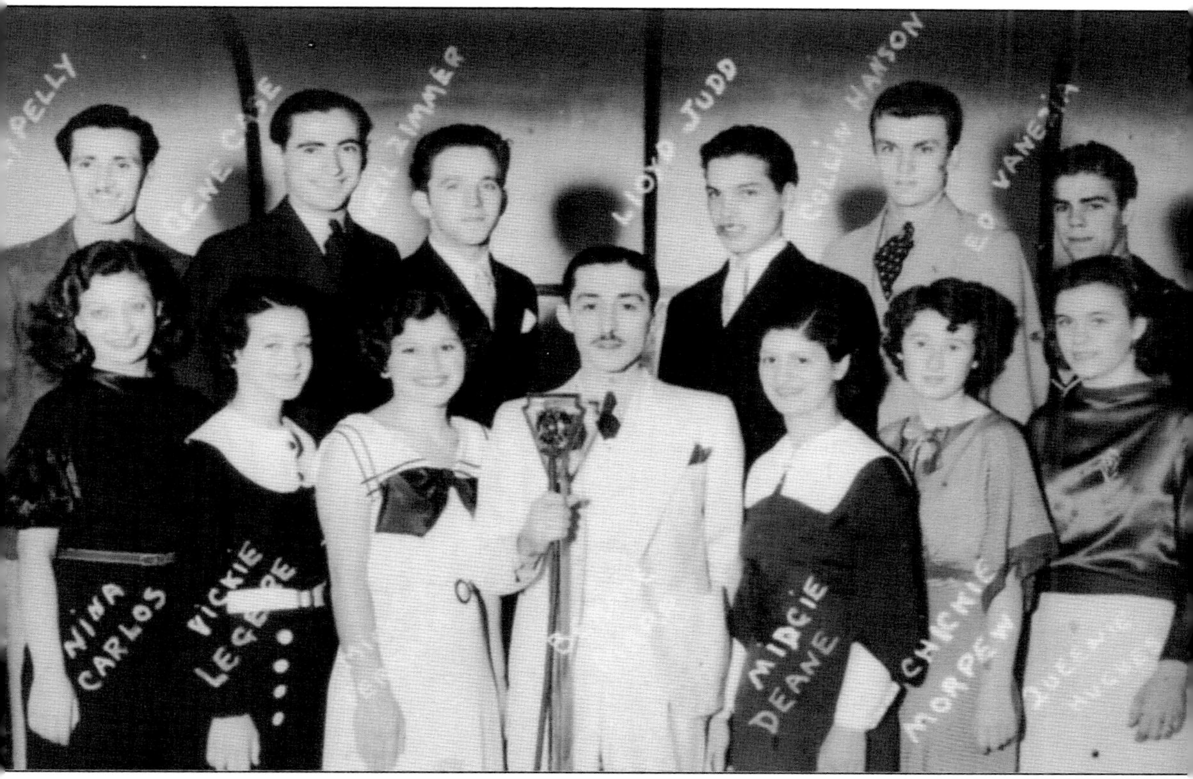


The first dance marathon held in Maine was in Old Orchard Beach in 1923. It was an outdoor affair, held in the Square. While the contestants danced to the phonograph, the sounds of the Salvation Army band playing nearby could also be heard. Five years later, on August 16, 1928, two bathing suit–clad couples danced their way from the First Parish Congregational Church in Saco to the Palace Ballroom in Old Orchard Beach, in 1 hour and 11 minutes. The winners were Irene Leger of Old Orchard Beach and Arthur Lambert of Biddeford. The marathon craze had caught on in Maine. A few days later, another marathon was held in the Palace Ballroom, this time not creating any traffic jams, as the previous one did. Maine's first real big marathon started on June 28, 1933. In Marathon Arena, 21 couples took to the dance floor that was located inside where the present-day Palace Playland building is. A $1,000 purse was at stake. First place received $500, second place received $300, and third place received $200. Mable "Bubbles" Everand of Brunswick and Ransom McNally of Old Orchard Beach came in fourth place, out of the money. This marathon lasted for 77 days, ending on September 12. The postcard above shows the contestants in the biggest and last marathon held in the Marathon Arena. This started on October 27, 1933, and continued 129 days, ending on March 4, 1934, for a total of 3,068 hours.

LIST OF CONTESTANTS FOR THE 1934

# *SPEEDATHON*

CIRCUS

| Team No. | Names of Contestants | Representing |
|---|---|---|
| 1. | Gene Case | New Hampshire |
| 2. | Lousia Marr | Rhode Island |
| 3. | George Lee | O. Orchard and Sac |
| 4. | Blanche Marcoux, Phil Poulin | Lewiston |
| 5. | Henry Trembley, Marion Young | Canada |
| 6. | Vickie Legere, Billie Joyce | So. Portland |
| 7. | Millie Phillips | New York |
| 8. | Katherine Sylvester, Billy Pelly | Massachusetts |
| 9. | Rita Tomaselia, Ken Tenny | Portland |
| 10. | Connie Morin, Jackie Muir | Rumford and Dixfie |
| 11. | Minnie Mouse, Mickey Mouse | Westbrook |
| 12. | Margie O'Neil, Ernie LaCass | Sanford |
| 13. | Irene Milliard, Lloyd Judd | Biddeford |
| 14. | Johnnie Hughes | Vermont |
| 15. | Dana Paulet, Johnnie Panchen | Connecticut |
| 16. | Margaret Maines, Arthur Maines | Brunswick and Freeport |
| 17. | Gene Hovey, Mickey Horan | Augusta & Gardiner |
| 18. | Al Piant | Waterville |

On December 10, 1933, in Hampden at the Paradise Dance Hall, during a raging snowstorm, 4 people died and 11 others were sent to the hospital after a raging fire during a dance marathon. After this, local authorities, clergy, civic leaders, and legislatures changed rules and regulations regarding dance marathons, eventually banning them. The above 1934 Old Orchard Beach "Speedathon," whose name was changed to circumvent the new laws, was held at the Palace Ballroom in 1934.

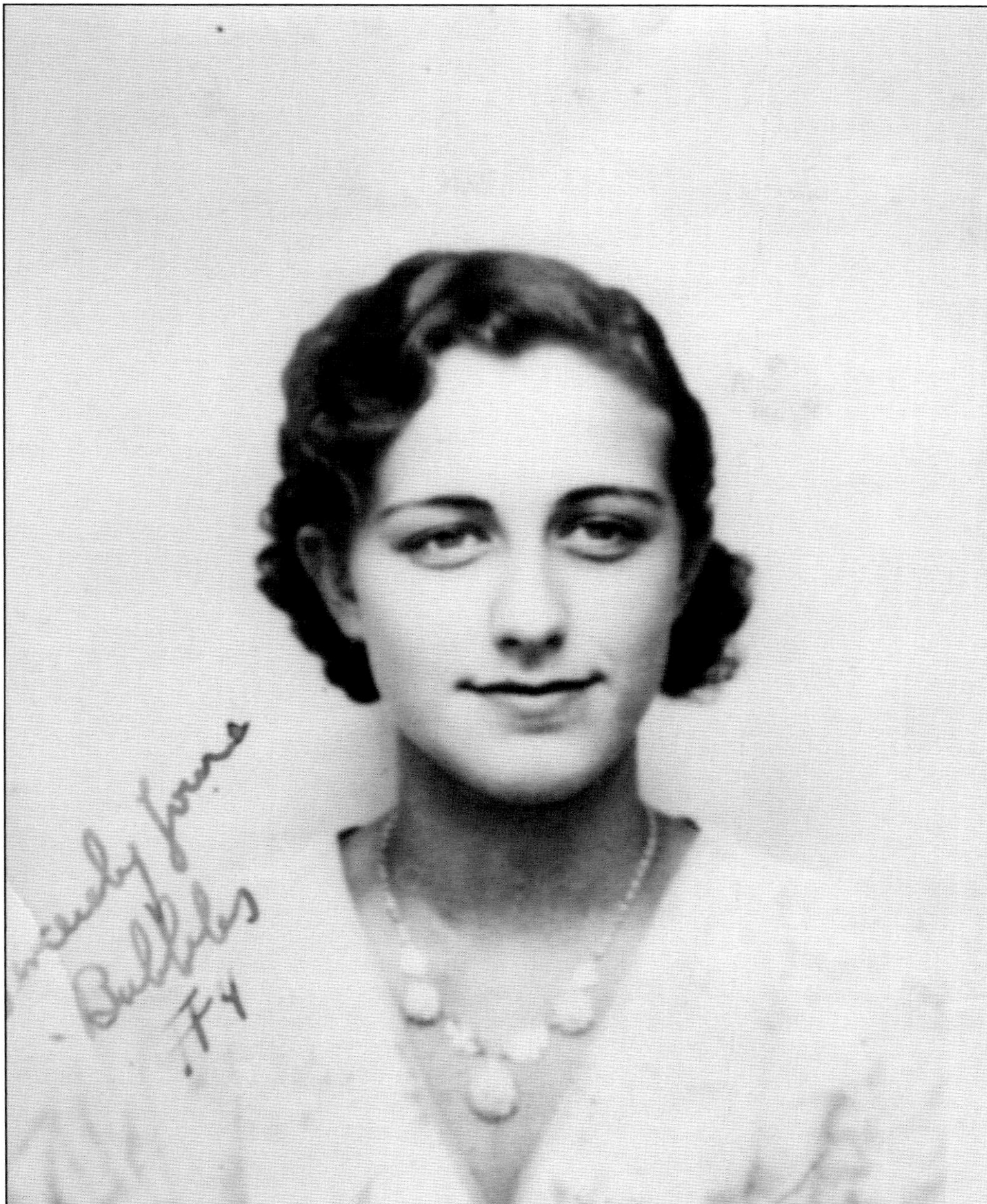


The above real-photo postcard (1934) shows Mable "Bubbles" Everand, who was the dancing partner of well-known local boy Ransom McNally. There were two marathons held in 1933 in Old Orchard Beach. The first started on June 28, 1933, and continued for 77 days. The second started on October 27, 1933, and lasted until March 4, 1934. The rules were 45 minutes of dancing, 15 minutes of rest. Unfortunately for Everand and McNally, they placed fourth, out of the money. Participating in the 3,068-hour contest (lasting 129 days), were 72 couples. Paying customers watched their favorite couple dance, and at noon the local radio station would give updates.

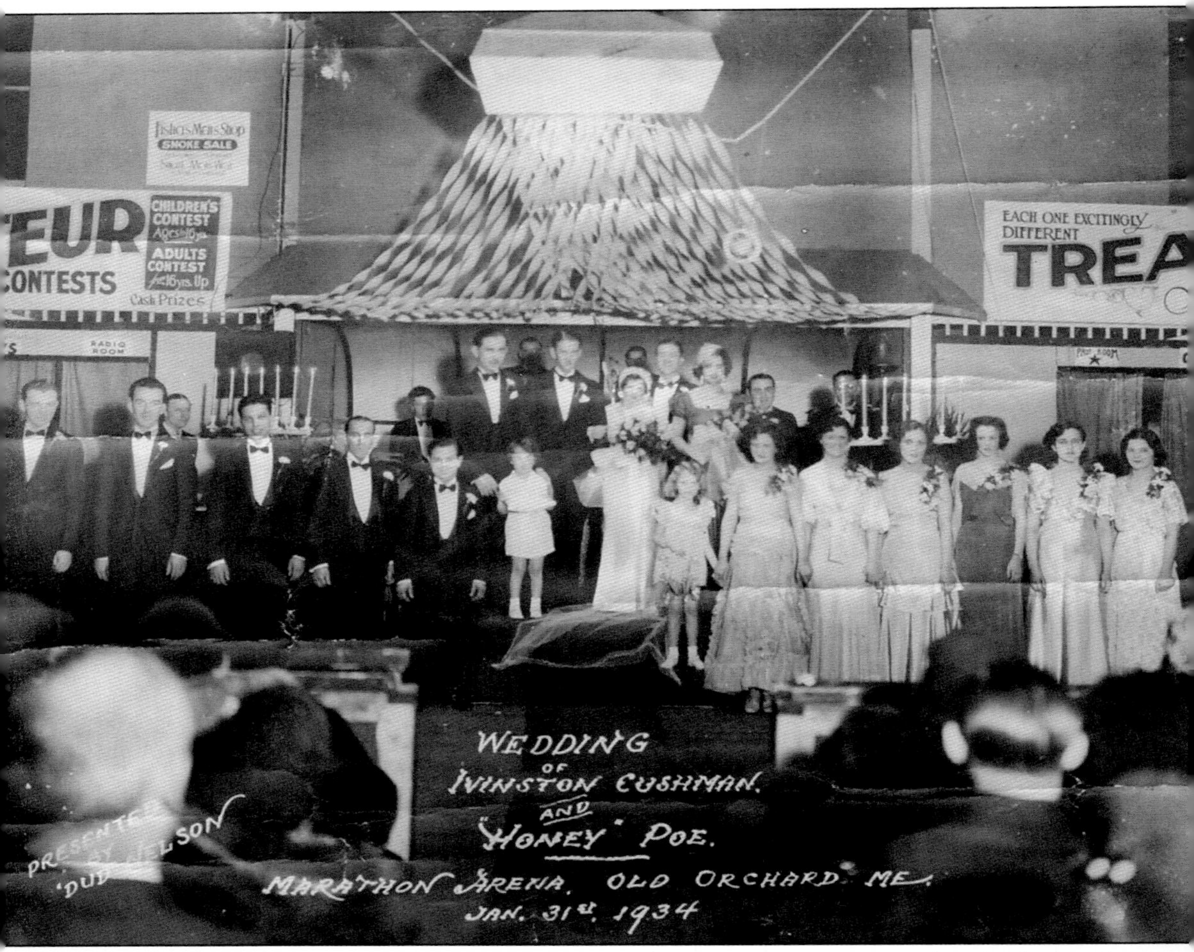


In every marathon or speedathon dance contest there were numerous novelty acts during the contest to keep the paying public entertained. One such novelty was the wedding of Winston Howland Cushman of Assonet, Massachusetts, and Margaret Theresa "Honey" Poe of Patterson, New Jersey, on January 31, 1934, at the Marathon Arena. The ceremony was performed by Judge Wesley M. Mewer of Old Orchard Beach. Besides the record for the longest marathon, at 129 days, there was also another wedding performed, in which the marathon couple actually got married while dancing, and the justice of the peace and attendants paraded around the floor with them, in step.

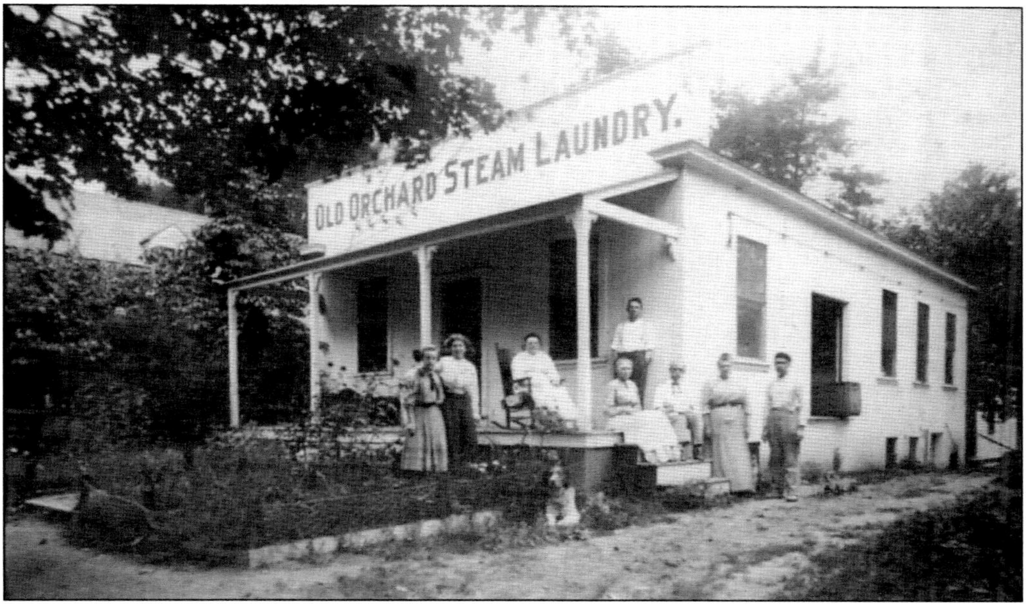


The Old Orchard Steam Laundry building located at 6 Pine Avenue is still standing in 2006 as a private residence. Many of the larger hotels had their own laundries, but the smaller hotels had their laundry sent out. Located in the campground section, many campers had their laundry done here also. The lady sitting in the rocking chair is Kate Stewart, mother of well-known town employee Henry.

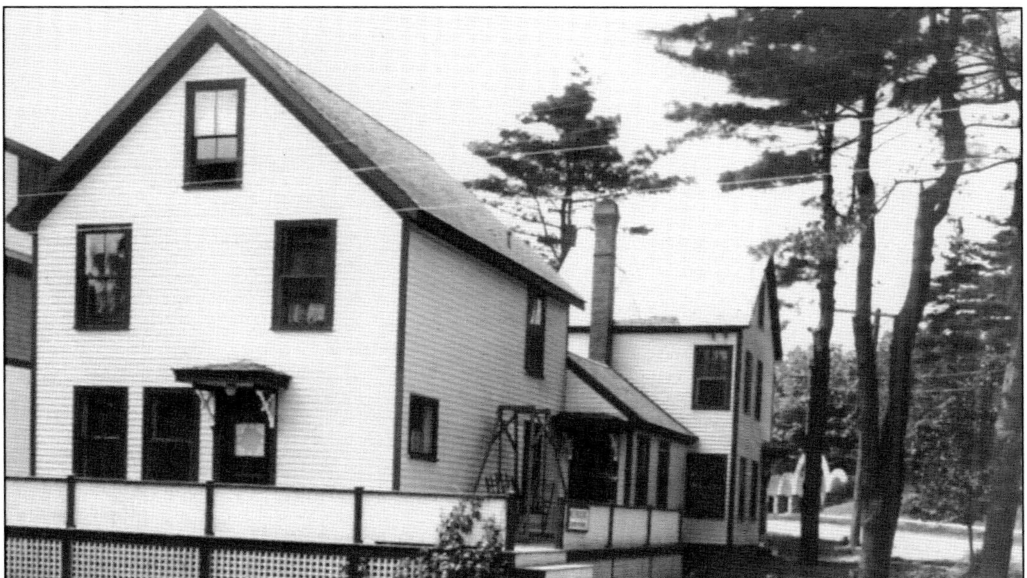

Local carpenter W. B. Spaulding's residence was this house, on the corner of Washington and Atlantic Avenues. This house later became Dickson and Simpson's Nationwide grocery store. On Tuesday, March 26, 1985, Dave's Market was destroyed in a wind-swept blaze. At the time of the fire, it was owned and operated by David Dardano. It was quickly rebuilt after the fire and is still a neighborhood grocery store with three apartments located above it.

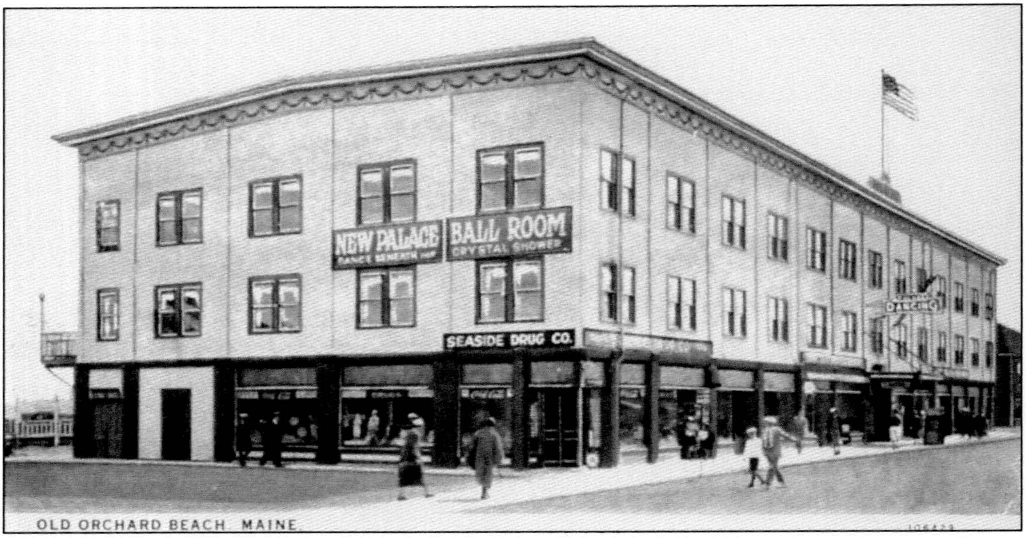


The new Palace Ballroom, also known as the Usen Block, is located on the corner of West Grand Avenue and Staples Street. The Palace Ballroom was officially opened on Saturday, June 28, 1924. Hundreds of big bands played the Palace Ballroom. Bill Haley and his Comets were featured here on May 28, 1957. The ballroom was sold out. The following year, a crowd of less than 100 came to watch Louis Armstrong play. Big bands were on the way out, and rock and roll was on the way in. The high school class of 1965 had its graduation on the second floor. Also in 1965, the world's drumming marathon record was set here when local drummer Roger Roscoe drummed for 50 nonstop hours. Two years later, the Palace Ballroom building was razed.

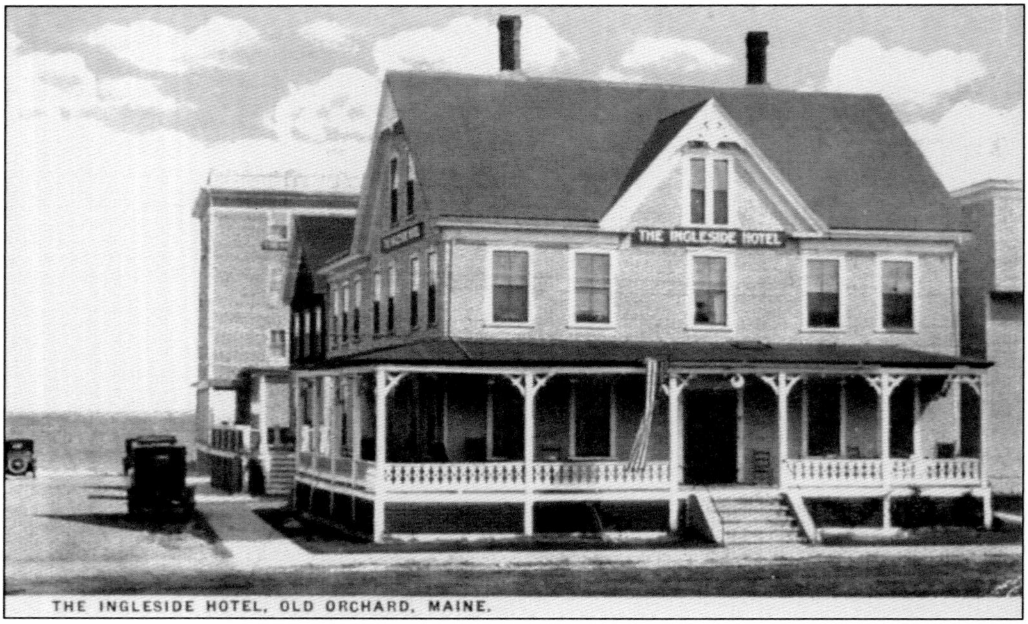


The Ingleside Hotel was built in 1883 by Mrs. E. Manson. It was on the corner of West Grand Avenue and Fernald Street. It was razed to make room for the two-story Brunswick Motel. In 1983, the motel was moved across the street, along the railroad tracks, and the name was changed to the Soho Inn. Today the lot is used for parking for the Brunswick condominiums.

*Nine*

# The Camp Grounds

The early postcard on the right with the beautiful poem by Jennie Lind Allen says it all. The Camp Ground section of Old Orchard Beach is one of the remaining treasures still in existence. With a stroll down Maplewood, Linden, Wesley, Zion, and many of the other narrow streets of the Camp Grounds, one can still see the many small cottages built upon former tent sites, which still retain much of the original architecture. One can still visit the sacred Camp Grounds, established in 1873. The narrow streets and small lots remind one of life as it was described in Allen's poem. Welcome to the Camp Grounds.

**OLD ORCHARD CAMP GROUND.**

**Our Father in Heaven we thank Thee**<br>
**For this sacred haven of rest;**<br>
**Where the burdened and weary hearted**<br>
**May commune with the unseen guest.**

**Where turmoil and strife are forgotten;**<br>
**Where quiet and peace reign within;**<br>
**Where gently the spirit is calling,**<br>
**"Come child leave the broad road of sin.**

**Where whispering pines wave their branches--**<br>
**As in benediction o'er all;**<br>
**While in nature's ampitheatre,**<br>
**We wait for the spirit to fall.**

**Where strangers from all lands are welcomed--**<br>
**To sit at a bountiful spread,**<br>
**Prepared for their use by the Master,**<br>
**A feast of God's own living bread.**

**Jennie Lind Allen.**

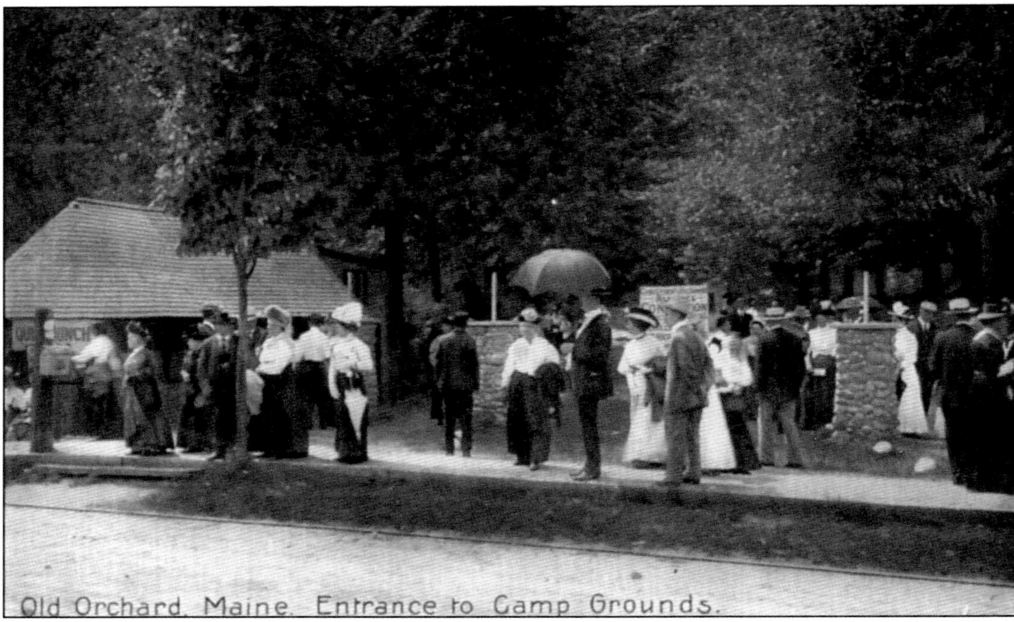


This *c.* 1909 postcard shows the entrance to the Camp Grounds, prior to the construction of the three arches leading into the main thoroughfare of the grounds. The arches were erected in 1910. In the foreground, one can notice the trolley tracks that ran down Washington Avenue, specifically to accommodate the thousands of daily visitors to the camp meetings.

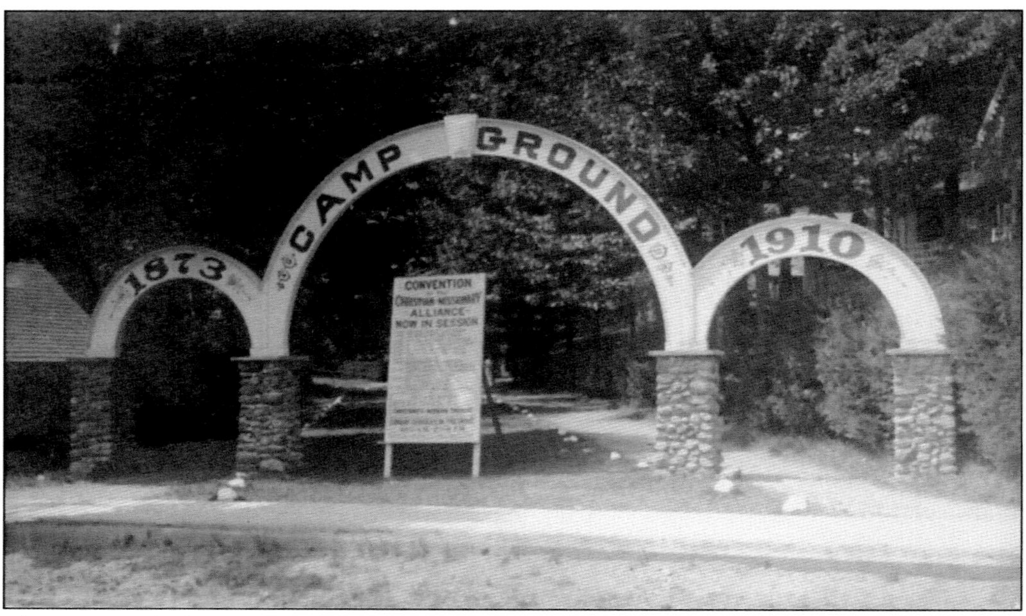


This 1915 real-photo postcard announces the coming of Dr. Albert Benjamin Simpson at the convention of the Christian Missionary Alliance. Reverend Simpson, successor to Dr. Charles Cullis, drew the largest crowds in the history of the Camp Grounds. His first appearance was in 1886. At one Sunday meeting, he received pledges of over $100,000. His faith-cure belief gospel was extremely popular, especially during the post–Civil War era.

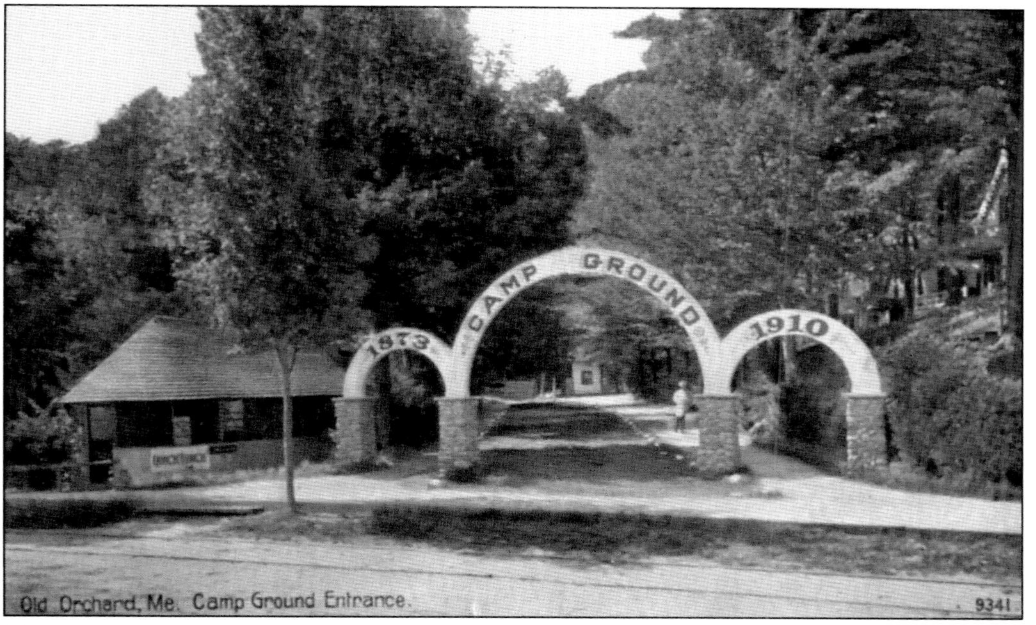


The Methodist Camp Grounds were formed in 1873 by the Portland Methodist District. It was one of the more popular meeting places in all of New England. All types of religious, reform, political, and temperance meetings were held. Early faith camp meetings were especially popular and largely attended. If Dr. Charles Cullis or the Rev. Albert Simpson were on the preacher's platform, one could expect a large crowd.

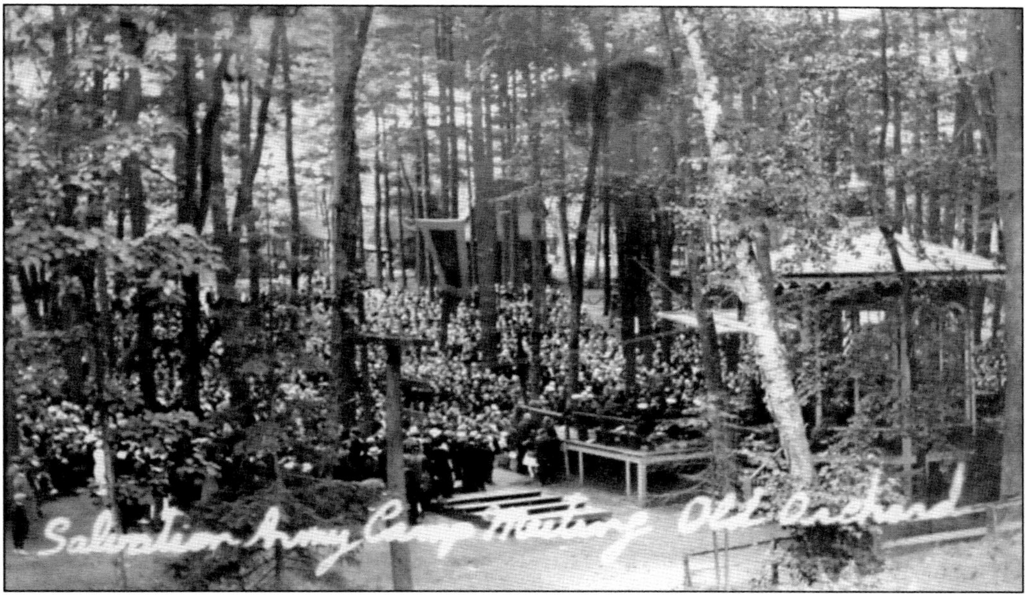


In July 1873, three ministers were looking for a better and larger camp meeting place than was presently being used in West Kennebunk. Rev. Israel Luce, of Old Orchard Beach; Rev. Daniel B. Randall; and Rev. Charles Munger bought 50 acres of the Jameson, Guilford, and Hardy Farms. This area roughly encompassed the land between Saco Avenue and the railroad tracks and Union and Atlantic Avenues. The Camp Grounds were established.

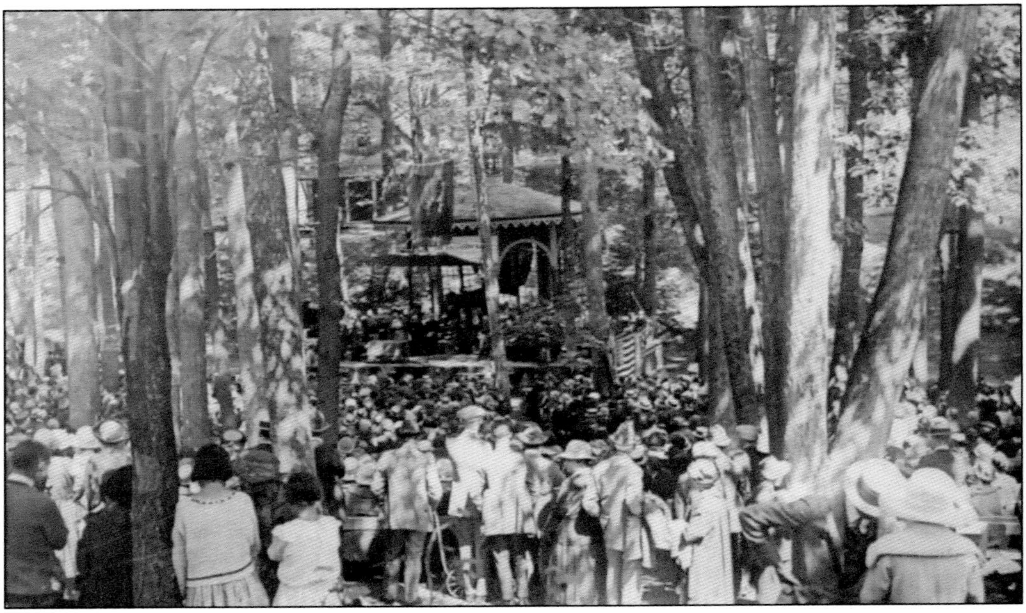

The above 1920s real-photo postcard shows a large group of Salvationists at one of their camp meetings. The Salvation Army held its first meeting in July 1885. With the exception of 10 years, 5 because of World War I, the Salvation Army has held meetings here regularly.

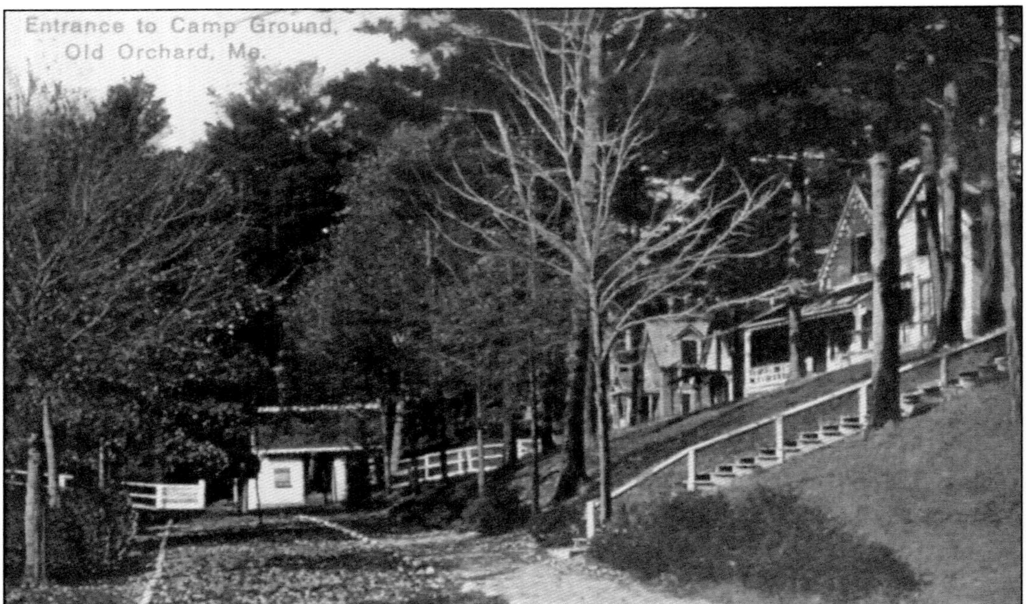


This 1909 postcard shows the main entrance to the Camp Grounds. In August 1904, Rev. Dr. Albert Simpson of New York raised $44,000 at one Sunday service, when the annual collection of the Christian Workers Alliance was taken. Many people threw watches, chains, rings, and all other kinds of jewelry into the collection basket. Some men rose and pledged their steam launches and other things of equal value, according to an article in the *Biddeford Daily Journal* of that year.

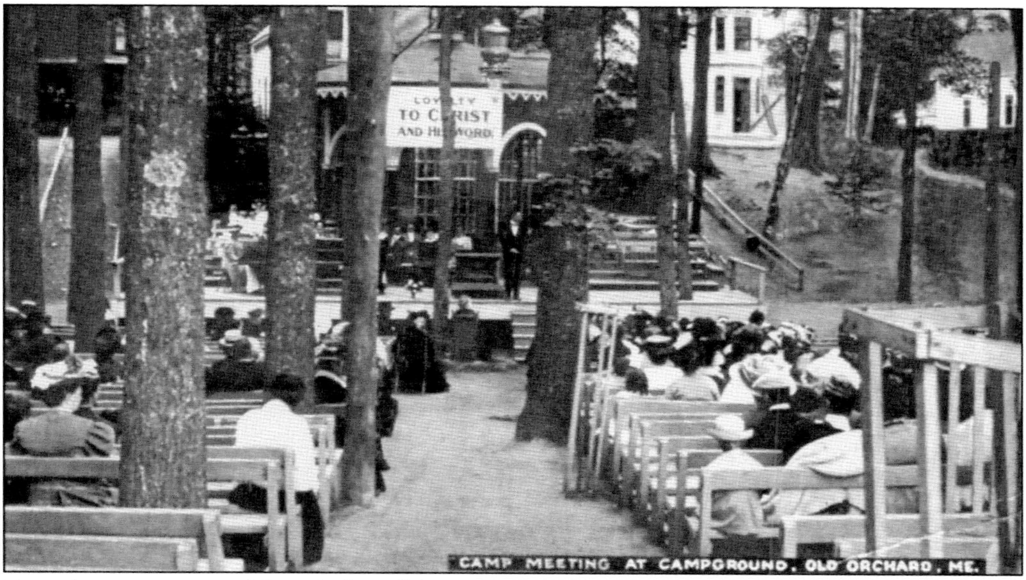


Over the years, many of America's well-known personalities have preached in the Camp Grounds: Dr. Charles Cullis, of faith-cure fame; Rev. Albert B. Simpson, founder of the Christian and Missionary Alliance; Francis E. Willard, leader of the Woman's Christian Temperance Union; Dr. L. B. Bates, head of the Christian Workers; Neal Dow, leader of the Maine Temperance Union; Congressman Thomas Brackett Reed; Honorable James G. Blaine, United States senator and secretary of state; 13 Salvation Army generals; and former president George H. W. Bush and former First Lady Barbara Bush. In 1879, then Pres. Rutherford B. Hayes and his wife were scheduled to speak, but it never materialized.

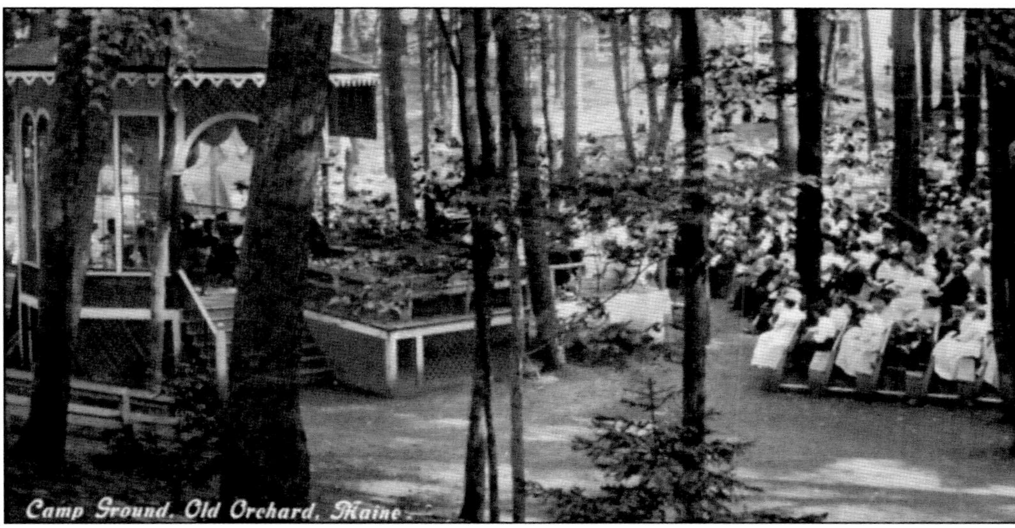


This postcard, dated 1911, shows a large crowd in the outdoor natural amphitheater with a seating capacity of 4,500. Originally tent lots were assigned to individuals or the churches and the Camp Ground Association. Each tent lot was 20 feet by 10 feet. Later platforms for the tents were constructed. This led to roofs, sides, and eventually, small cottages. A wooden sidewalk was run down Union Avenue to the Camp Ground train station. In 1879, the Camp Ground Association even sold shares for the construction of a pier and hotel at the foot of Union Avenue, but neither was ever built.

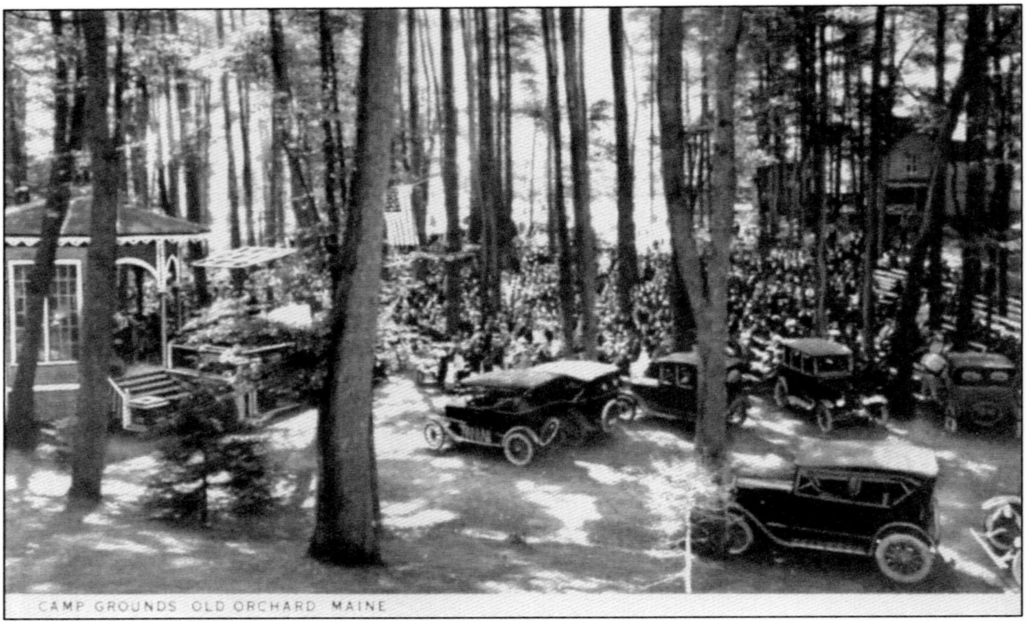


Groups as large as 7,000 people are recorded attending a single meeting. As many as 54 trains in one day were stopping at the Camp Ground station to load and off-load passengers. What a sight it must have been to see all the people walking up the wooden plank sidewalk to attend a daily service.

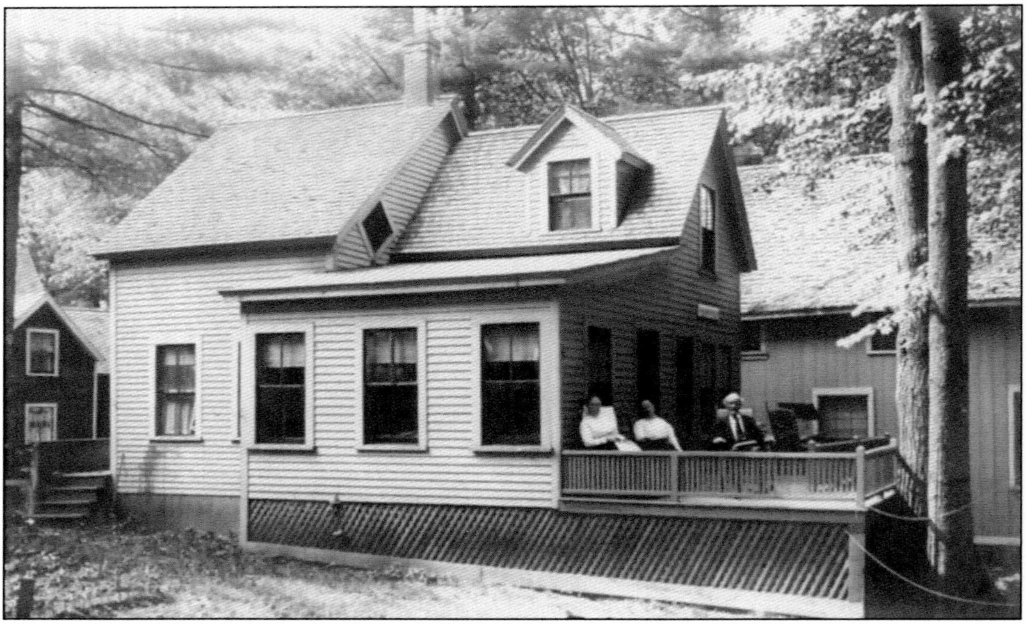

The above *c.* 1910 postcard shows Churchill cottage, located at 39 Society Avenue. In 1925, Alliance meetings were held here by Rev. H. E. Corthell of Portland. Society Avenue had the best seats in the house overlooking the speaker's platform. Today there are no houses on Society Avenue, as there is no Society Avenue. The Salvation Army has razed the cottages to expand its buildings, and Society Avenue is now just a paper street.

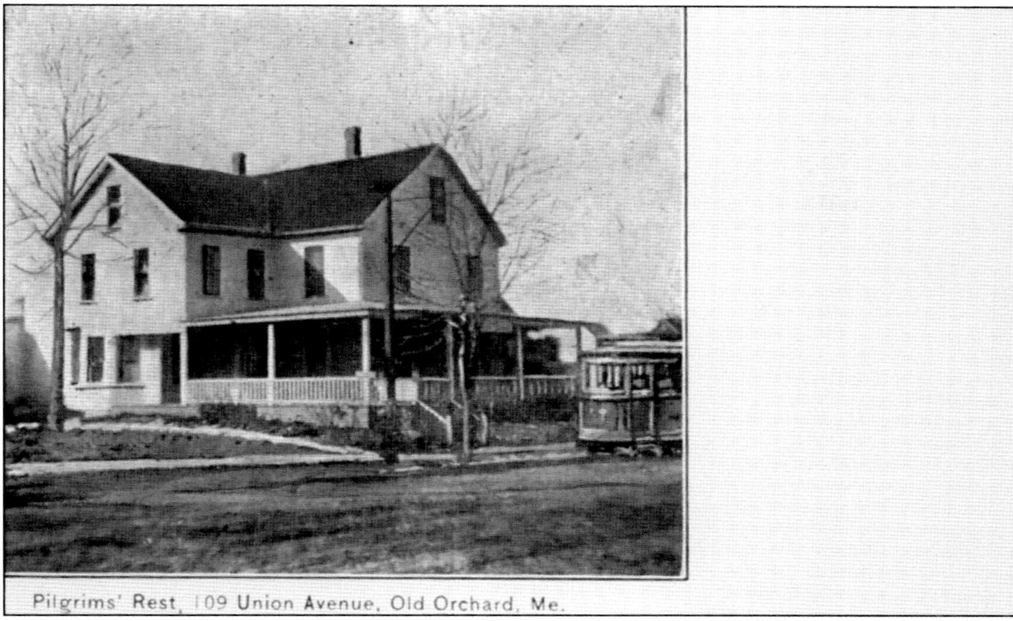


Pilgrim's Rest, at the corner of Central and Union Avenues, was a popular guesthouse, rented by people attending the camp meetings. Many homes and rooming houses in the Camp Ground section earned extra income, especially during the meetings.

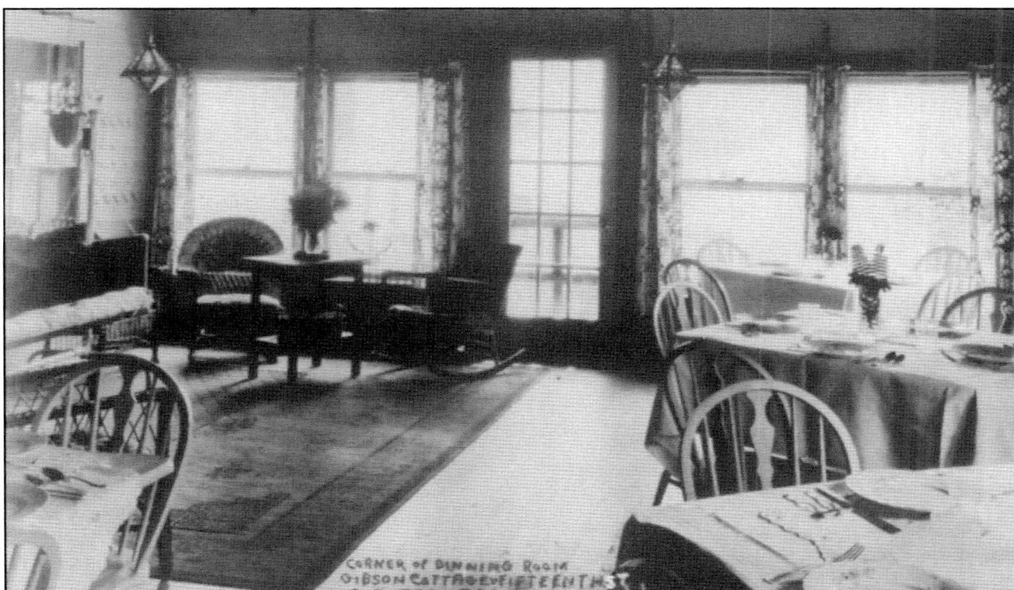


This is the Gibson Cottage, located at 47 Fifteenth Street and the corner of Oakland Avenue. This house is still standing today. It was later called the Augusta House. Many small rooming houses in the Camp Grounds had small dining rooms open to the public.

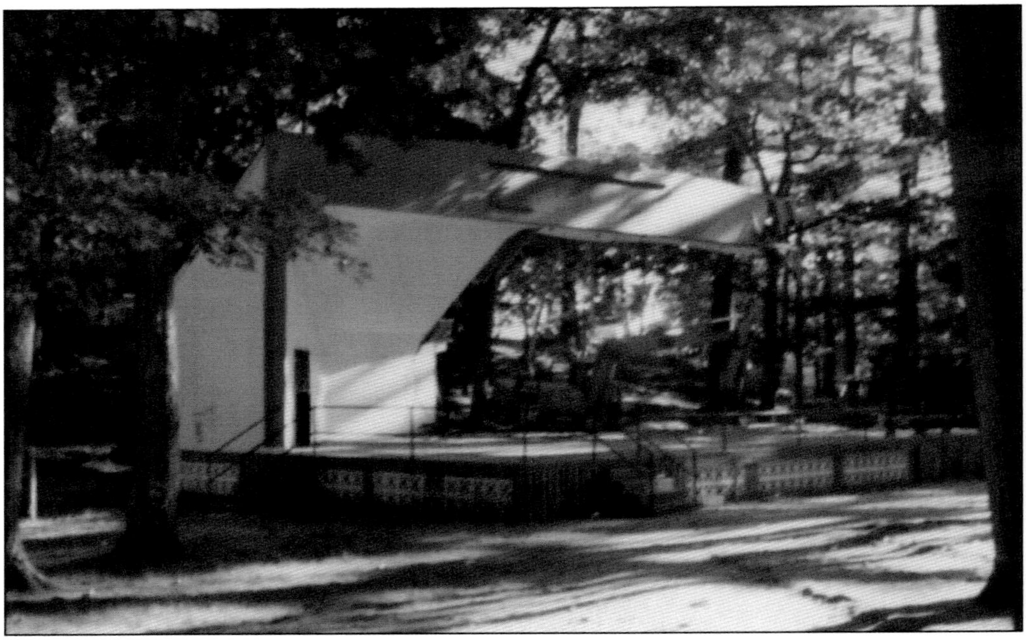

The photograph above, taken on September 24, 1997, shows the old 1954 pavilion being razed. It served for 43 years until the new pavilion was built. Many of the tall pines seen with red ribbons were removed to make room for the much larger pavilion being built.

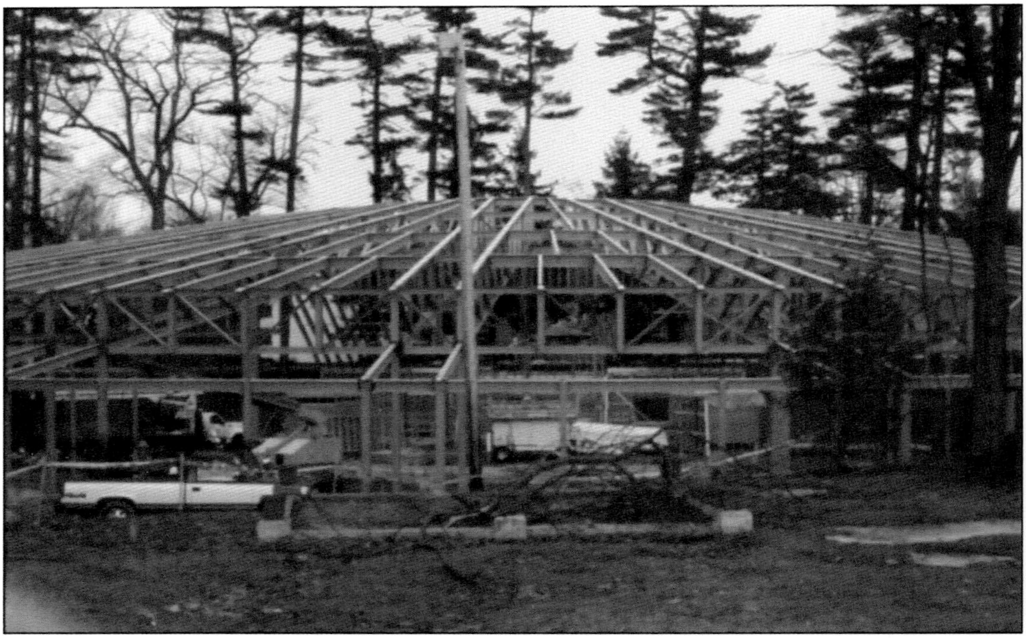

Construction of the new pavilion is seen in this February 21, 1998, photograph. The new 1,421-seat pavilion was dedicated on July 31, 1998. The autumn of 1997 saw the cutting down of 40 cathedral pines, making way for the $1 million pavilion. Amid early grumbling from a few neighbors, in reference to noise and concerts, many great venues have taken place; these were a welcomed pleasure to many.

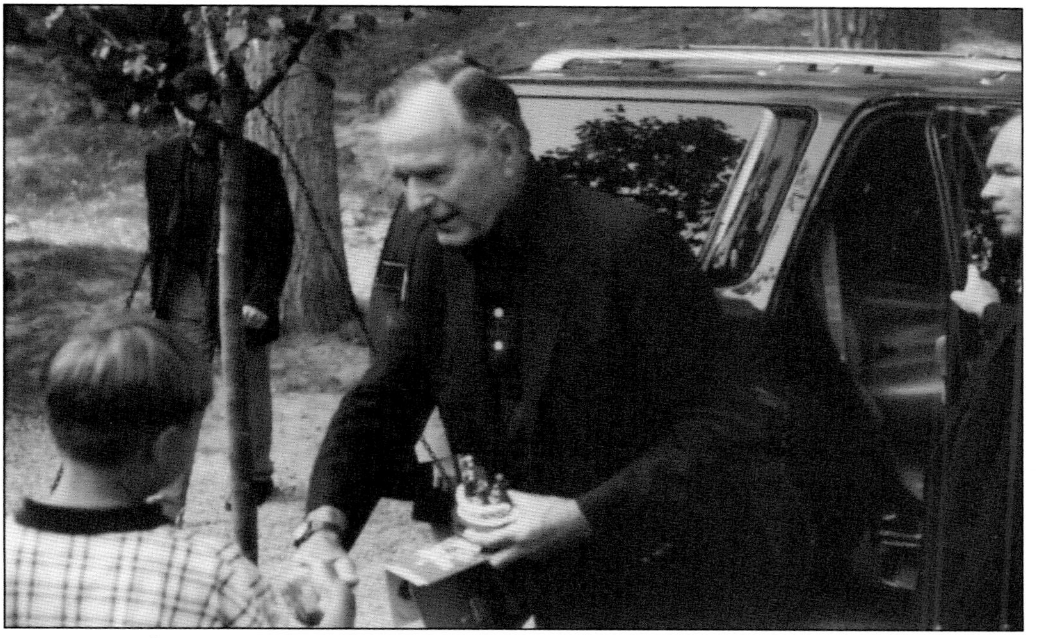

Former president George H. W. Bush shakes hands with a young boy on Saturday evening, August 8, 1998. A concert on the theme of "A Salute to America" was held with President Bush and First Lady Barbara Bush as honored guest speakers. A capacity crowd was treated to a beautiful evening of music and the presence of the former president in the new pavilion.

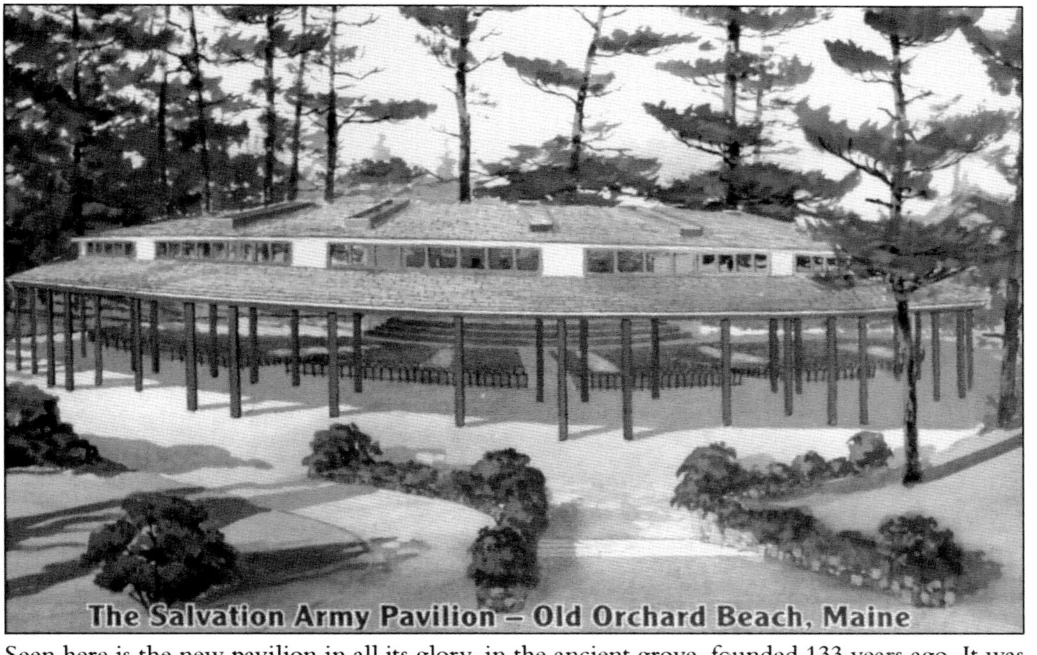


Seen here is the new pavilion in all its glory, in the ancient grove, founded 133 years ago. It was dedicated on July 31, 1998, by Salvation Army general Paul A. Rader and commissioner Kay F. Rader. Today many fine programs are held here along with the annual two-week Salvation Army camp meetings.